The boxes of our lives
don't have to be traps;
they can be
building blocks
for possibilities.

HOPE-FILLED
ENGAGEMENT

Other resources available from Ergon Communications:

Amundson, N.E. *Active engagement: The being and doing of career counselling.*

Amundson, N.E. *Metaphor making: Your career, your life, your way.*

Amundson, N.E. *The physics of living.*

Amundson, N.E. & Poehnell, G. *Career pathways.*

Amundson, N.E. & Poehnell, G. *Career pathways: Quick trip.*

Amundson, N.E., Poehnell, G. & Pattern, M. *CareerScope: Looking in, looking out, looking around.*

McCormick, R., Amundson, N.E., & Poehnell, G. *Guiding circles: An Aboriginal guide to finding career paths, Booklet 1: Understanding yourself.*

Poehnell, G. & Amundson, N.E. *Career crossroads: A personal career positioning system.*

Poehnell, G., Amundson, N.E. & McCormick, R. *Guiding circles: An Aboriginal guide to finding career paths, Booklet 2: Finding new possibilities.*

HOPE-FILLED
ENGAGEMENT

creating new possibilities
in life/career counselling

GRAY R. POEHNELL

NORMAN E. AMUNDSON

Library and Archives Canada Cataloguing in Publication

Poehnell, Gray
   Hope-filled engagement : creating new possibilities in life/career counselling / Gray R. Poehnell, Norman E. Amundson.

Includes bibliographical references.
ISBN 978-0-9784653-1-5

      1. Vocational guidance--Psychological aspects.
2. Personal coaching. 3. Counseling psychology.
I. Amundson, Norman E. (Norman Edmund), 1948- II. Title.

HF5381.P64 2011   331.702   C2010-907066-6

Published by Ergon Communications

To order this book or other Ergon Communication publications, contact:
      Ergon Communications
      PO Box 36033
      10991 No. 1 Road
      Richmond, BC V7E 1S4
      Tel./Fax. 604.448.9025
      Website: www.ergoncommunications.com

Text and cover design and illustration by Gray Poehnell
Open box illustration on cover © piki / Fotolia
Penny photo (p. 205) courtesy of Bruce McCaughey

Printed and bound in Canada by Hignell Book Printing, 488 Burnell Street, Winnipeg, Manitoba, R3G 2B4; Tel. 204.784.1033; Fax. 204.774.4053

Mixed Sources
Product group from well-managed forests and other controlled sources
www.fsc.org   Cert no. SW-COC-003438
© 1996 Forest Stewardship Council
FSC

Dedicated to my Mom, Blanche,

whose sacrifice broke the trail for me

and enabled me to go where she could not

and to my wife, Trish,

who has ever been my love and joy

and who has continually encouraged me

to be more than I thought I could be.

- Gray

Dedicated to the generations that follow:

my children Erin, Andrea, & Gus;

their spouses Andrew, Nick, & Jenna;

and my grandchildren

Emilia, Ezra, Felix, Jasper,

and those that are still to come

- Norm

Acknowledgments

So many have brought hope into my life; I can only thank a few. I thank God for speaking a word of hope in my heart when I was a confused, dysfunctional university student. He has walked with me for over 40 years and is still my Rock of hope. He has graced me with supportive friends and family. My Mom believed in me and sacrificed so I could have the hope of a future she only dreamed of. My dear wife Trish continually shows me the joy of life and has supported me in ways beyond counting. My precious daughters, Tabitha and Sarah, continually remind me to keep it real. I must also thank Tabitha for her invaluable editing of this book. Though I cannot name them all personally, many friends have been there for me throughout my life journey. Over the last several years, Dawn Schooler, as my counsellor, has helped me find hope as I'm working through painful leftovers from my past.

I have also been blessed professionally. The ideas in this book have been honed in hundreds of workshops and presentations with life/career practitioners and with a wide diversity of people. The people I have met in these workshops and in individual sessions have allowed me to learn with them; without them, this book would not be possible. I have also had the privilege of learning from many deeply committed career developers and trainers. In particular, Lynne Bezanson and Sareena Hopkins (Canadian Career Development Foundation) have taught me about the heart of counselling and Paul Stevens (Regent College) has taught me about the spirituality of work. Rod McCormick, one of the co-authors of Guiding Circles, has graciously shared of his experience and activities in Aboriginal healing and education. Trina Maher has walked much of the Guiding Circles journey with me on behalf of the Aboriginal Human Resource Council of Canada. Trina's insatiable hunger to learn and grow has helped me to think through so many concepts and activities. Without her ongoing support in administration and marketing Guiding Circles and its workshops, the Guiding Circles program would not be what it is today.

Finally, I must thank my mentor, partner, and friend Norm Amundson. It was Norm who initially opened the door to the career field for me 21 years ago and gave me direction at a time when I didn't know which way to turn. Over the years, I have had the incredible opportunity of working alongside Norm. He is the most generous person I know and I am a better person because of it; he has shared not only his ideas with me but his life as well. Norm exemplifies all that Hope-Filled Engagement is about; Norm not only teaches about an engaged life of hope, he lives it to the full.

- Gray, Richmond, B.C., November 2010

The foundation for this work comes from the opportunities I have had over the years to work in a number of different settings. First and foremost is the UBC Community Counselling Training Center in New Westminister, B.C.. This center provides free counselling service for the greater Vancouver area. The challenges that were put forward in this context were complex and did not fall neatly into categories, such as personal versus career counselling. People needed service from a holistic perspective; they needed service that focused on strengths (hope) as well as weaknesses.

I have also appreciated the opportunities to work in many different cross-cultural contexts in over twenty different countries and with outstanding community groups such as S.U.C.C.E.S.S. and the Aboriginal Human Resources Development Council. These experiences have shown me the importance of a culturally-sensitive employment counselling approach.

Lastly, I must acknowledge the importance of the Guiding Circles project in helping me focus on the importance of developing a hope-filled career counselling approach. Through this project I have shared ideas and learned from the wisdom of my colleagues, Rod McCormick and Gray Poehnell. I particularly want to acknowledge the extensive work that Gray has done in refining and extending the original Guiding Circles ideas. Gray has worked tirelessly in bringing this hope-based knowledge to teachers and counsellors in different sectors throughout Canada and Australia. It has been a joy to work with Gray and to see hopeful engagement take root in so many different contexts.

- Norm, Richmond, B.C., November 2010

Table of Contents

List of Figures

chapter one

INTRODUCTION

Welcome to a journey. For that is what Hope-Filled Engagement is—a journey.

It is a journey of exploration and discovery—a journey further into a world of creative career counselling that started in 1998 with the award-winning book *Active Engagement* (Amundson, 2009). Therefore, it is a journey of active engagement. Engagement not just for the people we work with, but also for our own selves, as life/career practitioners.

It is a journey of creativity in the face of a world of increasing change and uncertainty.

It is a journey of hope. The journey may not start with much hope, but it is a journey that generates hope the further along one travels. Hope for people who have been unable to see any hope on their life/career path. Hope for practitioners who struggle with despair and cynicism, who want to believe again that it is possible to help the people they are committed to.

There will be destinations along the way. But each destination is just a stepping-stone to the next stage of the journey. Our desire is much more than to just get people working. It is to equip them with hope as they discover that it is indeed possible to walk their life/career journey with a sense of dignity and value no matter where that path may lead.

In *Active Engagement,* some people are described as being "stuck in a crisis of imagination"; they just can't see their lives any different from what they are or have (Amundson, 2009). Many practitioners also seem to be "stuck in a crisis of imagination." They sincerely wish to help the people they work with but are not quite sure what to do.

There are no simple answers. It would be presumptuous to say that Hope-Filled Engagement will solve all the challenges that practitioners face today. All the issues involved are far too complex for any one book or approach to solve. But perhaps it will give you some fresh new ideas, new perspectives, and new strategies. Hopefully you will find some new motivation to be involved in the creative task of developing even more new tools and processes for the challenges of today and tomorrow.

We have found that there is usually more commonality between people than there are differences. No matter whether high or low economic status, young or old, male or female, a citizen or an immigrant, educated or uneducated, professional or blue-collar, many people struggle with the same issues in their lives. Many have questions about who they are and what they ought to be doing with their lives. Many struggle with personal and external issues that make it difficult for them to effectively answer these questions in practical ways that can be worked out in today's labour market.

We believe that people need to take responsibility for their lives and for the choices they make. There are some people out there who are stuck in their life/career journeys because of poor personal choices. But it is also true that many face barriers not of their making: age, sex, culture, socio-economic class, local labour market, lack of opportunity, to name just a few. This reality is becoming more common today as counselling becomes increasingly complex. For example, multi-barriered clients are becoming more common, and so practitioners need to be appropriately prepared. As practitioners, we need to do all we can to create an environment that is conducive to all people making good choices no matter the cause of their challenges. Thus, personal responsibility is not just something for people generally but also for practitioners and for those who create and maintain the structures and policies under which practitioners work. In this rapidly changing world, it is not only the people we work with who may need to change but also we as practitioners.

The need for this book became clear through the work we have done with the *Guiding Circles* program. The *Guiding Circles* approach started with a model of career development and some research that was conducted on the career decision-making needs of Aboriginal youth (McCormick & Amundson, 1997; McCormick, Neumann, Amundson, & McLean, 1999; Neumann, McCormick, Amundson, & McLean, 2000). This research supported the need for a career approach that would make career development more accessible to Aboriginal people and others. Working with Dr. Rod McCormick, we helped develop *Guiding circles: An Aboriginal guide to finding career paths, Booklet 1: Understanding yourself* (McCormick, Amundson & Poehnell, 2002), then *Guiding circles: An Aboriginal guide to finding career paths, Booklet 2: Finding new possibilities* (Poehnell, Amundson & McCormick, 2006), and finally a coaches manual (Poehnell, 2003). Since we will be referencing these frequently throughout this book, we will simply refer to them as *Guiding Circles 1* and *Guiding Circles* 2. We also entered into a partnership agreement with the Aboriginal Human Resource Council of Canada and this led to a national research project to test and validate the Guiding Circles approach with First Nations, Métis, and Inuit practitioners in different regions in Canada (funded by Human Resources and Social Development Canada - HRSDC).

Since 2002, thousands of workbooks have been circulated and over 1500 practitioners in Canada (as well as in Australia and New Zealand) have received training. The workshops have been held with reservations, Aboriginal organizations, non-profit organizations, government organizations, schools, colleges, and universities, and private businesses.

Though *Guiding Circles* was initially directed toward multi-barriered people, it soon became clear that the underlying approach had a much broader application. For example, several school boards have been incorporating it into their curriculum. As well, we have observed this approach helping people not only in direct career matters such as self-assessment and career exploration but also in building self-esteem and a greater sense of identity—essential building blocks for effective life/career development. We recognized that we were not so much training people in *Guiding Circles* but in the hope-filled engagement process that was being expressed in the workbooks. Practitioners kept asking for background material beyond what could be covered in the workshops. It is this appeal for greater elaboration of hope-filled engagement that we seek to address in this book.

This approach seems particularly well suited to

- people who don't fit into the mainstream world of school or work or who feel intimidated by traditional career counselling,

- people who come from a cultural background different from mainstream North Americans,

- people with low self-esteem,

- people who have lost a sense of meaning in their lives, and

- people who are unaware of their career potential.

It is our hope that *Hope-Filled Engagement* will assist you, as a life/career practitioner, in the ethical and practical development of knowledge, skills, and practices for working more creatively and positively with people. It is designed to provide practical help for the challenges you may be facing in your work—challenges such as finding ...

- creative approaches to help people increase their self-awareness and find realistic career possibilities in today's rapidly changing world,

- a flexible realistic framework to guide the counselling process,

- ways to involve community in the counselling process, and

- a counselling approach that is cross-culturally sensitive.

The *Hope-Filled Engagement* career development approach combines a holistic worldview (including spirituality, connectedness, community, values and life balance) with sound contemporary career development concepts. It is a creative approach that encourages flexibility and innovation. It is a person-centered, solution-focused, hope-focused approach that engages people where they are engaged with life and works from there.

In writing this book, it has been hard to know where to put what and what order to follow. There are challenges to face, themes to consider, activities to try. Because these are all so interrelated, we are dealing with a web of ideas. For example, when discussing an activity, it is possible that several challenges or themes might be considered. Therefore, as you read this book, you will want to reference and cross-reference different sections.

We have attempted to group the different inter-related parts of the *Hope-Filled Engagement* approach under 8 broad sections.

Chapter 2: Diversity and Challenges looks at the need to critically reflect upon our own assumptions and conventions in the light of the increasing diversity of people today. We wish to encourage the use of the most appropriate tools and processes.

Chapter 3: Key Themes that undergird the Hope-Filled Engagement approach: diversity, active engagement, mattering, the backswing, CareerCraft, imagination and spirituality, holistic life/career perspectives, values and life balance, career integrity, community perspective, and creative decision/action planning.

Chapter 4: Creativity, Spirituality, Imagination, and Hope are important elements in all aspects of the life/career counselling process. Such elements are needed in the light of the rapidly changing world of work which call for more holistic and flexible approaches, especially for those experiencing hopelessness.

Chapter 5 Self-Assessment must engage people in identifying and valuing who they are. It emphasizes finding the best starting points for self-assessment and then the facilitating of storytelling using proven questioning strategies.

Chapter 6: Storytelling is an effective and inclusive approach for self-discovery that can be used with a very broad range of people whatever their background, even if they are disconnected from the mainstream world of school or work and have a difficult time relating to many traditional life/career counselling approaches. This section will explore in depth both storytelling concepts and practical activities, especially finding the right starting points and facilitating storytelling through the use of effective questioning.

Chapter 7: Career Exploration applies the same *Hope-Filled Engagement* principles, tools, and approaches used in self-assessment to person-focused career exploration. Practical creative activities, such as the use of stimuli and brainstorming, can enable people to expand the way they view the world of work, to identify potential career fields flowing from their own potential, and then to fine-tune the possibilities in these career fields. We will also explore how to discover uncharted entrepreneurial potential. Finally, we will look at the process of getting the relevant career information needed to make effective career decisions.

Chapter 8: Creative Vision/Decision/Action Planning addresses the need for more creative, holistic, and communal approaches to vision casting, decision making and to action planning in today's ever-changing chaotic world. Practical activities are employed that will enable people to keep moving no matter the uncertainties or the barriers that they face.

Chapter 9: Keeping in Step with a Changing Career addresses the self-care of practitioners who are facing a changing job in a changing work environment in a changing world. In one sense, every career practitioner is only a step away from becoming a client himself or herself. We all are walking a life/career journey in a very uncertain world. We all need to find ways to engage with hope.

Whether you read *Hope-Filled Engagement* straight through or selectively, read with a spirit of exploration, honest self-reflection, curious experimentation, and creative adaptation. Let us know what you discover on your journey.

chapter two

DIVERSITY AND CHALLENGES

Our Stories

Personal Foundations of Hope

In the introduction, we mentioned the fact that this book has both personal and professional foundations. These stories embody some of the struggles that people may face in bringing hope into their lives. In presenting these stories, we are hoping that, as you read further chapters, you will be encouraged to look at your own story and the stories of the people you work with. Think of the challenges that you and they have had to overcome or still face. Examine your personal assumptions and conventions, which direct the way you practice life/career counselling. Commit yourself to exploring new ways to engage pcople with a sense of hope.

Gray's Story

As a child, I faced many challenges, which have profoundly affected my life. My dear mother was a Francophone Métis from Saskatchewan. She left school and started work at age 12, married at 16, and had five children in the next 10 years. Although at the time I did not see or understand that my family struggled with dysfunctionality, as I'm getting older, I am becoming more and more aware of the effects of that dysfunctionality upon myself.

There were times when, as a family, we struggled financially. Though my father was a highly-skilled craftsman, he, for various reasons, found it hard to maintain a consistent work life. My Mom always did the best she could; but still at times, we didn't always have the food or the clothes or the housing that we would have liked to have had. The situation was more challenged in my extended family; where many of my relatives struggled with alcohol abuse and even physical abuse.

My mother saw education as the way out of the family dysfunctionality; she believed it was the way to a better life. Unfortunately when I went to school, I seemed to have continual difficulty. My brother and I are visually impaired, but my Mom insisted that we both go to a regular school rather than a school for the visually impaired. She wanted us to have the best education possible and not to be set aside as different. I was always small for my age. I also struggled with learning disabilities and speech difficulties; as a result I always seemed to struggle with any classes involving language or reading or writing. One of my not-so-fond memories was a situation in grade 4 when the teacher stood me in front of the class at the blackboard for an hour because I did not know how to spell my name. She thought that by grade 4 a child ought to be able to spell his own name. After a considerable time at the board, I was still unable to spell my name, so I received a detention. After school I again stood at the board but was still unable to spell my name, so eventually I was sent home with a note to my mother asking why I was unable to do so. Rather than helping me discover why I had such difficulties with the language arts, I was in effect punished for not being able to do what the teacher assumed I ought to be able to do.

As I continued to go through school, I became more and more convinced in my own heart and mind that there was something wrong with me and that I was just stupid. By the time I graduated from grade 12, most of my self talk revolved around some form of telling myself that I was stupid, ignorant, or "retarded" in some way.

I finished high school, because my Mom saw education as the way out of the family disfunctionality. Although I could not seem to grasp the basics of the language arts, I was able to do mathematics. So I went to the University of British Columbia and enrolled in a bachelor of science degree (mathematics).

My entrance exams showed that I was functionally illiterate. This further convinced me that I was stupid. So aside for first-year English (that I almost failed) and a few other courses that I needed to meet my arts requirement, I did not take any other arts courses during my four years of university. Although I did manage to graduate with a degree, I still struggled in my heart and mind, for I still perceived myself to be stupid. My self talk still revolved around this very negative view of myself and I became quite crippled by low self-esteem, shyness, and introversion.

This came to a head between my third and fourth years of university. The inconsistency between my crippling low-esteem and constant self-depreciating self-talk and my seeming ability to make it in university resulted in a very deep personal crisis. I was absolutely confused as to why I was not happy and satisfied now that I was fulfilling the dream of getting an education. At this time I went through a profound spiritual experience, which enabled me to re-examine my life and begin the long process of changing my own self perceptions and my life. I decided that I no longer wanted the rest of my life to be controlled by the dysfunctionality of my childhood.

With much doubt and fear, I entered the next phase of my life journey. I went on for further schooling in which I would have to take several years of English. Again entrance exams showed that I struggled with basic literacy. Even though I had managed to earn a degree in mathematics, I still couldn't grasp the basics of English. I was put into the slow English section my first year. But I decided that I would start from scratch and do my best to learn. I committed myself to learn how to learn. To make a long story short, four years later when I finished this program, I was hired to be on faculty at this college. One of the subjects I was hired to teach was English grammar and later I became the head of the English department. I went on to teach ancient Koine Greek and to become the chair of the languages department.

Obviously I was not as stupid as I thought. My difficulties in language arts were affected by my life circumstances, my own perceptions and attitudes, and the inability of my earlier teachers to find ways to help me through them. Fortunately in many schools today, teachers have come a very long way in creatively working with students with learning disabilities, with physical handicaps, and with cultural issues.

In the years since then, I have devoted myself to finding creative ways to help people (including myself) learn things that they thought they could not learn or to do things they thought they could not do. I have given myself to the practical outworking of creating hope through equipping. This has been one of my passions both in my years of college teaching and in my years as a career practitioner.

So the concept of finding new ways to engage people in the career counselling process in order that the very process itself will enable them to find new hope is something that is very dear to my heart.

Norm's Story

Like Gray, I grew up in a home where there wasn't a lot of money. My father worked for the railway and my mother stayed home with the five children (I was the eldest). To make ends meet, my father always was supplementing his income with two or three part-time jobs. These involved running a concession stand at the ballpark, building houses, and doing some accounting for various small businesses in the community. There always was enough money but there was a lot of work to be done. I remember collecting bottles and stray golf balls as part of my contribution to the family enterprise.

Finances in the family became a very big issue and during my high school years there was a real crisis when the railway restructured. During that time my father was "bumped" from his position in the ticket office. While he kept his job with the railway, he found himself counting boxcars for minimum wage. The job was mindless and routine and was compensated accordingly. There also were some physical challenges and my father was hurt when he fell between the boxcars. My parents didn't talk much about their financial struggles but we all knew that money was tight.

From a cultural perspective, being an immigrant family was always very close to the surface. The small town in Saskatchewan where we lived had a definite social and political hierarchy, and there wasn't much opportunity for immigrants. Most of the extended family bought into this structure and yearned for some way to become a "somebody." My mother, on the other hand, completely rejected all this "nonsense" and repeatedly assured us that we were as good as anybody. In her eyes, all this snobbery was ridiculous. She had met my father during the war while playing the piano for the troops. She was an outstanding jazz musician that played in various clubs up and down the Eastern seaboard. There was no one that was going to tell her that she was somehow inferior because she married into an immigrant family.

As with Gray's family, education was viewed as the way out of poverty and one's social situation. We were all encouraged to consider post-secondary education. Of course, no one in our family had actually gone to university, so we didn't really know what was involved. What I did understand was that, if you were good in school, you could get scholarships and that would cover the financial costs. The prospect of earning money through grades at school was a great incentive, and I responded accordingly.

When it was time to go to university, my parents decided that this was also a good opportunity to move to a bigger city so that I could continue to live at home and go to school. It also made university more accessible for others in the family. As mentioned earlier, the job at the railway was becoming increasingly untenable. So the house was sold, and we made our move. My father quickly found another low-level job with the railway, but being on his feet all day selling tickets meant that he spent most evenings on the couch getting the swelling out of his ankles. He had some wartime injuries and these were aggravated by the work he was doing. But then our fortunes turned, and my father found work with a government agency as the head of purchasing. His salary improved and at one point everyone was in university, including my mother.

I went through university with good grades and kept moving ahead until I had my doctoral degree. My work experience during these years focused on the correctional system where I worked as a parole officer. In helping people to find their way back into society, I learned the importance of work as a stabilizing influence (money, social contacts, and structure).

I don't think that it is by chance that my research at the university has had as its focus the experience of unemployment, underemployment, and working life. Through this work, I have focused on the importance of context and culture. I also have looked more deeply at issues of emotion, mattering, hopefulness, and self esteem. Given the influences of my mother, it is not surprising that I also have a strong pull towards imagination and creativity as a base for the interventions that are being applied.

I am very committed to the idea of helping practitioners work with people on the "fringe" in new and imaginative ways. A few years back I called for a meeting of practitioners who worked with this population. The response was overwhelming and what I realized was that in many respects the "fringe" had become the mainstream. It is in this spirit that the material in this book is put forward.

The content of the upcoming chapters relates to theory and to good counselling practice. It also has as its foundation some of our personal life experiences.

Diversity

There are many challenges that practitioners and people face in the context of life/career counselling. One of the most pressing is the challenge of diversity.

Today more than ever before there is a continual need to examine and reexamine one's assumptions and conventions in terms of attitudes, perspectives, tools, and processes in the light of the diversity of people and, therefore, the diverse challenges that many face.

Some of the myriad diversity issues that practitioners and people may face today include:

- age
- sex
- cultural background
- nationality
- language
- socio-economic status
- location
- sense of personal identity
- spirituality
- disabilities

- level of self-esteem
- value systems
- personality styles
- learning styles
- communication styles
- coping strategies
- sense of individuality and community
- life experiences (family, learning, & work experiences)

Obviously this is not a comprehensive list, but it is representative. In addition to these issues, people may have many different perspectives on career issues (e.g., North America is interest focused, while Asia is opportunity focused).

This is made even more complicated by several realities. First, as our world is changing, so is the scope of this diversity. We are becoming more sensitive to increasing numbers of diversity issues. Second, usually there is not just one diversity issue but a combination of issues. Finally, the level of self-awareness on the part of people and/or practitioners is another factor. People may not be consciously aware of their own personal frames of reference on these issues, let alone the impact of these on the life/career counselling process. Unrecognized perspectives are not easily challenged or adapted.

Multiculturalism

There are many effective tools and processes currently in use in the life/career counselling field. But are they as effective with everyone? No one intentionally seeks to use culturally-inappropriate tools or processes; but it can happen unintentionally when mainstream career counselling assumes an understanding and acceptance of many "mainstream" values and perspectives that are not universally accepted by all peoples.

This is obviously an increasing issue in a country such as Canada, where multiculturalism is one of the main characteristics of our society. Such assumptions will obviously affect counselling relationships with many from other cultures or perspectives.

The shifting cultural landscape is reflected in many aspects of our society. For example, in 2007, Gray attended a 40th high school reunion. His 1967 graduating class in Vancouver had relatively few students who were not of European descent. Yet in 2007, within that school, there were 52 birth languages from 48 nations. This reflects a new reality in many communities across Canada

Such cultural differences can also be seen with Canada's Aboriginal peoples. As well, cultural differences may extend beyond that of race and language to include the culture differences reflected in all the diversity issues mentioned earlier.

In the early nineties, we worked on a New Canadian Job Link research project. The goal of the project was to explore the creation of a cross-cultural vocational counselling model for immigrants. We worked with about 250 Chinese, Vietnamese, and Hispanic immigrants, often with the assistance of interpreters. These clients were assisted through self-assessment, career exploration, and work search. There were many positive findings from this project; it especially revealed the need for culturally-appropriate career counselling material. For example, several self-assessment tools were translated into the 3 languages of the client groups. But just translating the words and having the clients read them didn't make up for the reality that these words represented concepts that were different for some. For example, one Vietnamese woman had only a few of years schooling, had only worked carrying vegetables from the family plot to the market, had spent 15 years in a refugee camp, had been virtually house bound since coming to Canada, and had not learned English while rearing her family. While she could read an interest inventory in her language, she didn't know most of the concepts behind them, because the Canadian world of work was almost totally unknown to her. It is true that this is an extreme case, but it does reflect some real challenges.

Since 2002, we have been working with *Guiding Circles* workbooks, designed initially for Canada's Aboriginal population but now proven to be effective with others such as minorities, multi-barriered people, or even mainstream people. In this project, we have again clearly seen the need for culturally appropriate life/career counselling tools and processes.

McCormick and Amundson (1997, p. 172), while arguing for the need for a culturally-appropriate life/career counselling model for Aboriginal peoples in Canada, wrote:

Worldview is the understanding that an individual has about how things and people relate to one another. To be effective, a counselor needs to understand the belief system and worldview of a culture before applying theories and techniques of healing.

A person's belief systems, decision-making strategies, models of problem solving, assumptions about how problems arise, and how change occurs are all connected to how he or she sees the world.

They go on to state that the effectiveness of counselling with Aboriginal peoples has been affected because the cultural differences between the mainstream Western worldview and the Aboriginal worldview have not been adequately taken into account.

Lack of knowledge of Aboriginal values, belief systems, and worldview can lead to faulty assumptions concerning the diagnosis of the situation and the strategies to be used. In the past, counselling services provided to Aboriginal peoples have been based on the wholesale adoption of Western approaches without regard to their applicability.

Cultural Embeddedness of Life/Career Counselling

This misguided assumption of the universal applicability of a Western perspective in life/career counselling can result simply from the fact that many do not recognize how culturally-embedded life/career counselling can be.

At the risk of oversimplification, it is clear that career counselling evolved out of the human resource world of business and is firmly rooted in the North American business culture. Therefore, it often reflects the worldview of that business culture (e.g., values, concepts, language, tools, and processes).

For example some common values of the Western business world, such as individualism, competitiveness, understanding of success, materialism (e.g., profit vs. people), secularism (vs. spirituality), and mobility, may not be understood or accepted by all peoples. In fact in some cases, such as with many Aboriginal peoples or people from various faith backgrounds, these values are exactly opposite to the things they held most dear. Such peoples would relate much better to a life/career counselling approach that recognizes and is sensitive to their own value systems.

The link between mainstream life/career counselling and the Western business world is most clearly seen in the technical language of career counselling. Mainstream career counselling does not always recognize that it uses very technical language that is not understood by everyone. For example, consider the invitation: *"Let's schedule a time for some self-assessment so that we can identify your marketable assets in order that you can sell yourself in the labour market more effectively; you have to become the CEO of your own career."* Such language may be effective with people who come from the mainstream world of work and business. But it is important to ask oneself whether or not the people you work with will understand this language (and the associated values, tools, processes) as you would.

As in any cross-cultural activity, the time may come when there will be a need to assist people to relate to the culture and language of the mainstream world of work. But does this mean that it is the best place to start? One must consider what is the impact upon people when they don't understand or accept the values being presented.

Effects of Culturally-Inappropriate Counselling

In our years of working in cross-cultural situations, we have seen the effects when practitioners don't recognize their need to challenge culturally-conditioned assumptions and conventions which work well in mainstream populations but which may do the opposite with someone from another culture or worldview. Some of the effects in people may include:

- confusion
- ineffective life/career choices
- discouragement
- the raising of unnecessary barriers
- lack of motivation

What to Do?

We have observed some effective ways in which practitioners have been successful in creatively addressing the diversity issues:

- recognize and adapt to this diversity;

- examine one's assumptions and conventions for any cultural bias;

- take time to get to know where people are coming from;

- don't judge; other values systems are not wrong, just different;

- challenge your assumptions (e.g., people appear reluctant; easy to assume disinterest but could there be other reasons, such as depression, confusion, lack of know-how, etc.);

- learn to examine your use of language, to become aware of how someone else might understand your words;

- acquire and/or develop additional tools and approaches which can be applied in differing contexts (e.g., read on cross-cultural counselling, find out about other cultural groups).

The issue of diversity and the need to learn how to work effectively with it is clearly one of the greatest challenges facing life/career counselling today. There is a need for much more to be done. *Hope-Filled Engagement* is an attempt to address this issue in practical ways.

Disconnection with Mainstream Structures

A second potential challenge for some people as they interact with life/career counselling is the usual starting points used in many mainstream career counselling. In a sense this is a specific form of the diversity issue; but, because it is such a large issue, we will treat it separately.

As a result of a shift in government policy in our province a few years ago, former financial aid workers were trained to assist their multi-barriered clients in preparing employment plans. Most of these workers had not had any formal training in career counselling. Gray facilitated a one-day training program for several groups of workers from an economically- and socially-challenged neighborhood.

When the workers were asked what would be the first question they would ask one of their clients to start the process of creating employment plans, the answers were very similar. Many of them responded with some form of four basic types of questions:

- *"What is your five-year plan?"* or *"What are your long-range goals?"*

- *"What is your work history?"* or *"What work experience have you had?"*

- *"What is your educational background?"* or *"What courses were you good at in school?"*

- *"What are your skills?"* or *"What are your interests?"*

These questions are all excellent questions in the right context. But when the workers reflected on them, they acknowledged that these questions were in fact irrelevant to most of their clients.

Most of their clients lived in Vancouver's Downtown Eastside, which unfortunately has the reputation for being the most troubled urban community in Canada. Despite the efforts of many, the Downtown Eastside continues to have many unsolved issues: homelessness; addictions and substance abuse; AIDS and other health issues; mental health issues; and criminal activity. Many have been out of the mainstream for sometime and live on social assistance; many live on and off the street. Tragically there are a disproportionate number of Aboriginal people.

In this context, it is not hard to see that these questions could be meaningless to many of these people. Often in these kinds of situations the same general answers are given: *"Dunno," "Not much,"* or the like. Is the problem with the clients or with the questions themselves?

Question: *"What is your five-year plan?"* or *"What are your long-range goals?"*

Typical Answers: *"I don't know." "I don't have any." "Not much."*

These people don't usually have long-range goals. They are just trying to survive the moment. At best they may be thinking of where they will get their next meal or where they will sleep that night. But most of them surely are not thinking about where their life is going to be in a few years.

Question: *"What is your work history?"*

Typical Answers: *"Not much." "Never had a job." "I can't keep jobs."*

Many do not have a typical work history. Some of these people may have worked in the past but these past experiences with work may not have been good. Some may never have worked at all.

Question: *"What is your educational background?"*

Typical Answers: *"I didn't do well in school." "I didn't like school." "I never fit in." "I never finished school."*

This question brings up similar answers to that of questions about work history. Some may have finished high school or college, but then something went wrong. Many may not have had good school experiences. Some may not have done well in school or even finished school.

Statistically a disproportionate number of the multi-barriered clients in Vancouver's Downtown Eastside are Aboriginal. Yet a 2006 report (Vancouver School Board, n.d.) about the education of aboriginal youth in the Vancouver school system showed that in "2003/04 the Aboriginal graduation rate was 14% ... compared to the non-Aboriginal rate of 86%." How would a question about educational background be understood by the 86% who did not graduate?

Question: *"What are your skills?"* or *"What are your interests?"*

Typical Answers: *"Nothing." "I don't know." "Not much."*

Since many of these people are dealing with various high levels of dysfunctionality and accompanying low self-esteem, they probably do not see themselves as having anything good in their life such as skills or interests.

We must ask ourselves: *"What do these kinds of questions mean to people whose lives are far from the mainstream?" "What message do these kind of questions send to them?" "What impact would such questions have on them?"*

Since the answers to such questions are all too often *"I dunno"* or *"Not much"* or similar hopeless answers, the workers in these training sessions readily admitted that these kind of questions would discourage rather than encourage their clients. Rather than engaging them in the process, the reality is that these questions would turn them off. Rather than building their self-esteem by reminding them of the good things they have in their life or in their past, such questions would just remind these clients of what they have lost or what they never had. The answers to all these types of questions, unfortunately isn't much more than *"Nothing! Zero!"* Though well intended, such questions just remind these clients that they're *"losers."*

So why ask such questions in the first place? These workers were not trying to give their clients a difficult time. Most had worked for many years in the community and were very committed to it and its people. The last thing they wanted to do was to discourage anyone. So why did they think of these questions to ask? Answer: *"That's all we know about career."*

Challenge of Typical Starting Points

These questions reflect the usual starting points for career in many people's minds. For example, in many government-funded programs, these questions are the usual ones on the computer screens. Also, most resumes reflect these four areas: something on future goals, work history, educational background, and lists of personal strengths.

Let us focus just on the starting points of educational and work background. Many of the tools and processes used in mainstream career counselling are based on people's self perceptions as they review their school and work experiences. This makes sense because these tools and processes have been designed for working people who for one reason or another are changing employment or career directions. These are excellent starting points for people connected to the mainstream world of school or work. But what if their lives have been disconnected from school and/or work?

This disconnection has some serious implications for career counselling. If people feel disconnected from school or work, then they could also feel disconnected from any tools or processes that are based on school and work. The tragedy is that these well-intentioned questions can have the opposite effect on people whose lives, no matter the reason, are disconnected from the mainstream world of school or work. Since these matters are irrelevant to some, when they are asked questions that focus on these matters, not only do they not have a good answer; but also the questions themselves may send a subtle message to people that this is not their world and they don't belong there. They can exclude rather than include. They can create a barrier in the mind of people who feel that they are on the fringe. People may become defensive and disengage further in order to avoid the sense of failure and hopelessness these questions engender. If they can't connect to the tools and processes that are the usual starting points for life/career counselling, if their answers to the typical initial types of questions are negative, it is not hard to see how this might reinforce a sense of hopelessness.

The reasons or causes for a sense of disconnection (real or perceived) with school or work and, therefore, with career are legion and may be centred in people or in practitioners. There may be issues of personality, depression, low self-esteem, past rejections, a sense of failure or shame, sexual abuse, difficulty coping with cultural differences, substance abuse, prejudice, inflexible systems, or negative relationships with those in the counselling or the social work professions. Though the reasons may vary, the effects are often similar.

It is important to note that not everyone is a long way from the traditional world of school and work. It is a spectrum. But it is clear that the further people are from that world, the more potentially challenging is the life/career counselling situation.

This situation has been further exacerbated by a tendency by some to exclude multi-barriered people from career counselling. Over the years we have observed some employment counselling services sending back as many as 75% of people sent to them by government social assistance agencies. The reason was simple. In order to maintain their contracts, they needed to get a certain percentage of people to work within a month or so after the job club ended. The further people were from being quickly employable, the less likely that they would find a job in the allocated time. So they were sent back to the government agency with the label of "unemployable."

Eventually, however, with a shift in economic conditions, there was a shift to getting as many people as possible back to work. Many who were previously viewed as "unemployable" were redefined by governments as "employable." This shift was a challenge for some practitioners because within the previous system, there was no need to develop relevant tools and processes for multi-barriered people. We have talked with many long-term practitioners who feel very tentative about working with such multi-barriered people simply because in the past they just had to send them back as "unemployable." They now are not only lacking in experience but also in actual tools. Fortunately there have been people and organizations that have found creative ways to work with people who are not mainstream. These alternative approaches will increasingly have to become the norm for many life/career counselling situations. More people will need to explore new tools and processes to reach a greater diversity of people.

Need for Alternative Starting Points

If these typical career starting points are irrelevant and/or discouraging to some people, then practitioners must look for alternative starting points. They must engage people where they are engaged in life and work from there. It must be a person-centred process not just a school/work-centred process. One of the goals of *Hope-Filled Engagement* is to suggest some alternative starting points and to encourage the development of new ones. We must develop tools and approaches that from the very start not only provide people with the essentials of life/career guidance but also in the process cultivate hope in people—hope that there is more in their lives than problems; hope that they indeed have been gifted with a richness of potential, that, once discovered and embraced, will enable them to find a meaningful life/career path.

Lack of Positive Focused Self-Reflection

The third fundamental challenge for mainstream career counselling approaches concerns one of the most fundamental skills needed for most career tools and processes: positive focused self-reflection.

Many career tools and processes require a measure of positive focused self-reflection before they can effectively be used. For example, during self-assessment, in order to recognize their assets from a checklist of skills, interests, values, or personality characteristics, people need to have already reflected on their life experiences, observed, and then taken ownership of these traits. Or if they haven't already done so, they need to know how to do this when asked. The completeness or accuracy of people's self perceptions are obviously affected by their ability to do positive focused self-reflection while completing the activity. But how easy is this for most people?

Several years ago, Gray facilitated an activity with 25 young adults from his church. They were a group of typical mainstream young adults. Some were just out of high school; some were in post secondary schooling; some were university or tech school graduates; some were working; some were unemployed. The ages ranged from 18 to 28. The discussion was focused on a question that had been raised by the group: *"Who am I?"*

At the start of the activity, each of them was asked to answer the question, *"Who am I?"* by completing the sentence: *"I am ... "* with as many descriptors as they could think of in five minutes. It was clear that some of them were having a difficult time writing down how they saw themselves.

The person who had the most answers had 25 things listed. However, about ten of the group had less than five answers. When asked why they had a difficult time stating who they were, the first thing they replied was, *"We are not used to thinking about ourselves in this way."* They may have been asking themselves the question about who they were; but they didn't really know how to answer the question. That is why they wanted the discussion in the first place.

To put the challenge into more formal language, they were not used to engaging in positive focused self-reflection. Just asking them to answer the question didn't give them the knowledge or experience necessary to answer it. But this often is the unspoken assumption with such activities.

We have tried different forms of this activity with other groups for many years, and found that many people (young and old, educated and uneducated, male and female, from different cultural groups) have a difficult time answering the question *"Who am I?"* Many reasons are given for this difficulty; but one of the most common is the same as that of these young adults, people often just haven't spent time reflecting on who they are or don't even know how to begin. Let's break this down into its component parts.

Self-reflection

People need to be able to think through their life experiences and reflect on themselves in these experiences. They need to be able to identify their personal characteristics. They need to see what they have done, what they enjoy, how they do things, why they do things, etc. They need to take ownership of what they have in their lives and value what they find. Such reflection does not come automatically for many people. It is something that must be learned, developed, and practised.

Positive

Not only must they be able to see their own personal characteristics but they must also be able to see the positive characteristics, the good things they have in their lives. People's lives are filled with incredible riches but that doesn't mean that people always recognize them. Many do not know how to use positive self-reflection. It is not that they totally lack self-reflection. Tragically it is often the case not that they don't do self-reflection but that the only self-reflection they do has a negative focus. They can't identify what is good in their lives, but they can certainly identify all that they think is not right. Many people find it much easier to talk about their faults and problems than their good points. We have found it amazing how much effort people put into avoiding seeing the positive thing in their lives. One of the goals of *Hope-Filled Engagement* is to present strategies for equipping people with the much-needed skill of being able to do positive self-reflection. We want to show people how to do it, not just ask them to do it.

Focused

Finally, people need to focus on those aspects of their life which are most relevant to the world of learning and work. They need to be able to see things such as their skills, interests, personality characteristics, or values. But many do not even know that they need to look for such things, let alone see them. In other words, we need to explore creative new ways to help people learn what to look for as they reflect on their life experiences.

Positive focused self-reflection is a foundational skill for life/career planning, but it cannot be assumed. In *Hope-Filled Engagement*, we will introduce several strategies that can be used to develop positive focused self-reflection skills as people are working on their life/career journeys.

Enculturated Humility

A fourth challenge that people face in life/career counselling situations is the fact that counselling is often a cross-cultural experience.

In the prior segment, we recounted the story of a discussion with young adults around the question, *"Who am I?"* Many of them found it difficult to answer this question about themselves. The first reason they gave for this was that they were not used to thinking of themselves in these terms. The second reason they gave was that, if they were to answer the question honestly, they would sound like they were arrogant or boastful in some way.

They were referring to a characteristic attributed to some North Americans. One of the strengths/weaknesses of North American culture is the ability of its people to be very forthright in talking about themselves and their perceived strengths. It is not surprising then that mainstream life/career counselling relies heavily on the ability to put oneself forward and to be able to talk openly about oneself and one's strengths. The notion of "selling oneself in the labor market" assumes this ability.

However this strength of being able to put oneself forward and to talk about oneself openly and freely is not culturally appropriate for many people. The basic assumption that, once people recognize personal skills or traits, they can easily talk about it to others is not one that can just be assumed. In many cultures, it is considered inappropriate to talk about yourself in this way, because it is seen as proud, arrogant, or boastful.

People learn from very young ages not to talk about themselves lest they be rejected in some way for being proud. This hesitancy to talk about oneself could be called "enculturated humility."

Even if people exercise positive focused self-reflection, recognize strengths in their lives, and take ownership of these strengths, it does not mean that they will automatically be able to speak openly of these strengths. They may have had a lifetime of experience, telling them that it is improper for them to talk about themselves. They may never have learned the difference between appropriate positive affirmation and inappropriate arrogant boasting. It is not easy for people to overcome such unrecognized cultural conditioning.

In scores of *Guiding Circles* workshops across Canada, we have heard people share stories of having been punished and humiliated because they drew attention to their strengths. Whether it was a verbal put down, a slap, a mouth washed out with soap, the effect was the same; people learned not to talk about themselves. So it is not surprising that, when some people are asked what they're good at in a counselling session, they respond with hesitancy and are unable to clearly talk about their strengths.

Enculturated humility is a characteristic of the Aboriginal subculture and also many faith-based groups. As we have travelled and worked in a number of different countries, we have observed some of the same cultural dynamics that we saw within some subgroups in North America. In Australia, there is the saying that the "tall poppies" should be cut off. In other words, it is better to be average and not stand out in any way. In the Scandinavian countries, there is reference to the "Laws of Jante." In 1933 the Norwegian/Danish writer Aksel Sandemose wrote a novel called *A Refugee Crosses His Tracks*. In his book, he portrays life in an imaginary small town called Jante and sets forth some of the unspoken social and cultural mores which govern how people interact. Though intended to emphasize social equality and fairness to all, it is not hard to see how the Jante Law could become abused and used as an unspoken way to control people and keep them in their place. (Landin, 2008).

The list below is one translation of the 10 laws of Jante:

1. You shall not think that you are special.

2. You shall not think that you are of the same standing as us.

3. You shall not think that you are smarter than us.

4. Don't fancy yourself as being better than us.

5. You shall not think that you know more than us.

6. You shall not think that you are more important than us.

7. You shall not think that you are good at anything.

8. You shall not laugh at us.

9. You shall not think that anyone cares about you.

10. You shall not think that you can teach us anything.

As we have worked with many marginalized people, we have repeatedly heard them say that they're not good at anything or that they don't think they are special or that they don't think anyone cares about them. Perhaps these laws of Jante go far beyond Scandinavia.

Enculturated humility is a very powerful influence and it can be a particularly difficult, yet unrecognized challenge in the context of life/career counselling. It is a subtle barrier to people being able to express clearly who they are whether in the counselling interview or in a job interview.

As life/career practitioners, we need to find ways to assist people to move beyond "enculturated humility" or the life/career journey process may be hindered. It is important to enable people not only to reflect positively on their strengths but also to equip them to be free to express who they are and what they have to offer.

Loss of Hope

When one considers the impact of the previous four challenges (diversity, lack of connection with mainstream school/work, lack of positive focused self-reflection, and enculturated humility) on people, it is not hard to see how the next challenge arises.

- If people were to come into a life/career counselling situation looking for assistance, and then find that they do not understand the language or concepts or the values being used, then what?

- If people were to come into a life/career counselling situation looking for assistance, and then find that the starting points for the help being offered are irrelevant to them in their lives, then what?

- If people were to come into a life/career counselling situation looking for assistance, and then find that they're being asked to do something they don't really know how to do, then what?

- If people were to come into a life/career counselling situation looking for assistance, and then find themselves in the embarrassing place of having to share personal things about themselves, then what?

The responses of people often come across in some form of the following: hesitancy, reluctance and resistance, embarrassment and shyness, or defensiveness. When people feel uncomfortable and possibly even threatened, it is very natural to respond in some of these ways. In order to protect themselves, they raise barriers of various kinds to resist the very process which is intended to help them. The practitioner then tries to apply some strategies to overcome people's reluctance. Used appropriately, these strategies may be quite effective but tragically sometimes people just become more resistant. The unfortunate thing is that while these tools and processes are intended to draw people in, they may do exactly the opposite and result in people putting up additional barriers to protect themselves.

The point is that people may not see the process as helping. Perhaps there is more at work here, and there may be value in approaching the situation from other perspectives. It may be that people are not so much reluctant as experiencing feelings of hopelessness.

Perhaps the most crippling challenge of all is the perspective of *"What's the use!"* If people do not see any hope of things ever changing, they will act accordingly. *"What is the point of trying at all?"* To do so is just to try and fail again. Nobody wants to fail, but the perverseness of hopelessness is such that people may passively fail to avoid trying and then failing again.

Hopelessness is truly inclusive; it can affect anyone, no matter the age, gender, race, religion, or socio-economic status. It can creep up on you or slam you in the face. It takes many forms and is like a weed—it will take root and thrive in almost any environment. There are numerous factors which are especially conducive to hopelessness:

- **Internal Environment:** fear, failure, fatigue, personal flaws, broken dreams, low self-esteem, health issues, bad choices, bad habits, lack of self-knowledge, disabilities, inappropriate assumptions, busyness, lack of resources, inertia, depression.

- **External Environment:** imperfect, changing chaotic world, racism, status quo, abuse, misleading myths, overwhelming responsibilities, negative paradigms, family issues, disconnectedness, lack of role models, sexism, prejudice, others' words and actions, socio-economic issues, inappropriate help, exclusive structures, tools, and processes.

We have all encountered or possibly even experienced hopelessness ourselves. The problem is not when there are isolated incidences of hopelessness that pass through our life but rather when hopelessness settles down and takes up residence. It may settle down slowly and then take over or it may be a quick emotional coup.

A look at some of the synonyms of hopelessness reminds us of the impact that hopelessness can have upon a life or lives (Hopelessness, n.d.):

> at one's last gasp, beyond remedy, broken, despairing,
> forlorn, given over, given up, hopeless, ill, impracticable, in
> despair, inauspicious, inconsolable, incorrigible, incurable,
> irreclaimable, irrecoverable, irredeemable, irremediable,
> irreparable, irretrievable, irreversible, irrevocable, not to
> be thought of, out of the question, past cure, past hope,
> past mending, past recall, remediless, ruined, threatening,
> undone, unpromising, unpropitious, pessimistic, cynical,
> dejected, in despair, despondent, gloomy

It has been said that there's no such thing as a perpetual motion machine, but hopelessness can be an extremely powerful perpetual motion emotion. Once hopelessness takes root, it is often tenacious, debilitating, and contagious. Hopelessness can go on and on, even from generation to generation. It seems to have the ability to feed upon itself and even to twist and distort any help given in such a way that it can feed off it as well. It is like a black hole that sucks the life out of a person.

The effects of hopelessness in individuals and groups are legion:

- it drains meaning and purpose;

- it blocks creativity and obscures options, possibilities, or choices;

- it dominates thinking;

- it distorts reality and perceptions;

- it masquerades as truth and insight:

- it cultivates a victim mentality that can be defensive and contrary;

- it destroys motivation to try to start;

- it gives up, sometimes even to the point of suicide;

- it robs people of their future.

It is a challenge to help people in the grips of hopelessness. It is even more challenging if the very tools and processes that are intended to help instead exasperate a sense of failure. If the help offered fails, then where is the hope? If they cannot start at the starting points presented to them, then it's easy to come to the conclusion that the life/career counselling can't really help at all. Many a practitioner has led people to water, but hopelessness has kept them from drinking.

But hopelessness is not hopeless. In fact, when looked at from the proper perspective, it can be the starting point for hope.

> At the heart of despair is a sense of isolation, impotence, and an immutable future, and yet it may give rise to new purpose or a new understanding and acceptance of life with its possibilities and limitations. (Beck, et al, 2003, p. 339)

We believe that it is possible to challenge the tyranny of hopelessness. We believe that people have been created to be people of hope. It may be very difficult to see hope in some lives; it may be hidden beneath layers upon layers of hopelessness laid over the years, as if they were layers of wallpaper or paint. But it is there. One just has to look at young children to see that hope is a gift given to us at birth. Hopelessness is fundamentally the "loss of hope"; and in order to lose it, you have to have had it in the first place; and if you have had it, you can have it again.

Hopelessness may be contagious, but hope is infectious. Sometimes we are so focused on hopelessness that we lose sight of hope. It is important to intentionally focus on hope and ask some basic questions: *"What kind of environment encourages hope to take root, to grow, to flourish, and to bear fruit? "What kind of an approach do we need?"*

If we are going to address the issue of hopelessness in the life/career context, we must consider several aspects:

- We need an approach that knows how to reignite hope and then how to keep it burning in people's live.

- We need a "subversive" approach that enables people to be surprised by hope before hopelessness has a chance to rear its ugly head.

- We need an approach that is acutely sensitive to the words, actions, structures, or attitudes that could possibly trigger defensive mechanisms maintained by hopelessness.

- We need an approach that is more than merely thinking positive thoughts without substance. Our approach must be realistic. It cannot be based on self-defeating myths or feel good cliches which just set people up for more failure. We need a process that provides people with a basis for their hope. A process that helps people see that each thing they have been richly gifted with is a starting point for hope.

- We need an approach that is inclusive, that does not in any way unintentionally exclude people because they do not meet some unspoken assumption or convention. An approach that is people-centered, that works with them where they are and not where someone or some system thinks they ought to be. Finally it is must be seen as doable by the people who are being helped by it.

It is our intention that *Hope-Filled Engagement* will reflect such an approach and will stimulate the development of other tools and processes in the years to come. Our intent is not only to provide some new tools and processes, but also to stimulate your own thinking in this area. How can you create a counselling environment that is more inclusive, holistic, balanced, mattering, positive, spiritual, realistic, simple, engaging, creative, imaginative, and flexible?

In all of our years involved with life/career counselling, we have met many who have been able to be agents of hope in situations that seemed hopeless. We wish to build on this rich heritage.

chapter three

KEY THEMES

Diversity, Assumptions & Conventions

Active Engagement (Amundson, 2009) encourages the critical examination of the assumptions, conventions and traditions associated with life/career counselling.

Having assumptions or conventions is not the problem—having unrecognized assumptions or conventions may be. Not all assumptions and conventions need to be changed, but we do need to be aware why we are making the choices we are making and the impact of these choices on our counselling effectiveness.

The issue of assumptions and conventions becomes even more critical when we consider the diversity challenge previously discussed. More and more people don't fit the profile of the classic mainstream client or student. Therefore, we can no longer assume that people before us will fit any standard profile. An important part of a positive working relationship with people is that we need to be informed about them and be able to use tools and processes which will be most effective with them. The more diversity we work with, the more we will need to diversify our concepts, tools, and processes. In order to do this, we will need to be more intentional in examining our assumptions and conventions.

The very concept of multi-barriered people assumes that there are challenges to bypass. Some are centred in people themselves. Some are centred in matters outside their control. Some of these may be centred in the assumptions and conventions of ourselves as life/career practitioners.

Remember that many elements of career counselling are based on a North American business model which may not be understood or valued by some people. The tools and processes in the mainstream are very effective with people who come from that world but not necessarily so for others, such as many Aboriginal peoples or immigrants. Assumptions and conventions either support or inhibit the counselling process.

The issue of assumptions and conventions is a particularly challenging one to address, because they are so often unspoken, if not completely unrecognized. We may have learned them through very conscious formal training, but we are just as likely to have learned some of them unconsciously through informal means.

The failure to recognize this can potentially have a very negative impact on the effectiveness of our counselling relationships with people. It is easy to fall into the trap of unconsciously thinking that we could work with people if only they looked like "[fill in with whatever profile we feel comfortable with]." When this type of thinking is present, it is easy to think that people need to change before we can work with them. We, in effect, believe that the problem is always the people—*"if only, they'd …, then we could …"*

Such an attitude may quickly trigger the kind of defensive barriers discussed in the last chapter. This can be minimized by using language, tools, and processes designed to bypass possible barriers, designed to surprise people before they put up defenses.

The reality is that increasingly we are working with people who don't look like [a specific profile], and it is we who may need to change first in order for us to be able to work effectively with them.

We must not only have self-awareness but also tools/process awareness. If we use a particular tool or process, we need to exercise critical reflection on that tool or process. It would be helpful to ask questions such as,

- *"Who designed this tool or process?"*

- *"Who was this tool or process designed for?"*

- *"What assumptions does this particular tool or process reflect? What does a person need to know in order to use this effectively?"*

- *"What message will this tool or process send to someone who is from a completely different background than those for whom it was designed?"*

- *"In what context did I learn this tool or process? When and where have I used it in the past? Are the circumstances different with the current people I'm working with than with those in the past?"*

- *"Is it the appropriate tool or process for this person?"*

Let's consider one example of how unrecognized assumptions and conventions could result in communication that is exactly the opposite of what was intended and, thereby, raise unnecessary barriers.

A few years ago in a workshop Gray was facilitating with teachers, one of them defined the concept of a "skill" as a *"strength or something someone is good at."* This is a popular understanding of what a skill is; one that we use at times. But what does this really say to those who hear this definition? Does everyone hear the same thing?

Gray drew a scale from 0-100% and wrote the word "skill" near the top of the scale. He asked the group to state at what point on this scale does someone become "good at something." The teacher responded by saying 75%, because in her province the education ministry tells parents that if their child gets 75% or above, they can succeed in that area. Gray then drew a line under the word "skill" at 75%.

But this understanding of skill raises a serious question, *"If a skill is something between 75 and 100, then what is everything in the range of 0-74%?"*

Obviously if the skill is above 75 then everything below 75 must not be a skill; it could be interpreted as a big "zero." While no teacher or school board would ever want students to believe that they have no skills, the assumption or convention that a skill is "a strength, something someone is good at" unintentionally may send the message that those whose grades under 75% have in fact no skills. It is no wonder that many students and adults who have struggled in school will state that they have no skills, when they're asked about them.

But this definition really does not define what a skill is. A "skill" is something that a person can do no matter how well. A "strength" refers to how well a person does it. So in fact there is a confusion between recognizing a skill and determining at what level a person uses that skill.

Furthermore there is another more subtle assumption in this misleading definition. There is the assumption that all skills need to be expressed at a high level of competency in order for success to occur. But in many work situations, many skills are employed which do not require a high level of competency.

We use an image from the world of music to illustrate this. The digital bars that bounce up and down in the front of an amplifier reflect the different levels of sound related to the music. If we were to adjust the system so that all these levels were raised up to 100%, we would no longer have music; we would have noise. If we were to screen out all those sounds that didn't meet a certain level, we would certainly lose the melody. It is precisely the different levels and types of sounds arranged together that produces a melody.

Each person has a melody of skills at any time in their life. Some skills will be highly developed; others less; others somewhere between the two. An accurate and complete picture of each person must include the entire melody not just the skills that are high. The skills that are lower are just as much a part of a person's melody as the high ones and thus are capable of being used. To cancel out skills as irrelevant because they are too low runs the danger of leaving out important aspects of a person's identity. To be true to a person, we must recognize all of the skills and how they interplay with each other.

The same is true for jobs; each job has its own melody of requirements and expectations. Some skills need to be more highly developed than others; but all may be needed no matter the level.

This means that no person ever needs to be left with the impression that they have no skills, because they have not met some arbitrary standard. Rather, people should be encouraged to recognize and value all their skills no matter whether they are high or low. The task is to help people discover where their unique melodies fit into life/work.

Examining assumptions and conventions is not a one-time activity. It is a continuous process that involves reflecting on and knowing ourselves; the people we work with; the world in which we both live and work; and the language, tools, and processes we use and the assumptions and conventions behind them.

It is not enough just to be aware of our assumptions and conventions. In order to be effective, we need to embrace life-long learning and develop increasing creativity, flexibility, and adaptability in our assumptions and conventions. We need to develop a wide range of concepts, tools, and processes. We need to be able to put ourselves in the place of others, in their skin so to speak—to see, hear, and feel what they see, hear, and feel.

Active Engagement

Active Engagement (Amundson, 2009) emphasizes the need for both life/career practitioners and the people they work with to be actively engaged in the life/career process. This is especially important when either find themselves stuck in a "crisis of imagination." They cannot see the situation other than the way they see it currently and so believe that the situation is hopeless. It is no surprise, therefore, that active engagement is one of the foundational themes of *Hope-Filled Engagement*.

When we consider the challenges set forth in the previous chapter, the need for active engagement is greater than ever. As we have already mentioned, it is easy for people to respond defensively in the context of a counselling process they do not understand, do not relate to, do not value, and especially do not see as having any hope. If people are stuck when they came into such a situation, it is possible that they will be even more stuck when they come out. Every time they try something new that does not work, their hopelessness deepens.

There is truth in the old saying *"you can lead a horse to water, but you can't make it drink."* When people feel hopeless, it is difficult for them to "drink the water" that life/career practitioners are offering. We cannot make people drink when they do not want to drink. We cannot directly change peoples' past experiences, present circumstances, or their attitudes towards themselves. But we can develop an environment in which it is easier for people to engage.

In *Hope-Filled Engagement,* we will explore further implications and applications of the key principles set forth in *Active Engagement*. These include an emphasis on imagination, creativity, and flexibility; a more active communications approach; a person-centered, cognitive behavioral approach; mattering; the backswing; a solution-focused, strength-based approach—all in the context of a dynamic helping relationship.

The basic principle of the Active Engagement model is that it is important to ensure that both people and their helper are actively and creatively engaged in the entire process. Though it may be expressed in diverse ways depending upon the situation, such an approach always calls for the questions, *"How are people being engaged in this process? How am I and my organization engaged?"*

In particular, throughout *Hope-Filled Engagement*, we will be exploring the key principle that it is essential to engage people where they are engaged in life—that is, finding the right starting points to begin the life/career counselling journey with people.

For example if people are struggling with life issues, they may be focusing on the mess that their life is in. But when asked to talk about their favourite things, they are reminded that there is probably more to their lives than their problems or failures. If they are really engaged in education or work, they will bring it up. If not, then these types of issues can be probed once a good working relationship is established and they have become engaged and committed to the process.

Such life-oriented activities can be non-threatening ways to start thinking of life. Such an approach also reflects a fundamental principle of learning: people learn by connecting the unknown to the known. By drawing out what people understand on any particular concept or activity, they will be better able to link all the new things that they will discover about themselves and the world of work.

They are also effective in developing meaningful relationships between people and life/career practitioners. We are asking them to let us into their lives so we should start where they are living. We need to go where they are and not just expect them to come to where we are. As we find common points to connect life to life with people, it will be easier for them to trust us as we seek to bring them into a more effective relationship with the world of education and work that we represent.

One other aspect of active engagement that we wish to emphasize is the need to recognize the connection between diversity and active engagement. The type of diversity that we discussed earlier calls for a diversity in terms of the tools and processes being used with people. The most effective starting points in their lives will be reflected in their diversity.

For example, consider the diversity of learning styles. Initial starting points for engagement might be radically different depending upon whether one is working with people who are visual learners or auditory learners or hands-on learners or book learners.

As you read the different concepts, tools, and processes set forth in *Hope-Filled Engagement*, take some time to reflect how each uses the active engagement of both people and practitioners to cultivate an atmosphere of hope.

Mattering

Another essential theme of *Hope-Filled Engagement* is that of developing a "mattering climate" in which people feel that they matter. This may be cultivated in many practical ways, such as the choosing of activities, the attitudes of practitioners, the way they address people, and the atmosphere they create in the counselling room.

Mattering addresses the issue of exclusion. The feeling of being excluded can contribute greatly to a sense of hopelessness. When people feel excluded because they do not fit into preconceived ideas of who or what they ought to be or be able to do, we may be sending a message that we do not value who they are. If we don't value who they are, then why should they? This creates a context, which affects people's self-esteem and the counselling relationship itself. A sense of rejection evokes rejection back—a cycle that can be very self-perpetuating.

> When people feel that they matter, they feel better about themselves, they feel connected, and their sense of human agency is enhanced ... When people feel that they do not matter their interpersonal connections are weakened and usually there is also some form of withdrawal and lowering of self-confidence. (Amundson, 2009, p. 43)

Mattering addresses the challenges set forth in the previous chapter. Lack of recognition of the issues related to diversity and disconnection can result in people feeling like they don't fit and, therefore, that they don't matter. This can result in people struggling with any sense of motivation. If there is no point, if it doesn't matter, why try?

Mattering addresses directly the nineth law of Jante that states you should not think that anyone cares about you. When we extend mattering to people, we demonstrate that we care. We care because we see value in their lives and the potential within them. They may not know how to do positive focused self-reflection, but we do. We see for them and show them how to see the good in their lives and how to value it.

One of the tragedies of enculturated humility is that it sometimes goes way beyond controlling inappropriate pride and arrogance to erasing people altogether. People may lack arrogant pride but they may also lack self-affirming pride so necessary to a healthy sense of identity.

A sense of mattering is directly related to one's level of hope. If people feel that they do not matter to anyone, including themselves, then that leads to thinking that there is no point to their life—that is no hope,

Mattering occurs at many levels (Amundson, 2009, pp. 43-44), which are important for people who have multiple barriers. For example:

1. **Visibility: recognizing their presence and ensuring they feel welcome.**

When people have been in "the system" for a long time, they sometimes begin to feel invisible. Just a "number" to be processed. This can be exacerbated, when practitioners struggle with an excessive work load that they feel they have to "plow" through. Taking some time just to recognize people and create some common ground as a foundation for a good working relationship speaks loudly that they matter.

2. **Valuing: listening to people and showing that they are important.**

It is important to actively listen to people, to hear their stories. It is even more important to take the time to demonstrate to people that their stories contain value whether or not they are related to the mainstream world of education or work.

We need to offer people the opportunity to assume more responsibility in the counselling relationship so that there is a rebuilding of their self-confidence. As practitioners assist people to tell their stories and to reflect on their stories, people will be able to see what they have in their lives from new perspectives. The *Hope-Filled Engagement* approach is a strength-based approach, designed to draw out that which is positive in lives rather than focus on what is wrong. There will be a time to identify what needs to be fixed; but by first identifying that which is positive, it will be easier to deal with problems later. Finding these positive things will show the areas where people are doing things "right." Using strategies such as "strength challenge," practitioners can show people that they do have positive traits to contribute in the counselling relationship itself and in the world of education and work.

3. **Establishment of a personal as well as professional relationship with their practitioner – connecting at a level of personal caring that involves empathy, genuineness, unconditional positive regard, and flexibility.**

People may come across as reluctant at different times. Don't jump to conclusions as to the reason for this reluctance. Not all reluctance is the same. It may be that they are being inappropriately resistant, but there may be many other reasons as well.

It may be that they are not ready, because some life issues need to be addressed first. If this is the case, you may need to refer them to more appropriate help if possible. Some are reluctant simply because they feel intimidated by the counselling process itself. They may not understand the process or the language or the values. Be empathic and remember that career counselling is a cross-cultural activity for many.

Reassure people by encouraging them that you will work with them to find a process that will work for them and that will equip them with the attitudes, perspectives, and skills needed for their life/career journey.

Throughout *Hope-Filled Engagement*, you will find concepts, approaches, and activities, which can be used to demonstrate mattering to people. As people learn to accept that they do matter, a firm foundation for hope is being established.

The Backswing

Another key theme is the "backswing." This metaphor, introduced in *Physics of Living* (Amundson, 2003), refers to the principle that often we need to go backwards before we go forward. Whether swinging a hammer, using a broom, or hitting a ball, some form of backswing is needed.

In workshops, we sometimes demonstrate this concept by using the image of hitting a home run. A piece of paper crumpled up into a ball represents life's opportunities. A participant is asked to be the pitcher; the facilitator is the batter, and a workbook is the bat. The facilitator holds the bat at chest level. When the ball (an opportunity) is thrown towards the bat, the ideal would be to hit a home run. This represents making the most of an opportunity that comes our way. The facilitator asks the pitcher to throw the ball at the workbook; and, each time the ball is thrown, the facilitator does something different with the workbook.

The first throw, the facilitator moves the bat out of the way of the ball and lets the ball hit his/her chest and fall to the ground. This represents people actively avoiding an opportunity. On the second throw, the facilitator lets the ball hit the workbook but does not move the bat and the ball again falls to the floor. This represents passivity and still no home run. The third time the ball is thrown, the facilitator hits the ball with a half-hearted bunt. There is some forward movement here, but it is limited. Again there is no home run. Finally, the facilitator takes a full swing at the ball and hits the ball across the room. *"Why was there a home run this time?"* Answer—the backswing. It provided power, momentum, direction, and control. These are all necessary to hit a home run.

The backswing enables people to be equipped and to be ready to make the most of the opportunities that come their way. This requires taking the time and effort to learn necessary skills or knowledge, to deal with any barriers to moving ahead, and to be actively doing what needs to be done when the opportunity comes. When people take the time to be prepared, they are much more likely to be able to hit the home run. Of course, people have to avoid the opposite problem of people who spend their lives indefinitely preparing for life but never living it. A good backswing is short, focused, and has release and follow-through.

This concept is important for both practitioners and the people they work with. People often want to move ahead but do not wish to take the time to make themselves ready to do that effectively. People may say, "*I don't have time to take a three week self-assessment program. I need a job right now.*" But when asked how long they have been unemployed, they may respond, "*Five years. That's why I need a job right now.*" If people have been unemployed for this length of time, it is likely that they may have been pursuing employment in an ineffective manner. It would be worthwhile to take the time to equip themselves so that, when they start to look for work again, they will be more effective.

Practitioners sometimes are under pressure to move people along and so they push people beyond their readiness level. While this might result in some activity, it often serves only to make a situation worse. Practitioners may also need their own backswing. As we have already discussed, assumptions and conventions may need to be examined; new tools and processes may need to be acquired. Instead of pushing people to take the next step, it is important that practitioners take the time and energy to better understand them. Practitioners must ask themselves questions, such as "*What does this person need to know or be able to do in order to move ahead?*", "*Are there any self-defeating perspectives which are feeding a spirit of hopelessness that need to be addressed?*", and "*What do I need to do in order to help this person be ready for the next steps?*"

Hope-Filled Engagement activities often involve some form of the backswing for both parties involved in the helping relationship. When practitioners tell us that they don't have time for the backswing, we answer, "*You don't have time not to do the backswing.*" When time is short, effective preparedness is even more important.

Holistic Life/Career Counselling

The theme of holistic life/career counselling is getting increasing attention. Writers such as Donald Super have argued that career is much more than a job; it is the sum total of all life roles (1990, 1992). Issues related to life balance and its impact on such matters as retention have resulted in holistic perspectives being explored with more regularity.

As we have discussed, life/career counselling has traditionally come from a North American business perspective. Unfortunately, North American business has not been known for its emphasis on holistic life/career issues, although this is changing in some areas. There is value in looking at life/career counselling from other cultural perspectives which reflect much more of a holistic approach, such as traditional Aboriginal views.

There are no simple answers to crafting a life/career but there are concepts and approaches which may help. The "circle" is one such concept; it is a unifying metaphor which can inform the life/career journey. Metaphors are important. It is often said that a picture is worth a thousand words; and a metaphor is a picture.

The "circle" is a natural metaphor, a culturally significant image for many peoples (including many Aboriginals), which conveys much about the concepts, feelings, and perspectives that should undergird holistic life/career counselling. *"When you think of the concept of a "circle," what thoughts and feelings come to mind for you?" "What do you think it would evoke in the people you work with?"*

In our workshops, practitioners usually answer with ideas such as cycles of life, seasons, wholeness, unity, balance, wellness, connectedness, community, continuity, centredness, equality, respect, and participation. Concepts such as these should inform the entire life/career counselling process. These concepts inform the themes and activities in *Hope-Filled Engagement*.

The "circle" ought to encourage us to keep the big picture in view. The "circle" reminds us that people's life/career paths aren't linear but circular. Career is not a destination but a journey. The goal ought to be not just the next job, but an understanding of ourselves that will enable us to discover and follow life/career paths that will help lead to a whole life, a balanced life that will promote health and well-being for ourselves and our communities.

Holistic life/career counselling recognizes diversity and encourages mattering and active engagement. It reminds us that we are not alone, that we are part of broader family and community. It encourages us to connect with our world at many levels and to embrace the privileges and responsibilities that come with these connections. It takes seriously the issues related to the life/career journey, as we go through the different stages of life or as we travel along a path of multiple career possibilities and work situations.

Career Integrity

A theme closely related to holistic life/career counselling is career integrity. It addresses the issue of how to be true to oneself in the midst of a chaotic world of work in which things are often less than ideal.

During a workshop with some Aboriginal people in Alice Springs, Northern Territories, Australia, some of the workshop participants talked about their work opportunities in Alice Springs. The local Aboriginals had used money from land claims settlements to purchase one of the two malls in Alice Springs. Although they owned the mall, none of them worked there. When asked why not, the response was that those jobs were "shame" jobs. After some discussion, it became clear what they meant. They had very little exposure to mainstream western work contexts. Their skills and life experience were related to living off the land. As a result, the only jobs available to them in the mall were very menial jobs cleaning up after the "white" people. Because of past experiences, they were very sensitive to being put back into menial subservient positions. Therefore, they perceived such jobs as shameful.

> *If you have integrity,*
> *nothing else matters.*
> *If you don't have integrity,*
> *nothing else matters.*
> - Alan Simpson

When a job appears to have little perceived status or value, it is easy to understand how people can feel that they have little status or value. Yet, there is a subtle trap here, that of equating who they are, their identity, with the work they are doing.

This is a particular struggle for people who, because of life circumstances, may not have many career possibilities before them. For many reasons, people's ideal jobs may just not be available to them. *"If people take less than ideal jobs, are they then "failures"? Are they not being true to themselves?"*

This is even more difficult for people who have grown up in situations where there has not been a history of meaningful work experiences. There are people who, in order to move themselves and their families ahead, must blaze the trail by taking less than ideal work in order to open the door for others to follow after them. Such "trailblazers" sometimes find resistance not only from the mainstream but also from their own people. They work hard to improve their life situation but may then be criticized by people within their own community for doing so.

Gray's mother, for example, had only a grade 6 education and no formal work experience. She saw herself as someone without much value in the world of work; but when her youngest child went to school, she decided to work in order to provide for the financial needs of the family. She also wanted to demonstrate that one could work steadily and break free from the type of family dysfunctionality that she had experienced. The only thing she thought she could do was laundry, so she took a job in a laundry and worked there until her retirement. This was far from being an ideal job for her; intellectually she was a very bright woman and an avid learner; physically she struggled with arthritis, which was aggravated by the humidity in the laundry; and socially she often felt belittled in her job.

> *A little integrity is better than any career.*
> - Ralph Waldo Emerson

But there was no "shame" in what she did. *"Was it shameful that she wanted to provide for her family? Was it shameful that she wanted to show a different way to her children? Was she not true to herself?"* An emphatic *"NO!"* to all of these. She was very true to who she was and broke trail for all her five children, all of whom went on to work in the mainstream. She sacrificed so they might have the opportunity to live better than she had.

It is this kind of career integrity that we need to encourage more in our times. It is something important for all who struggle with being unemployed or underemployed, who struggle with their sense of value because they don't perceive their work as being what it should be. This can be a struggle no matter what social economic class people come from. It is also something that many practitioners struggle with, when, because of life's realities and limited circumstances, they have to encourage people to take jobs which are less than ideal. They know that this is the best thing, but it can still be very frustrating as they empathize with those they counsel.

So the question must be answered: *"What is career integrity and how does one live it?"* We must start by defining what we mean by "career" and by "integrity."

We understand career to be more than a succession of jobs; career is the sum total of all of life's roles. If this is true, then career integrity is found not only in formal jobs but also in all of the various other life roles.

The word "integrity" is derived from the word "integer," a complete entity that is derived from a Latin word meaning "undivided" or "whole." The verb "to integrate," derived from the same Latin word, means to bring together into a unified whole. It is not surprising then that the word "integrity" refers to the state or quality of being whole or complete.

So what is "career integrity"? We would like to suggest the following understanding of career integrity:

> Career integrity involves a life/work balance in which people can live and work in a manner consistent with who they are, with what is most important to them and with a sense of hope.

Before we explore this further, we should consider the question, *"Is career integrity even possible today?"* We sometimes ask practitioners if they know of people they believe demonstrate career integrity in their lives. We ask them to identify personal characteristics they see in these lives that reflect career integrity. The answers are usually very similar: honest, open, humble, focused, knows what is important, can say *"no,"* generous, balanced, happy, sincere, and consistent. No one ever states that the personal characteristic they remember is related to a particular job or education that they have or to their power or socio-economic status. It always has to do with personal traits and values possessed by people. Such people demonstrate that career integrity is indeed possible.

> ### *This above all;*
> ### *to thine own self be true.*
> \- William Shakespeare
>
> ### *Don't compromise yourself.*
> ### *It's all you've got.*
> \- Janis Joplin

However one difficulty in discussing career integrity is the confusing messages in popular media today about what it means to be true to one's self. There is an overemphasis today on certain life/career myths:

- **Find your passion and follow it:** Passion is significant but it is not the only key factor to consider.

- **You can be whatever you want to be:** This greatly overstates the challenge for people to do the best they can in their circumstances. It is blatantly untrue because everyone has limitations of one sort or another.

- **You can have it all, and you can have it all NOW:** This encourages unrealistic consumerism and breeds an impatience that causes people to try to rush life's journey like the proverbial donkey trotting after the carrot on a stick.

All of these myths may set people up for unrealistic expectations and for failure. They imply that in order to be true to yourself, you must find that "ideal job" which will fulfill all your passion and provide you with everything you want in life. This does not match life reality for many people. *"What happens if circumstances beyond a person's control (such as sickness, disabilities, racism, labour market conditions, political instability, family needs, etc.) make it impossible for them to get the ideal job? If people don't get those ideal jobs, does that mean they lack career integrity and are failures?"*

Another potential confusion is misunderstanding about a concept often used as a means to help people understand the connection between self-assessment and career exploration: "who I am" points to "what I can do." This is a good fundamental principle if used with discernment; but there is the danger that when it is used in isolation then career integrity may be reduced to nothing more than the "ideal job." *"What about people who are not able to access their 'ideal job'?" "Does 'what I do' automatically define 'who I am'?"* The answer is clearly *"no."*

> *Every job is a self-portrait of the person who does it. Autograph your work with excellence.*
> - Author Unknown

"Who I am" also points to other aspects of a person such as "why I do what I do" and "how I do what I do." Career integrity often is found in being true to oneself in these areas. People may have an "ideal job" but if they are doing it with the wrong motivation or in the wrong manner, then career integrity is lost. Yet people may have jobs that are far less than ideal but do it in such as way as to remain true to themselves.

Perhaps it is more correct to say that we should strive to find our passions and then find ways to express them throughout the different spheres of our lives, no matter the circumstances.

What if finding career integrity is related not so much to the "ideal job" as it is to the intentional choice to know oneself and to find creative ways to express the "real self" in all of the various life roles? This opens up career integrity to everyone. This means that people may be unemployed or underemployed and still live with a sense of career integrity that enables them to live with a measure of dignity.

This does not mean that there are not real challenges to cultivating career integrity in our lives. Some are personal and others are more external. First of all, in order to be true to ourselves, we must first know ourselves. Second, while seeking to sort out our lives, we often struggle with conflicting values, with many voices telling us what is important. We can become confused by the clutter and lose our way. Third, fear may be an issue. Parker Palmer (1998, 2000) suggests that in order to achieve integrity in work, it is necessary to bring yourself to it; you, therefore, become vulnerable because criticisms of your work can easily be seen as criticisms of you. In order to avoid such vulnerability, people put on masks to protect themselves, but this can become a trap in which they lose sight of who they really are. Finally, cultivating career integrity faces the challenge of trying to sort out who we are and living accordingly in the midst of an imperfect, every-changing, and increasingly imperfect world.

> *If a man is called to be a street sweeper, he should sweep streets even as Michelangelo painted, or Beethoven composed music, or Shakespeare wrote poetry.*
> *He should sweep streets so well that the host of heaven and earth will pause to say, here lived a great street sweeper who did his job well.*
> - Martin Luther King, Jr.

Let us suggest a tentative model for what is involved in a life/career counselling approach that promotes career integrity. There is a need for further development in this area. What are some of the key concepts to consider when seeking to cultivate career integrity?

There are three essential pillars in our career integrity approach (Figure 1: Career Integrity Model):

1. **Self-discovery** (*Who am I?*) is important because, unless people know who they are, it is hard to be true to themselves. The discovery process must enable people to self-discover in order that they can ownership of and value their true identity.

2. **Values** (*What do I really want?*) is important because not everything that people discover is of equal value, and so they must discern what is most important to them. A clear knowledge of values will promote motivation and wise life choices.

Figure 1: Career Integrity Model

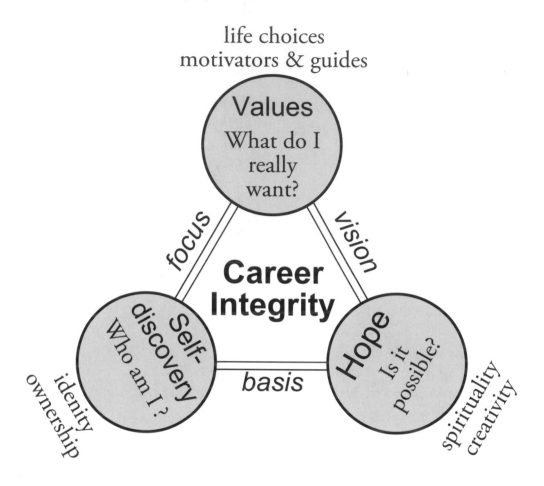

3. **Hope** (*Is it possible?*) is important because, without a sense of hope that it is indeed possible to be true to oneself, hopelessness will trap people into thinking either that they have to fake their way through life in some way or that there is no point in trying in the first place. But hope grounded in spirituality and creativity believes that things are possible and, therefore, worth trying for.

These three pillars are closely interconnected and support each other. Values provide needed focus to self-discovery. Hope provides life-giving vision to values. And self-discovery gives a basis for hope. All of the personal assets people discover in their lives point to hope; if it is there, then it is possible to express it in someway.

Throughout *Hope-Filled Engagement,* we intend to explore concepts, tools, and processes which will reflect these three pillars (self-discovery, values, and hope). These concepts are relevant both for people and for the practitioners who work with them.

Values

Values are one of the central pillars of career integrity. In today's changing chaotic world, it is increasing difficult to sort out values and to live consistently with them. In light of this, values may need to be given even more attention in life/career counselling contexts than ever before.

At one level, the concept of values is simple. Values answer the question *"WHY? What is important to us in our lives?"* The ideal is to find a balance of all our values in life and to find means of fulfilling or expressing them whether it be in paid work or in other life activities.

At another level, values are very profound and challenging. They are an essential element of people's life/career journeys, especially for practitioners who are concerned not just with getting people into jobs but also with work maintenance. People sometimes take jobs because the opportunity arises or it is something they think they can do or enjoy. They speak of the new job as if it were the greatest thing. But then these same people, when talking of the job in a few weeks or months time, see it as "the job from hell." This turn around often revolves around value issues; some value is violated and people struggle in contexts where their values are not upheld.

Values perform two essential roles for people as they walk their life/career journeys. First, they motivate people; when people value something, it ought to motivate them to start moving towards it. Then, once people are motivated and start moving, values guide people as they make life/career choices along their journey (Amundson & Poehnell, 2004). If people are unclear about their values or how to express their values, then motivation and life/career choices may be compromised.

When people violate their values, they usually struggle with guilt and/ or anger; this further compromises their motivations and choices. They may struggle with fragmentation, inconsistency, overload, frustration, and more. This can become a vicious cycle that traps people.

Challenge of Values

Though values play such a defining role in people's attitudes and actions, they are often unrecognized, inconsistent, conflicting, and unrealized. Life/career practitioners and the people they work with both face several common challenges when they attempt to work with values.

- **Different definitions**

One challenge is that there are many different definitions as to what a value is. Some use a very broad definition and include anything a person thinks is important in life. Others see values as narrower and would say that something is a true value only if it is acted upon.

- **Lack of self-knowledge**

Discovering values can be a challenge simply because people may not know what values are, let alone what their personal values are. Many people have not developed the life skill of intentional positive focused self-reflection; as a result they are often unaware of their own values. After a discussion on values in a workshop, one practitioner came back quite shocked. She had gone home and talked about the discussion with her daughter who was going through some problems while attending university. The practitioner was absolutely stunned when her daughter told her that she had never heard of the idea of values before and thought they sounded like a good idea. Some people are unaware of their values simply because of the lack of positive focused self-reflection discussed earlier, others because of more systemic issues. For example, exploring values with Aboriginals in Canada can be even more challenging for some because of historical issues.

As a result of the process of forcible assimilation of
Aboriginal people, it has become difficult to connect with
traditional family, community, and cultural values. Not
knowing how to connect with values and meaning or not
having the strength to reconnect causes anxiety. Although
anxiety can lead to constructive action to seek out meaning,
too often it is dealt with in a negative way, such as through
substance abuse, suicide, or other self-destructive behaviors.
(McCormick & Amundson, 1997, pp. 171-79)

- **Dynamic**

Another challenge is the dynamic nature of values; they can evolve
with time and changing circumstances. What people value at 20 years of
age may be quite different from what they value at 30, 40, 50, 60, or older.

- **Different, often conflicting, sources**

Some experience "values clutter"; through life's experiences they
consciously or unconsciously acquire a "clutter" of differing values from
many different sources. These values can be inconsistent with one another
and result in fundamental values conflicts that can seriously inhibit
people's ability to realize their values. People can get "stuck" because they
lose the ability to decide what really is important and how to choose it.

Chang and Jun (n.d.) state that though the conflict of values has
been a challenge throughout human history, it is becoming an increasing
challenge in our modern culture. When one considers values in light of the
Connections Circle discussed in Chapter 5, the reason for this is clearly seen.
When asked from which of six spheres (self, family, community, culture,
natural world, and spiritual world) do values come from, the answer is that
values come from all of them. When people lived in relatively homogeneous
communities, the values across these different spheres tended to be more
or less homogeneous. But in a world that is pluralistic and relativistic, the
values presented within each of these spheres may be increasingly different.

Chang and Jun demonstrate that values conflicts today are distinguished by four characteristics: **(1) extensiveness**, the conflict of values has extended beyond the moral realm into every area of life; people today are faced with an unparalleled number of choices and options in every sphere; **(2) complicatedness**, the interweaving of an increasing number of different values systems in our pluralistic and ever-changing society results in a confusing puzzle of complicated issues which seem to have no easy answers; **(3) profoundness**, historically established value systems through which people understood the difficult issues of life are now open to questioning and differing perspectives in our culture; **(4) continuousness**, the conflict of values is so extensive, there is a sense in which people can not escape this sense of continual conflict; once they settle one issue there are a plethora of new ones to take its place.

This is further complicated by the fact that people tend to unconsciously assimilate values from all the different spheres of the Connections Circle. This may result in people's having a clutter of values systems in their minds that they are not even fully aware of. This assimilation of values can be described as a "values smorgasbord." But it is not a smorgasbord in which only you choose what to put on your plate. Rather it is more the case that when you are young, others decide what you should have on your plate. As a result, you may have all kinds of stuff heaped on your plate to the point that it becomes overwhelming. You may be unaware of the inconsistency and confusion that comes from not being able to sort out all of the conflicting voices that arise.

For example, in our workshops the situation of children reared in foster homes is often brought up. Teenagers who have been in the system since they were young children may have lived in ten or more homes by the time they reach high school, they may have lived in several different communities, they may be influenced by many different cultures (racial, religious, socio-economic, sports, education, music, TV and movies, etc.), they may be hearing the different sides of the environmental debates, they may go to a church on Sunday, a yoga class on Monday, and a traditional ceremony on Tuesday. Obviously the value systems they are assimilating from all these different sources probably won't be consistent; in fact many of them may be contradictory. It is no wonder that so many in our day are confused as to what is really important in their lives. Which voice or voices should they listen to and what do they do with the other voices which are then condemning them for not following their direction?

- **Inconsistency**

Another challenge is that often even if people identify the values they wish to follow, it is a struggle for people to live consistently with them. However values are defined, at a practical level it is true that people may have idealized values that don't match the actual values they are acting upon. People are not perfect and even at the best of times they struggle to balance conflicting values.

When people have values that they don't recognize or don't live up to consistently, there may be issues of intentionality, especially an unwillingness to pay the cost of their values. This is seen in the middle class male whose family has left him and who says, *"If I had it to do all over again, I would do it differently because I love my family more than anything."* But the problem is that he wasn't willing to pay the cost when it needed to be paid. The very word "value" implies cost; and when people choose a value to follow, they should be willing to pay the cost to live consistently with that value. It may cost such things as money, time, energy, or even relationships. Sometimes part of that cost is taking the time to sort out conflicting values and finding ways to balance them. This concept may be lost when people overemphasize the myth that you can have it all and you can have it all now. Unfortunately this concept strips the concept of value of its value. If there is no cost, there is no value; if no value, than no meaning; if no meaning, then there is no point to things.

- **Hope**

Finally, as mentioned in the segment on career integrity, there is the challenge of values and people's level of hope. Unfortunately, it happens that people may really want something very badly but, if they don't think it's possible, they still won't try. People sometimes say that they would really love to do something, but they just don't think they can. Insult is added to injury when people then feel guilty because they don't fulfill their values and then give up even more in response to the guilt.

Clear values are crucial on the life/career journey. If they are unclear or compromised in some way, both motivation and decision making will be affected negatively. In light of this and the increasing challenges of sorting values out, we, as life/career practitioners, must develop a wide range of tools and processes that will assist people in the area of values to do the following:

- to recognize the values that they have assimilated in life and to be aware of their influence,

- to identify the personal individual values they wish to live by and then cultivate a sense of hope that they can find ways to express them meaningfully,

- to silence the unwanted voices from unwanted values that have been assimilated throughout life,

- to prioritize and balance the diverse values that people choose,

- to identify any inconsistencies between their stated values and their lifestyle and choices, and

- to know how to use values effectively in their life/career journey.

In the activity on Resolving Conflicting Values in chapter five, we will explore some strategies for addressing this need, but there is a need for far more to be done in finding ways to assist people with this challenges associated with values.

Life Balance

Balance is an essential aspect of a holistic life/career journey, especially for identifying and living consistently with one's values; therefore, it is an essential theme of the *Hope-Filled Engagement* approach.

It is such an important theme, that we have revised one of our fundamental tools, the Career Circle (Figure 12, p. 137) to include balance as one of the eight components essential in life/career counselling.

Some people, including some practitioners, may not recognize the importance of working with balance in life/career counselling. Multi-barriered people may protest that they're just trying to survive and can't afford the luxury of life balance. So why look at balance?

Life balance is much more than an esoteric ideal; it is a very pragmatic life skill that can make all the difference for the quality of people's lives throughout all phases of their life/career journeys.

We must keep the big picture in view. People's struggles with life balance may be keeping them from moving ahead on their life/career journey. Their lives may to too imbalanced even to consider actually taking a job. People's finding work is not the ultimate goal. Rather, it is equipping them to discover and follow life/career paths which will help lead to an integrated, healthy life, in which they will not only be able to find work but to maintain themselves in that work.

If balance is necessary for well-being in life, it is obviously essential to consider the impact that one's work or lack of work can have upon life balance and vice versa. The ever increasing impact of stress-related illnesses on work maintenance and retention speak very loudly to the need to integrate life balance into life/career counselling. Different people require different life balances for health. Different careers reflect different life balances. Obviously there is a greater likelihood that people will succeed in their careers if their careers are able to match their life balance needs.

When working on self-assessment and career exploration, rather than setting up false expectations that "all that a person is" can be fulfilled solely by finding the right career, it is more realistic to encourage people to find a balanced expression of themselves in all of their life, whether paid jobs or other unpaid activities.

Life balance may be looked at using many different approaches. Each may have value depending upon which aspects of life people are wishing to keep in balance. For example, in our workbook *Career Crossroads* (Poehnell & Amundson, 2001), balance is examined using a Life Balance Wheel, composed of four sets of contrasting factors: work and play, physical and spiritual, social and personal, emotional and intellectual.

In *Hope-Filled Engagement*, we focus on the balance as expressed in the traditional Aboriginal Medicine Wheel. It emphasizes balance in the context of health and well-being.

> The Medicine Wheel provides the best illustration of First Nations people's holistic view of well-being. The Medicine Wheel shows the separate entities of the emotional, mental, spiritual, and physical part of humankind as being equal and part of a larger whole. Healthy living is essentially ensuring that all parts of self work in harmony with all of the other parts of self. The Medicine Wheel represents the balance that exists between all people and all things (e.g., animals and humanity are brothers and sisters). The goal in working with First Nations people is to help them seek balance and equilibrium with everything around them... Traditional First Nations medicine incorporates the physical, social, psychological, and spiritual selves. (McCormick. & France, 1995, p. 28)

In particular, we will examine life balance from four spheres:

- **Physical**: anything related to the body, such as exercise, eating, grooming, energy and physical stamina.

- **Mental**: anything related to thinking (formal or informal), such as self-reflection, self-talk, learning, planning, or decision making.

- **Emotional**: recognizing and expressing emotions appropriately.

- **Spiritual**: metaphysical perspectives (formal or informal); being inspired by concepts and activities, such as meaning, hope, faith, forgiveness, or prayer.

It is no surprise that these four spheres of balance are increasingly being given more attention in life/career contexts. For example, the call for life-long learning addresses the mental sphere, the need for emotional intelligence addresses both the emotional and mental spheres, the emphasis on physical fitness in the work place addresses the physical sphere, and finally there are repeated calls for people to draw upon their own inner spiritual resources for matters of identity and meaning.

Obviously, we as life/career practitioners, in the midst of our increasing workloads and increasingly difficult counselling situations, also need to reflect on our own life balance for our own self-care.

In *Hope-Filled Engagement*, we will present activities that can be helpful in introducing people to the concept of life balance, in providing opportunities for them to examine their own life balance and its impact on their current life situation, and finally to encourage people to consider ways to come into a healthier life balance where necessary.

Interconnectedness

Another key theme related to holistic life/career counselling is interconnectedness. One of the goals of *Hope-Filled Engagement* is that people can discover and value themselves as they connect to the world around them.

Remember that the people you work with as clients or students are not alone; they are part of a larger whole, whether they recognize or acknowledge it. The communal perspective in this approach recognizes that people's identities must be seen in the context of their world of connections (Neumann, et al., 2000). If people feel disconnected from themselves and the world around them, their sense of identity, purpose, and motivation will be affected. It is important that people have a sense of identity in context rather than in isolation.

It is not our aim to explore metaphysical debates about interconnectedness but to look at the practical realities of interconnectedness as it impacts life/career counselling. Our hope is to provide opportunities for people to address any sense of disconnection they feel from their world and to assist them to re-connect in meaningful ways as a means to greater self-motivation and support.

This interconnected approach also ensures a fuller and more realistic perspective throughout all phases of the life/career journey. We recognize the essential need for people be intentional with respect to interconnectedness and the meaning and support it brings to all phases of life/career counselling.

In particular, we will explore the value of interconnectedness in self-assessment and career exploration. In self-assessment, people will reflect on their being part of the larger world, especially their roles and their potential sources of support and meaning. They will seek supportive feedback from others to gain a more complete and more accurate picture of themselves. Connections will also be employed in generating, researching, and evaluating career possibilities. In decision making, connections will assist people in recognizing and working with the various influences on the choices they make.

In the area of life-long learning and work search, they can provide important networks of people for finding and contacting learning and employment opportunities. Connections can point to the practical supports many need to be able to go to school or to maintain a job.

Interconnectedness is especially important in light of the challenges addressed earlier. North American culture has tended to follow a paradigm of "rugged individualism" that stresses independence and self-reliance in establishing and pursuing life goals. This individualism is reflected in many of the conventions of mainstream life/career counselling. For example usually individuals are counselled with little or no consultation of the significant others in their lives. Yet diversity reminds us that many come from cultures that emphasize a communal rather than an individualistic approach to life.

There must be a healthy balance between independence and interdependence. Too much independence can lead to dysfunctional isolation; too much interdependence can lead to passivity, emotional dependence, or toxic control. People need to take personal responsibility but not to the denial of fundamental interconnectedness.

This is especially pertinent when people feel a deep sense of disconnection from the mainstream world of learning and work and so don't see any reason to be involved in that world. Remember that some people may have experienced primarily only negative relationships. They may have developed a very defensive posture against interconnectedness because they have lost sight of the positive side and can now only see the negative. In such situations, the tragic results of unbalanced individualism is that people can become isolated and lose a sense of context, which in turn can make difficult circumstances even more difficult.

When people state things such as, *"What difference does it make?"* or *"So what?"*, they are subtly undermining any sense of purpose or meaning in what they do. If it really doesn't make any difference, then what's the point. If there is no point, there is no purpose or meaning in what they do. It is no wonder that in our western culture that so strongly emphasizes individualism, there is also a struggle on the part of many to find value, purpose, or meaning in their lives.

When people think that they do not need anyone else's help or that no one else cares, they are also inadvertently shutting themselves off not only from unwanted negative influences but also from legitimate support from others. As they shut others out to protect themselves from being hurt, they also fall into the subtle trap of shutting themselves in.

Sometimes others sincerely want to help but often, because they don't know how to do that effectively, they do it in ways that do the opposite of what is intended and turn people off. It is important to provide a framework and a process that enables people to be intentionally involved in helping each other effectively.

Of course in all of this there must always be a note of caution to guard people against toxic relationships. The forms of toxic input are legion (e.g., misunderstandings, distortions, put downs, negative voices, indifference, lack of empathy, lack of practical support, loss, or abuse).

As you work through *Hope-Filled Engagement*, think through the various concepts and techniques for honouring the interconnectedness of people and explore how you can use these ideas and strategies as means to assist them to intentionally draw upon their connections as they walk through their life/career journeys.

The Life/Career Conversation

Life connections implies that crafting a career involves a conversation, a dialogue between people and their world (Figure 2). People and the world they interact with both have their own worldview, culture, customs, language, expectations, and so forth. The challenge is for them to be able to communicate in a manner that is effective for both.

Figure 2: The Life/Career Conversation

There are two starting points for this conversation. My world (e.g., life/career practitioners, employers, etc.) may set forth their expectations — *"Here's what we need you to be able to do. Show this to us."* or people may start— *"Here's who I am and what I am capable of doing. Let me show you."*

This conversation is not always understood. If at any time there is only a monologue or the perception of a monologue, there is the danger of distortion. For example, if people do not clearly hear the input from others, they may be unrealistic about their potential and possibilities. Too often, we hear stories such as the following: a First Nations reserve in an isolated community has three women who are very passionate about hairdressing so they are sent off for training. When they return to the reserve there is not enough work to support them. The end result is three unemployed hairdressers. Even though they followed their passion, they did not take into account the other side of the life/career conversation—they didn't think about what their world needed and could support.

On the other hand, if people think that what they say is irrelevant and that only what the world around says is what is important, there may again be distortions. Tragically some people live in circumstances where people put them down all the time. They can become victims of such abuse and, as a result, begin to believe that they have nothing to offer. They may not even try for certain work because they don't think that they fit employers' expectations. They don't realize that with the career conversation, there is always room for some negotiation. Or if they decide to take work which doesn't really fit them, they may attempt to be someone or to do something that doesn't fit who they are. They may be able to fake it; but at a certain level, if the work doesn't engage them or is beyond them, they may experience boredom or be unable to do the work at all.

There may be distortions as well when practitioners or employers view the life/career process as a monologue—their monologue. They can also be unrealistic or too rigid and inflexible. They may fail to see people's full potential and lose good people as a result.

This dialogue is especially important when the cross-cultural factor in life/career counselling is in effect. People need to be able to know and value who they are and what is in their lives in the context of their own cultural understanding and language. But when they are interacting with others, they may need to translate their expression of who they are into the culture and language of those they are interacting with. In the same way, practitioners and employers may need to translate who they are and their expectations into the culture and language of those they are wishing to engage. It is clear by the number of companies across Canada that are seeking to develop greater cross-cultural sensitivity to immigrant or Aboriginal communities that the awareness of the need for this dialogue is increasing.

Whether working on behalf of the company (HR department) or for people (employment or guidance counselling), one of the tasks of practitioners is to facilitate bringing people together with their world and the subsequent conversation. We cannot assume that either people or employers fully understand the dynamic nature of this conversation nor what is needed for an effective conversation that will result in a win-win situation for both. Ideally two needs (peoples' and employers') meet and as a result of an effective conversation, both needs are met.

There are several elements of the conversation that people, practitioners, and employers need to be aware of. Crafting a career may be a cross-cultural experience for many people. As such, basic communication skills such as active listening, effective questioning, paraphrasing and the like, can be most valuable. It may also help to develop some knowledge of the cultural backgrounds of everyone involved, so that communication barriers may be anticipated.

At a deeper level, it is important to develop discernment skills in order to be able to read between the lines, to hear what is implicit in other's communication. For example, Angel and Harney (1997) emphasize the need for people to be able to discern employers' real concerns and needs even if they are not stated explicitly.

Finally, flexible and creative negotiation skills must be developed. In this life/career conversation, there is often a need for people, practitioners and employers to find a middle ground between who a person is and what employers are looking for. For example, understanding this conversation leaves room to fine tune a work position to specific individuals in such a way that the work is most effectively accomplished by them.

This conversation affects all aspects of the life/career counselling process: self-assessment, career exploration and decision making, lifelong learning, work search, and work maintenance. Throughout *Hope-Filled Engagement*, this conversation will be explored from many of these different perspectives.

Creative Vision/ Decision/Action Planning

Throughout the counselling process, it will be important for people to choose to take some concrete actions.

This may be more challenging than one would think. In light of the types of challenges already discussed, such as diversity, the need to re-examine assumptions and conventions, and the changing and chaotic nature of today's world of work, it is important to re-examine the assumptions and conventions associated with decision making and action planning.

In the workshops we have conducted, we often enquire about how practitioners use action plans with people. Though many state that they use action plans, when asked whether they believe people will actually follow through on the action plans, it is surprising how many say that they don't fundamentally believe people will follow through. When asked why they use action plans at all then, they usually say that they have to in order to meet funding requirements of some sort. This ought to alert us to the reality that the way action planning is often done may not be as effective as hoped. It is worthwhile exploring some reasons for this.

We will discuss this in more detail in Chapter 8 on Creative Vision/ Decision/Action Planning. For now, it is enough to note that when we critically examine traditional action planning in terms of its strengths and weaknesses, it is clear that it is not adequate for today's rapidly changing and uncertain world. Though there are many good aspects to it, traditional action planning does reflect the reality of a time when things were much more linear and static.

There is a need to develop new approaches that maintain the strengths of traditional action planning while supplementing it with more creative and flexible elements essential in today's world. Therefore, we would propose a revision to the traditional action-planning model that would draw from the best aspects of the traditional model and then address some of its weaknesses. The use of a non-linear creative vision/decision/action planning model will better equip people to navigate through the uncertainties of a volatile labour market. This *Hope-Filled Engagement* approach should give people a sense of hope that they will be able to face whatever confusing twists and turns they encounter on their life/career journeys.

chapter four

CREATIVITY, SPIRITUALITY, IMAGINATION, AND HOPE

CareerCraft

We have written about the challenges that many people face today as they try to engage with today's dynamic (potentially chaotic and uncertain) world of work. Because of the increasing diversity of people and especially an increasing disconnection that some have with the mainstream world of education and work, we have encouraged the examination of the assumptions and conventions which guide our approaches to life/career counselling.

Part of this reexamination should include taking a good look at the metaphors we use for life and career. Metaphors by their very nature are culturally informed. This has profound implications when working with an increasing cultural diversity. We would suggest that one reason why some people are stuck with a crisis of imagination as they look down the road of their life/career journeys is that the primary metaphor currently used for career may not be the best starting point for them.

Many career counselling concepts have evolved from the business world, including the widely-used metaphor of "career management." This metaphor has influenced the language of career and many of the approaches, activities, and tools. In some respects this metaphor is useful and has many important and essential associations. However, there are some limitations to this metaphor and we will present an alternate perspective.

When we introduce CareerCraft in workshops, we ask practitioners to brainstorm the first five words that come to mind for the word "management" and then for "craft." Their thought associations are then listed on a flip chart; Figure 3 summarizes typical results.

When asked to compare and contrast such lists, there is recognition that there is some overlap. Beyond this, however, participants also report that the term "management" tends to elicit negative feelings while "craft" elicits more positive feelings.

Figure 3: Management and Craft Word Association

"MANAGEMENT"		"CRAFT"	
organize	marketing	craftsmanship	practical
step-by-step	logical	skillful	magical
planning	status	expertise	unique
control	conservative	creative	artistic
bureaucracy	rules	beauty	personal
action-oriented	fearful	hands-on	glue
decisive	focused	feelings	passion
conservative	realistic	art	relaxing
guiding	driven	specialist	money
influence	productive	competence	imaginative
disciplined	reports	paint	functional
regulated	cognitive	proficiency	innovative
leadership	order	inventive	patience
creativity	policy	flair	noble
business	vision	love	stimulating
policy	"suits"	well-wrought	original
strategy	responsibility	flexible	inspiration
formal	structure	good	concentration
boss	slow	pleasure	fun
greed	power	social	talent
commitment	out of touch	maternal	material
time	stress	tradition	family
expectations	"better than you"	immersed	touchy-feely
hard		messy	leisure

There are many perceived contrasts between the two terms: structured and rigid vs. flexible; impersonal vs. personal; external vs. internal; "boxed in" vs. freedom. These contrasts are obviously not the case in all instances, but they are common perceptions. If these associations are expressed by life/career practitioners, how much more would they be true for people who feel alienated or disconnected from the mainstream world of education and work? These associations can unconsciously exacerbate the sense of disconnection people may have and result in feelings of suspicion and distrust.

What then is the impact of the metaphor of "career management"? Will not some of the same associations be present even if only at a subconscious level?

We have suggested that the metaphor of "CareerCraft" may be a more accessible metaphor to complement the typical "career management" metaphor (Poehnell & Amundson, 2002). Most people are involved in some sort of craft in the broadest sense. Sometimes they don't recognize it because they have a very narrow definition of craft. But craft can be more than knitting or carving; it can include gardening, cooking, tying fishing lures, writing, outdoor craft, or countless other activities which people do. A craft metaphor can provide an effective alternative that is easily understood and accepted by a wide diversity of people.

Such a shift will provide new perspectives, new associations, and fresh creative tension and energy that could prove to be invaluable in the face of current career realities.

We believe that "craft" complements "management"; it does not replace it. A quick glance at the previous lists of associations shows some overlap. The paradigms of "management" and "craft" are not mutually exclusive. A focus on CareerCraft and creativity seems to be well timed in light of the fact that businesses are increasingly embracing creativity concepts as they face the growing complexities of the business world.

It is not only the world of business that is fundamentally changing. So too is the world of work. If the business world is recognizing its need for more creative approaches, how much more is this a need for the field of life/career counselling which works with people being influenced by the same growing complexities. This rapid change demands a greater emphasis on holistic approaches that utilize creativity, flexibility, optimism, and imagination.

As the business world is addressing its changing world with an increasing interest in creativity, so too the career world could benefit from such a shift in perspective. The new perspectives and skills associated with a craft metaphor enable people to see themselves and the world of work in new ways that create a sense of hopefulness and also to find new solutions to old or new problems. There are three fundamental characteristics of the "craft" metaphor (Figure 4: CareerCraft Model):

Figure 4: CareerCraft Model

1. Function

Craft is very functional; it is purposeful and practical; it combines creativity and beauty with the everyday practical things of life. So too in today's evolving labour market, there certainly needs to be a synergism between creativity and practicality as people craft their careers. Craft is also "hands-on." People actually craft something themselves rather than expecting someone else to do it for them. Unfortunately, in career matters, some people want others to do it all for them. This can be a trap that some multi-barriered people fall into when they become overly dependent on government assistance. Such "hands-on" involvement doesn't mean that people are on their own; they are still interdependent with others. When people perform crafts, they often involve others in what they are doing; but they still take responsibility for their part of it.

2. Skill

Craft also suggests skill and workmanship; this involves learning to use the right **materials**, **tools**, and **processes** effectively to produce the desired product. So too, as people craft careers, they must know their materials. What are the materials out of which they can craft a career? These materials are the personal characteristics set forth in the Career Circle (skills, interests, personal style, values, balance, learning, life/work roles, and work connections, see Figure 12: The Career Circle), and the sources of strength, meaning, and purpose set forth in the Connections Circle (self, family, community, culture, natural world, and spiritual world, see Figure 13: Connections Circle). Using the appropriate tools (e.g., assessment tools, resumes, cover letters, etc.), people weave these characteristics together in different ways for different life/work roles and contexts. The weaving together of these elements takes place through the different career processes, such as self-assessment, career exploration, decision making, life-long learning, work search, and work maintenance (Figure 5: CareerCraft Processes). Unfortunately, some people are unaware of the materials they have in their life to work from, let alone the tools and processes of crafting a career.

3. Creativity

Finally, a craft requires much more than the mastering of all the technical specifications of materials, tools, and processes. These must be combined in a creative process that produces a unique item of beauty and function. So too career calls for creativity and many related concepts such as individuality and uniqueness, passion, and imagination. There is no one magic solution that will work for everyone as they walk their life/career journeys. There may be general principles but these must certainly be applied creatively and flexibly in each case. We must also beware of stereotyping people in such a way that we lose the ability to see each person's uniqueness. The potential impact of creativity upon people will be expanded more in the next segments.

Creativity is essential for everyone but especially for those who are multi-barriered. Creativity directly addresses the high levels of hopelessness and dependency as it frees people to draw on their own inner resources, both spiritual and intuitive, and to open their lives to new possibilities.

When people feel hopeless, they often take a very defensive posture that keeps them from taking any risks. Fearing further failure, they don't even try. Yet in the world of craft, these same people will often do exactly the opposite. Throughout the 1990s, Gray attended a local weavers' guild. At their monthly meeting, there was always "show and tell." The accomplished weavers would show the beautiful work that had been done. Those who were just learning were encouraged to bring their attempts at weaving, even when things didn't work out. These would be shown and the question would be asked—*"What went wrong?"* There was no shame or defeat in the misshapen weaving. *"Why not?"* The answer is simple. Failure is viewed differently in craft.

Failure is not something to be avoided but to be embraced as part of the learning process. People were willing to try and fail because they were learning to do a craft. This is an attitude that is sometimes missing in the management metaphor where people fear failure because they fear some form of rejection or ridicule. This is certainly an attitude that effective life/career counselling needs to cultivate in people as they craft their unique careers and lives.

Figure 5: CareerCraft Processes

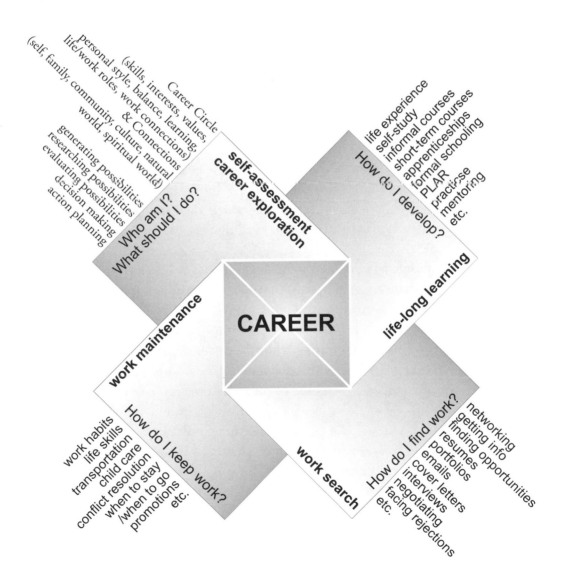

CareerCraft: Creativity

In the last segment, we presented CareerCraft as a new paradigm to assist people to understand what is involved in crafting a career in today's rapidly changing and uncertain labour market. This complementary metaphor to "career management" generates hope through a holistic approach that emphasizes function, skill, and creativity.

In this chapter we will expand the discussion on creativity and explore three key ways in which creativity can help people.

The challenge in suggesting creativity to many people is that they don't think they are creative. It may be better to use creative approaches without explicitly saying that is what is being done. It may be better to lead people through experiences in which they re-discover their innate creativity rather than to try to convince them beforehand that they are creative.

The problem is that many equate creativity with being good at art or music, yet these are merely areas in which creativity is applied. The reality is that everyone is creative in countless ways.

Creativity is about creating "choices" rather than following "habits." Siler (1999. pp. 76-81) in his book *Think Like a Genius* defines creativity as "any unconditioned response or interpretation" as "choice" rather than "habit." A "habit" is like a long narrow highway with no exit. It is a common occurrence for people to live much of their lives following habits, customs, and traditions which have become second nature because they are pre-conditioned responses. This is not necessarily a problem. But when those habits are self-defeating—such as negative attitudes, distorted self-perceptions, low self-esteem, victim mentality, or inappropriate actions—then there is a problem. In such instances such habits can breed hopelessness and people can be stuck in a "crisis of imagination" that traps them in forms of dysfunctionality.

The challenge is to identify and disarm any self-defeating pre-conditioning and to assist people to discover that they do have choices. "Choice" is like a road with "a fork in it," with an alternative route. It is creativity that enables people to see that there are forks in the road ahead, alternative ways to respond or, if necessary, to create them.

When a painter paints in a new style, it is seen as creative, because he/she is showing an alternative way to paint that is different from what has been done in the past. In the same way, when people see themselves no longer as those without anything to offer but as people with a wealth of personal assets, they are being just as creative. Or, when people change their thinking that there are no jobs to realize that there is a wide variety of work that they could do, they are taking a creative step.

It is the facilitation of this creative step that lies at the heart of Hope-Filled Engagement. Our goal is to assist people to see themselves and their world in new ways that are not self-defeating.

There are at least three key ways in which creativity can enhance people's involvement in their life/career journey; it will engage, energize, and empower them (see Figure 6: CareerCraft Creativity).

1. Engage

First, creativity helps people to engage more holistically in the entire life/career process. One of the foundational themes of hope-filled engagement is an "active engagement" approach. As discussed in the last chapter, "active engagement" calls for a counselling relationship in which both practitioners and the people they work with are fully engaged.

It has been our experience that practitioners who have been most effective with multi-barriered people are those who find ways to motivate them to take new steps. They can recognize when people and/or the counselling relationship is stuck and are creative with their attitudes, tools, and processes.

Figure 6: CareerCraft Creativity

It is difficult to engage people in areas that they don't understand, have no interest in, or don't know how to do. When we engage people where they are engaged in life, people often have the "flow" experience that Csikszentmihalyi (1991, 1997) describes in his research on the "psychology of optimal experience," where creativity and everyday life meet.

As well, it is in these places that people often demonstrate their own innate creative abilities to deal with life and its problems. Someone may never have done well in school or the world of work and, as a result, will struggle to see themselves as creative in these contexts. But in some other life role, they may be demonstrating creativity with life skills and abilities that could be transferred into the world of learning and work.

2. Energize

When people are actively engaged, they usually also feel very alive and full of creative energy. The opposite is also true, when people are not engaged, they can feel very passive and lethargic. Many practitioners have seen this resigned passivity in the attitudes, thoughts, and actions of some people who live in a cloud of hopelessness.

Rather than viewing present circumstances as a barrier to future career goals, it is possible to be energized and to use this power to pursue opportunities for creative movement towards desired goals. It is not that people totally lack energy, it is that unfortunately the energy they do have is drained away in self-defeating actions and reactions. They think their situation is hopeless so they respond with frustration, anger, bitterness, and guilt; sometimes they lash out at those around them, especially to those who would seek to help them. Life is too short to drain life's energies this way but sometimes people know no other way.

Yet a creative approach can reveal alternatives. The very energy that is being drained away may be redirected not to reacting to the problems but to finding solutions for them. This is the dynamic effect of creativity as explored by Fritz (1989) when he suggests that there is always a tension between people's present reality and where they would like their lives to be. This tension energizes people. People can choose what direction they direct this energy. Responding as "victims," people can exhaust themselves in negative reactions or they can transform this tension into creative energy that commits itself to finding solutions. As mentioned earlier, crafts people whose projects don't work, usually will just take them apart and try again.

3. Empower

Finally, creativity empowers people by freeing them from mental blocks and habits and by opening up new perspectives, new connections, new possibilities, and, thereby, new choices.

a. Empowering by freeing from mental blocks and habits

If you haven't already started one, you may wish to keep a running list of the diverse self-defeating mental blocks and habits that control people's thoughts, decisions, and actions. The list could include issues such as low self-esteem, lack of opportunity, victim mentality, inaccurate views of the world of work, passivity, hopelessness, to name just a few. In order to help people and ourselves get unstuck, it is clear that some of these barriers may need to be set aside.

vonOech (1990) suggests that people often develop such blocks as survival mechanisms when they are young in order to survive in an adult world. However these same survival mechanisms become self-defeating in adulthood because they trap people into ways of thinking that blind them to seeing new possibilities. He identifies the following ten "mental blocks":

1. the right answer

2. that's not logical

3. follow the rules

4. be practical

5. play is frivolous

6. that's not my area

7. avoid ambiguity

8. don't be foolish

9. to err is wrong

10. I'm not creative

He further argues that "often we have integrated these mental blocks so well into our thinking and behavior that we are no longer aware that we're being guided by them. They have become habits. The danger of habits is that a person can become a prisoner of familiarity. ... You get stuck in how you already think about things" (pp. 12, 14). It interesting how many of these can be seen in life/career counselling contexts.

It is being "stuck" in "crises of imagination" that blocks people from being able to see, generate, or follow alternative paths in their life/career journeys (Amundson, 2009). Such mental blocks, whether in multi-barriered or mainstream people, are particularly harmful in today's rapidly changing world of work which often requires bold new creative steps.

vonOech (1990, p. 14) suggests that we occasionally need a "whack on the side of the head to shake us out of routine patterns, to force us to re-think our problems, and to stimulate us to ask the questions that may lead to other right answers."

b. Empowering by opening up new possibilities

It is not enough to free people from mental blocks or habits which have been hindering them. It is also essential to empower people by assisting them to recognize or generate new possibilities and equip them to attempt to follow these new paths.

This leads us to the positive side of creativity's empowering approach. As we have discussed, creativity helps us to see new perspectives; then new perspectives reveal new connections, new connections present new possibilities, new possibilities enable new choices, and new choices bring new hope. Filled with new hope, people are more willing to try new paths.

CareerCraft:
Re-discovering Imagination

Creativity engages people in hope by removing blocks and revealing new possibilities. Creativity works through imagination yet many do not think that they are imaginative. Yet when people feel stuck in their journeys, they are experiencing "crises of imagination." They experience a resigned passivity in which they feel boxed in (Figure 7).

Figure 7: Feeling Boxed In

Imagination is often unrecognized and undervalued, if not outright denied. It is common to hear people say, *"I don't have an imagination."* Yet nothing could be further from the truth. Imagination is an innate ability which everyone possesses. In this and the next two segments, we will explore the potential of re-discovering, harnessing, and cultivating imagination.

What is imagination and how does it work? The concept of imagination is difficult to define. It is derived from the Latin word *imago*, meaning a copy or likeness. It refers to our ability to form mental images. It is easier to describe than to define. Wujec and Muscat provide one of the clearest and most practical descriptions in their excellent book *Return on Imagination* (2002). They set forth four key aspects of imagination:

1. Representation: Seeing with the Mind's Eye

People have the ability to see with their mind's eye. They can visualize in their minds both themselves and their world, things real or imaginary.

2. Connection: Compare and Contrast

The imagination takes the images we create and compares and contrasts them to our previous experiences and images. It then connects them to these past experiences.

3. Emotion: Responding to the Mind's Theater

Once images (real or imaginary) are formed and connected, we respond emotionally to these images according to how we perceive what we see.

4. Interpretation: Deriving Understanding and Meaning

It is through the imagination, that our minds seek to derive understanding and meaning by looking at the connections we have made and then looking for patterns that make sense of it all. In a certain sense, it is our imagination that to a large extent determines the reality of our lives.

How we view ourselves and our world will influence how we will live. It is therefore much more important than most of us realize. Thomas Moore (1997) suggests that the life we make for ourselves is only limited by our imagination. Therefore, the vitality of our imagination will directly impact how we make our world.

Three helpful implications arise from this understanding of imagination. First, it shows that we all have imagination and our minds are constantly creating and recreating imaginations (positive and negative), though we may not realize it. People may lose their awareness of their imagination but they haven't lost their imagination. The question is not whether we have an imagination or not, but how conscious we are of our imagination.

> … we can't not use our imagination; [there is a] constant
> stream of images and words that create a personal sense
> of the world. We imagine all day and all night—why our
> loved one is late for dinner, how to triumph in tomorrow's
> presentation, what route we'll take to the grocery store…
> We actively use our imagination to make sense of our
> lives… (Wujec & Muscat, 2002, p. 11)

Second, this understanding of the imagination helps us understand why people can have radically different responses to the same circumstance. It is not always the reality of a situation that determines our emotional responses; it is our perception of the situation as created by our imaginations. After an accident, one person, reviewing it over and over in the mind's eye, is uncontrollably shaken, while another finds peace in thinking of God's hand of protection. When a teenager is not home late one evening, one parent, thinking there has been an accident, is worried sick; the other, thinking that the teen has just lost track of time while enjoying friends, is completely calm. After a downsizing, one former employee thinks life is over and walks away in fear and depression, while another walks away with a sense of relief and anticipation. One person, thinking only of their lack of a high school diploma, feels like a "dummy" that no one will want; another with the same educational level, focuses on the informal learning he/she has accumulated and feels confident.

The question is not whether we have an imagination or not but rather how healthy is our imagination; how well we work with it; and how well we harness its perception-forming power. Unfortunately many people are unaware that they even have an imagination, let alone thinking about its health. It is always hard to convince some people that their perceptions are too self-defeating. What is needed is to take a step back and use the backswing to equip them to challenge and change such perceptions.

Third, this understanding of imagination suggests that though people may not always be able to control their circumstances, they can, to some degree, control their responses. "Everything can be taken from a man but one thing: to choose one's attitude in any given set of circumstances, to choose one's own way" (Victor Frankel, as cited in Bissonnette, 1994, p. 5).

Ultimately we can't totally control our imaginations, but we can learn to cultivate a healthy imagination and to work with it effectively. When people are stuck in their life/career journeys because of barriers that they face, it is essential that we facilitate the re-discovery of their imaginations. This will be a key aspect of equipping them to more effectively change the way they perceive their current situations and their future possibilities.

How we use our imaginations will not only determine how we perceive our reality; it will also enable us to see beyond it, to see outside the box. We will explore this more in the next two segments.

CareerCraft:
Harnessing Imagination

Everyone has an imagination that is working all the time. The challenge is to harness this innate ability in the most effective manner possible. In particular, there are three aspects of the imagination people can learn to use. We will explore them using three easily understood metaphors:

A. A Window of Discovery: The imaginative exploration of ourselves and our relationship to the world

The imagination can be a window of discovery that, when opened, enables the imaginative exploration of ourselves and our relationship to the world. This is a crucial aspect of the life/career conversation. "The imagination is a discovering faculty, a faculty for seeing relationships, for seeing meanings that are special and even quite new" (Merton, p. 357).

Sometimes people are stuck in their life/career journeys, because they are stuck in the way they perceive themselves and their circumstances. Trying to change people's perceptions can be challenging; the backswing can help. Rather than trying to change their perceptions, it might be more effective to first equip them with the ability to change their own perceptions. If we can facilitate their seeing themselves and their circumstances in a more positive light, they may begin to make progress on their journeys.

Zander and Zander (2002) refer to two opposite ways of responding to life circumstances: through problems or through possibilities.

There are those whose starting point is their problems (Figure 8: Living with the Whirlwind of Problems). Like a dog tethered to a stake, they just go round and round them and cannot see beyond them. No matter what you say, there is always some sort of reply like, *"Yes, BUT you don't understand my [blank]."* You can fill in the blank with any number of common responses: my life, my problems, my family, my circumstances, my community, my past, my disability, and so forth.

Figure 8: Living with the Whirlwind of Problems

In their imaginations, they are trapped in the proverbial box, powerless and hopeless. People in this mode experience the same repeated depressing messages over and over again until they become natural to them and they can't see that they are caught in a whirlwind of deception that is sucking the life out of them.

Zander and Zander suggest that there is an alternative approach (Figure 9: Living with Possibilities). Instead of problems as the starting point, use reality as the starting point. Reality contains not only problems but good things as well.

This completely changes the perspective. People in the "problem mode" never fully explore what is possible within the box of their circumstances because they don't see any point to trying. People who start with reality recognize that there is more to their lives than their problems. Instead of saying that things can't be done because of their barriers, they ask themselves what can be done from the point they find themselves. Rather than becoming depressed and defeated, they allow themselves to be energized by the possibilities.

Figure 9: Living with Possibilities

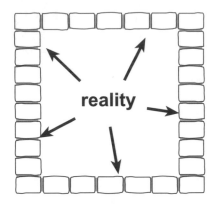

With a possibilities perspective, not only do people explore all that is possible within the box, they can look at the box itself, and then possibly even look outside the box. As they examine the barriers they think are boxing them in, they discover that not all walls are as they seem. In a problem mode, people perceive all their barriers as permanent, unmovable walls; yet there may be at least four different kinds of walls (Figure 10; Kaye & Jordan-Evans, 2002):

Figure 10: 4 Kinds of Walls

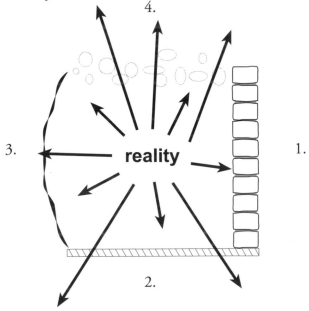

Wall 1: Some walls are like brick, rigid and difficult or impossible to change. There some unchangeable realities, such as physical disabilities, sex, race, and so forth. Some careers have unchangeable requirements, such as a medical degree, a driver's license, a language proficiency.

Wall 2: Some are like glass: strong & sturdy, but if hit in the right place in the right way at the right time, they will break. In the last generation or so, many women have been able to challenge the so-called "glass ceiling." When someone is the first in a family to go to university or to find a full-time job, he/she is breaking a glass wall. Events like these shatter barriers and open the way for others to follow.

Wall 3: Some walls are made of rubber; thick and strong but have some give when pushed in the right way. Many people who lack formal education have been successful in having their informal learning acknowledged through prior learning assessment and recognition. Many employers are flexible and willing to negotiate job descriptions to mold a position to suit a particular employee more effectively.

Wall 4: Sometimes the perceived wall is nothing more than smoke and vapor; it looks solid but isn't really there at all. When tested, such beliefs, assumptions, and perceptions are seen to be totally false, nothing more than a creation of our minds. Some people think that they have no marketable assets, even though a thorough self-assessment reveals a wealth of assets. Some perceive there are no jobs when there may be lots of employment opportunities.

When people have the ability to test the walls they perceive as barriers, they may discover that they can do much more than they ever anticipated. Their barriers become challenges to be faced and opportunities for creative solutions. The illustrations of this are legion: disabled athletes who perform in the Paralympics or disabled performers who seem to do the impossible; or young disadvantaged single parents who find a way to finish high school, go to college, and craft careers.

B. A Dream Maker: The ability to create images of the future and to be energized by possibilities

The imagination also enables people to look beyond their present circumstances to create images of the future and to be energized by possibilities. The incredible fact that we are hardwired for imagination means we are also hardwired for hope. Though people may think that they have lost their imagination and the ability to hope, nothing could be further from the truth. They haven't lost their imaginations, they are using it all the time. Nor have they lost the ability to hope; they have just misdirected it.

> *"It is only through imagination that [people] become aware of what the world might be."*
> - Bertrand Russell

When people say that they have no creativity, no imagination, no faith, no hope, you can simply ask them if they worry or fear. Everyone who worries demonstrates that they have an imagination, that they can believe what their imagination creates, and that they can be impacted by that imagination and faith. They are using their innate God-given imagination, but in the wrong direction (Figure 11: Hardwired for Hope).

Figure 11: Hardwired for Hope

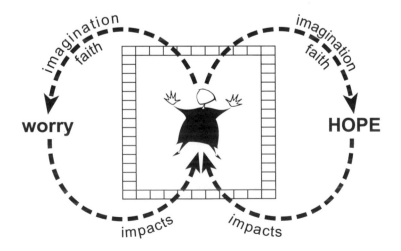

Everyone who worries proves that they can hope. Just as people can imagine and believe negative thoughts, worries, and fears, so too they can imagine and believe positive thoughts that can encourage them to step out in life with hope.

C. A Bridge to the Future: The turning of possibilities into realities by the mental rehearsing of positive change

One form of the backswing is the imagination's innate ability to envision possibilities and then to turn possibilities into realities by the mental rehearsing of positive change.

> Seeing all possibilities, seeing all that can be done, and
> how it can be done, marks the power of imagination.
> Your imagination stands as your own personal laboratory.
> Here you can rehearse the possibilities, map out plans,
> and visualize overcoming obstacles. Imagination turns
> possibilities into reality. (Imagination, n.d.)

The sports world for some time has used visualization as a means to improve performance. Countless studies have demonstrated that when athletes perform an activity in their mind prior to the actual event, they usually perform the actual activity better.

In the same way, people can learn to use their imaginations to be more effective in overcoming the various challenges they face. This is at the heart of *Hope-Filled Engagement*. As people are engaged in using their imaginations to see themselves and their world from new perspectives, to recognize not only the challenges they face but the possibilities as well, and to use their imagination to create bridges to a more positive future, the very process fills the present with hope. This hope in turn begins to create a healthier environment for the imagination for new perceptions, new possibilities, and new bridges to the future. So instead of a process that spirals people's spirits and lives down, the process lifts them up. Such a hope-filled engagement will invariably generate new levels of motivation and action.

CareerCraft:
Cultivating Imagination

Assisting people to rediscover and begin to work consciously with their own imaginations will help them move towards greater self-sufficiency.

This may seem like a daunting task in and of itself, because the imagination itself cannot be controlled. But it is possible to create a healthy environment in which to cultivate a healthy imagination. This may seem somewhat circular in nature and it is. We either create environments that bring down our imaginations and our lives or we create environments that cultivate healthy imaginations and healthy lives. We start where we are and where the people we work with are at.

A good starting point for cultivating our imaginations is to examine how we perceive our imaginations. Reflect on the following four questions:

- *Are you imaginative? If yes, describe your imagination?*

- *How often do you use your imagination?*

- *When was the last time you used your imagination?*

- *What stirs your imagination?*

Your answers to these questions will help you assess your perception of your imagination, suggest some strengths to build on, and challenge some areas needing some conscious improvement.

What can we do to create an environment for a healthy imagination? There is no simple list of things to do to create such an environment but there are several concepts which can give direction to the process.

A. Permission

It is important to challenge any assumption that implies that we do not have very active imaginations and to give ourselves permission to recognize and to be comfortable with our imaginations.

One major reason why some people don't try to change the way they think is that they believe that their thoughts are static and unchangeable. But this is far from the truth. Recent studies into the area of brain plasticity have shown that our minds are not static but dynamic. We have the ability to change our neural pathways and change our thinking.

> Muscles become stronger when exercised… Neuroplasticity responds to the full spectrum of mental activity by enhancing whatever mental faculties we use, and always in proportion to how vigorously we use them. Neuroplasticity is a built-in response mechanism that does not significantly diminish with age. Developing rigid patterns of thinking is not a physical manifestation of aging; it is entirely a matter of willful choice. (Bono, n.d.)

When people are especially discouraged, suggest that they give themselves permission to explore new paths. Allow people to discover their innate imaginative ability indirectly through the process. We may need to hope for them when they cannot hope for themselves. Hope can be infectious; sometimes people just need someone who believes in them. By believing in them and giving them a process that is accessible to them, we will facilitate their re-discovery of imagination.

The concept of strength challenge (Amundson, 2009) may be used to help people find where they are already using their imaginations. How quickly the mind says *"no!"* And for all kinds of reasons: fear, habit, lethargy, lack of know-how—to name a few. But if people can say *"no!"*, they can also say *"yes!"* People can challenge their self-talk and use it to give themselves permission to use their imaginations in new areas of thinking and living.

B. Time

Giving ourselves permission involves giving ourselves the time necessary to get to know our imaginations. Cultivating healthy environments for our imaginations is something that will take time. We need to make space in our hectic lives for imagination to flourish. It is important not to jump too quickly, lest people try to jump too far and fall too hard. People can be encouraged to make time in their lives to consciously cultivate their imagination through creative activities.

It takes time because it takes time to change thought and life patterns. Studies on brain plasticity have shown that it typically takes three months to create new mental pathways. Richard O'Conner (2008) draws from recent developments in psychology and science to assist people to identify and enjoy the positive aspects of life by learning how their brains work.

> Here's the good news: We can change our own brains
> And here's the bad news: It takes longer than we want
> it to. Some researchers recently taught a group of
> college students to juggle and, using the latest high tech
> neuroimaging equipment, observed their brains as they
> learned. After observing three months of daily practice,
> the researchers could identify measurable growth in gray
> matter in certain areas of their subjects' brains; after three
> months of no practice, the growth disappeared. Life
> experience changes the structure of the brain itself. Just
> like juggling, happiness is a set of skills you can learn;
> and, just like juggling, learning to be happy is work that
> requires dedication and practice (pp. 8-9).

The time invested to replace negative habits with positive ones is well worth the time and effort. Once people have put in the effort to overcome habits that foster unhappiness, it doesn't take much effort to maintain the new habits that foster a sense of happiness.

C. The Beginner's Mind

Sometimes the biggest hindrance to freeing our imaginations is that our minds are just too cluttered; we may be just too busy. "As well as strategies to foster the imagination, we need ways to stop the busyness that prevents the deeper imagination from flowing… The pressures keep our imaginations busy, crowded, and engaged, so that we have little room to let the deeper ideas emerge" (Wujec & Muscat, 2002, pp. 20, 25).

Our minds may be full of things (e.g., assumptions, self-perceptions, fears, etc.) which may be very misleading and limiting when it comes to the imagination. For example, we may think we already know all there is about ourselves and our world and, as a result, be closed to new perspectives. Or we may have a "been there-done that" attitude that produces a passive skepticism that jumps to conclusions or makes snap decisions without all the facts (*?What If!*, 2002).

The idea of the beginner's mind is that we accept with humility that we don't really know everything and then temporarily set aside all that we think we know to make room for new ideas. We can then assume the position of learners who approach things with an innocent eye, suspending all preconceptions and criticism for a time and allow ourselves to be open to learning and trying new things (Henson, n.d.).

At a practical level, this may be as simple as people being willing to try a new activity even if they don't fully understand it. It may be that understanding only comes through the experience itself.

D. Play

One thing that characterizes our workshops is laughter. This is because people are having fun. And when they are having fun, they become engaged and their innate creativity and imagination kicks in. Why is this? Michael Michalko (1998, p. 261) in his excellent book *Cracking Creativity* explains the important link between play and creativity.

> An environment of playfulness and humor is highly
> conducive to creativity. Playfulness relaxes [people]. In
> a state of relaxation, individuals show less fixation and
> rigidity in their thinking… When we play, we become
> childlike and begin to behave in spontaneous creative ways.
> Play and creativity have much in common. In particular,
> play often involves using objects and actions in new or
> unusual ways, similar to the imaginative combinations of
> ideas involved in creative thinking.

This is especially important in the case of people who are struggling
with hopelessness. Through playful engaging activities, people have the
opportunity in a non-threatening context to explore themselves and their
world from new perspectives. A few minutes of play can melt mental
barriers that may only harden under other approaches. It can be very
powerful to surprise people with who they are and what they can do
before they consciously realize they are even learning such things.

E. Break out of the box

We have looked at the metaphor of people feeling trapped in a box.
Helping people break out of the boxes they feel trapped in is essential
to cultivating a healthy imagination. Sometimes all that is needed are
activities that are outside the box.

A highly successful graphics design teacher Richard Wilde (Davis,
2001) tells of his frustrations during the first few years of teaching. He
felt his students weren't very creative. He would give them problems to
solve, and the answers he would get back were very typical, clichéd, and
unimaginative. It was only after much reflection that he realized that it
was his lack of creativity and not his students that was the issue. He had
been asking typical questions, questions within the box, which already
had well-established answers. As a result, he received back from his
students well-worn answers. He realized that if he wanted his students
to think outside the box, he had to ask questions that were outside the

box, questions for which his students didn't already have pre-conditioned answers. When he changed his approach, the work he received from his students displayed new levels of imagination and creativity. Because they didn't have answers to these problems, they had to create their own.

This certainly applies to career counselling, especially with people who have been in the system for some time. When such people sit before us, we must remember that we are probably not the first person they have talked with about their life and work situation. They have probably been asked the same questions countless times before and have learned unconsciously how to answer them. By breaking out of the box, by engaging them with fresh activities that they have no experience with, we are giving them the opportunity to start fresh with a beginner's mind and to discover new insights that they would never have thought possible.

F. Stimulus

The most basic way to facilitate people's breaking out of the box is the use of some form of stimulus. What is a stimulus?

> Stimulus is any experience that is new to you or outside the boundaries of the problem you are dealing with. This is important. Stimulus is not a new idea in itself but the raw material of the creative process. In our experience, if you've got good stimuli, you won't be able to stop yourself from being creative - the unique connections will just flow from that (*?What If!*, 2002, p. 5).

A stimulus distracts our brains from its usual thought patterns by directing it to something else which then enables us to find new perspectives on the problem we are facing.

In a sense, the concept of a stimulus has been effectively used for years in life/career counselling. There are many stimuli which are traditionally used to assist people in self-assessment: life/work experiences, stories, dreams, role models, assessment tests—to name a few. In career exploration, practitioners have used stimuli such as books on labour market information or informational interviews to help people see new perspectives. But these are not the only stimuli that could be used.

There are a gold mine of ideas that can be adapted for use in life/ career counselling situations. They can be used as icebreakers with a purpose. They can be used as backswing activities for the development of creativity and imagination. They can be adapted for formal activities. For example, in the upcoming chapter on Career Exploration (Chapter 7), there is a segment on the use of a common wooden pencil as a tool to inform people about the world of work and its possibilities. Our use of the pencil in career exploration was originally stimulated by an activity on object linking in *Five Star Mind* (Wujec, 1995). There are many books written on creativity and imagination, in which you will find activities which provide stimulus for new ideas. In addition to books cited in the reference section, you will find others in the section on Additional Cross-training Resources at the end of the book.

Throughout the next chapters of *Hope-Filled Engagement*, you will find many practical activities with utilize different types of stimuli. But this is just the beginning; there is no end to the type of stimuli you can adapt or create. Collect as many as you can; you never know what will work for any particular person. Play with these different stimuli and explore what creative juices will flow both for you and for those you are helping. As creativity and imagination are released, new perspectives and possibilities will arise which in turn will draw out new hope.

chapter five

SELF-ASSESSMENT

Who am I?

Self-assessment revolves around the question *"Who am I?"* It may be a very simple question, yet it is very profound and challenging. It includes several other important questions, such as *"Who have I been?"*, *"Who am I becoming?"*, and *"Who do I want to be?"* How people answer such questions will certainly affect the other life/career counselling processes.

The question *"Who am I?"* is directly linked to *"What should I do with my life?"*, to a sense of identity and purpose. If people don't know who they are, they don't know where they fit. The opposite is also true: if people don't know where they fit, they won't know who they are. Through a dynamic life/career conversation with their world, people negotiate their sense of identity and purpose; this in turn affects their self-esteem and sense of hope.

Also *"Who am I?"* is not a neutral question. People do not come to the question with a blank slate. Their previous experiences on their life/career journeys may create perceptions that affect their ability to answer this question completely and accurately.

Multiple Questions, Answers, & Perspectives

This reality suggests that the way the question *"Who am I?"* is asked should bypass or remove potential barriers. There are many different kinds of barriers, so it may need to be asked many different ways.

Just as there are many different ways to ask the question, there is also never just one answer to it. Each person is a unique creation with a unique combination of aspects. Looking for one answer easily becomes looking for the "right" answer and results in creativity being hindered. Better to look for multiple answers, because when people are freed from the pressure of finding the "right" one, they are free to take more risks and to look at other possibilities. Learning to see ourselves from different perspectives is one of the most effective ways to generate these multiple questions and multiple answers.

Remember that *"Who am I?"* is a not a static question that can be asked and answered only once. Rather it is a dynamic, life-long question with a life-long answer. As people walk their life journeys, some aspects of their lives will remain relatively stable, others will change, others will disappear as new aspects appear. Unfortunately, some people are stuck in perceptions formed at an earlier time in their lives, even though life circumstances have changed.

Identity in Context

Finally, answering the question *"Who am I?"* is more than generating a list of personal assets. They do not exist in isolation but in a "web of interconnectedness" in which each asset is naturally connected to all others. For example, people's personal style will influence how they express their particular skills. People's skills and level of skills will influence how they may express their interests. This "web of interconnectedness" also enables people to see where they fit in their world. This dual perspective (personal assets and interconnectedness) is essential for a sense of "identity in context." Without this, people may discover their personal characteristics and yet not value them because they see no point to them.

In the segments to follow, we will be emphasizing this holistic multi-faceted "identity in context" through the Career Circle (Figure 12)and the Connections Circle (Figure 13), as well activities on Values and Balance which explore fitting everything in our lives together in a life-energizing sustainable way.

Activity: Point of View

The Point of View activity developed by Richard Wilde (Davis, 2001) can help prepare people for self-assessment using multiple perspectives. It can be used with small groups or adapted for individuals.

Overview the Activity

Introduce this activity by informing people that looking at things in many different ways is a very helpful ability when they are seeking to explore who they are and what they could do in life. The following activity is a fun way to begin looking at life from different perspectives.

The "Filling in the Blank" activity is based on the following sentence: "a [something] from the point of view of a [someone or something] is _____ ." You complete the activity by repeating the sentence and filling in the blanks as often as you can in the time allowed. There is no right or wrong answer. Think outside the box. Have fun. Provide an example by asking people to complete sentences such as the following; leave a few blanks empty for them to practice on:

a car from the point of view of a   driver   is transportation .
a car from the point of view of a car dealer is income   .
a car from the point of view of a   teen   is cool   .
a car from the point of view of a   dog   is _____ .
a car from the point of view of a _____ is _____ .

Small Group Activity

We typically use the "telephone" for this activity, but other things could be chosen if more relevant to people. Once they understand the activity, ask people to think about the question, *"What is a telephone?"*

and to brainstorm on the "telephone" from as many points of view as they can in 3-5 minutes. Ask them to list their ideas to be shared later:

"A telephone from the point of view of a _____ is _____."

You can assist their brainstorming by encouraging them to ask questions to generate different points of view. For example:

- *"What about different age groups? A baby? A teen? A senior?"*

- *"What about different occupations? A telemarketer? An interior decorator? A 911 operator?"*

- *"What about different life roles? A parent? A friend? A lover?"*

- *"What about different companies or organizations? A telephone company? An insurance agency? A charity?"*

- *"What about animals? A dog? A bug?"*

- *"What about inanimate objects? A table? A piece of paper?"*

- *"What about imaginary people or things? Superman? A ghost?"*

This could be even more interesting if you turn it into a mild competition by asking individuals or small groups to see who can come up with the most ideas.

Debrief the Activity

Ask those involved to share their answers. Ask them to think about what they have learned about the telephone through this activity. Did it expand their view of what a telephone is and does? We have found that people always realize that they thought they knew what a telephone was (usually a telephone is "something to talk to others with") but that there is much more to it than they ever imagined. Each one of these answers reveals aspects of what a telephone is and each of these aspects points to possible uses for the telephone.

How does this apply to self-assessment? *"If something as seemingly simple as a telephone can be and do so many things for so many, what about us, as people?"* We certainly have more aspects to us than a telephone does. *"If we were to look at ourselves from many different points of view, how would this change the way we answer the 'Who am I?' question?" "How would this expand the possibilities for what we could do with our lives?"*

In *Hope-Filled Engagement*, we illustrate this process with different activities that facilitate people looking at themselves from different perspectives. For example, the Career Circle (Figure 12) helps people to see themselves from the perspectives of skills, interest, personal style, values, life balance, learning, life/work roles, and work connections. The Connections Circle (Figure 13) enables people to look at themselves from the point of view of the different contexts that make up their life. The Favourite Things activity (Chapter Six, Figure 20) provides another set of different points of view. Each of these provides different perspectives. All of these emphasize a holistic multi-faceted perception of identity. Each of these circles is like a different lens for a kaleidoscope; as people look at their lives differently, they are able to see more things than they every imagined and also to see how the various aspects of their lives flow together to make a unified whole.

The Career Circle

In the process of self-assessment, people need to understand both what to look for and how to look for it. The "circle" is a culturally significant metaphor for a holistic life/career counselling process. One of the circles we use extensively is the Career Circle (Figure 12). It encourages looking at lives from multiple perspectives. It provides a visual framework to collect and organize insights about eight components essential for a proper understanding of oneself and for establishing career goals.

Over the years, we have adapted the Career Circle for different contexts, such as *Career Pathways* (Amundson & Poehnell, 2004) and *CareerScope* (Amundson, Poehnell, & Pattern, 2005). The most recent version from *Guiding Circles* has several adaptations designed to make it even more inclusive. It addresses the challenges and themes presented earlier by integrating components that are important to a holistic worldview (e.g., interconnections, balance, values, life roles, gifts) with more traditional career counselling components (e.g., learning, work experience, interests, skills, personal style, and labour market options) (Amundson, 1989; Amundson & Poehnell, 2004). The Career Circle has several key parts: the eight components, two rings, and the centre. We will examine these parts in more detail.

Eight Components

The Career Circle has eight components: skills, interests, personal style, values, balance, learning, life/work roles, and work connections. Issues such as diversity should alert us to the danger of potential misunderstandings of these components. It is important to ensure that practitioners and the people they work with have a similar understanding of these eight components.

Figure 12: The Career Circle

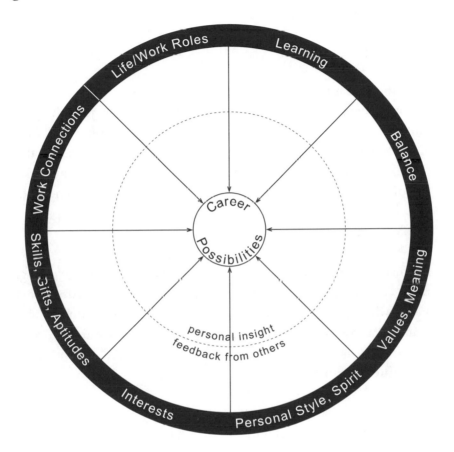

• **Skills, gifts, aptitudes:**

People have skills, gifts, or aptitudes that may be already mastered, in development, or still dormant. They may be "work related" or not. A "skill" is something people are capable of doing no matter how well. Skills should not be confused with "strengths" that refer to how well a person does something. Skills are usually expressed by action verbs (e.g., cook, teach, drive, remember, etc.). Watch for actions that contain other actions. For example, suppose people plan a party for friends. Obviously planning is a skill they have. But if you were to go to the next level and ask how they planned the party, you would probably discover many more skills (e.g., motivation, communication, organization, budgeting, cooking, decorating, etc.).

• **Interests**

The emphasis is on what people like or don't like, enjoy or don't enjoy. Watch for people discounting interests. Sometimes people don't think their interests outside of work have any career relevance. Sometimes they discount them because they don't think they can do them or because they don't think they are important. People may never be musicians, but it is still important that they enjoy music even if they are not proficient at it.

• **Personal style, spirit**

Personal characteristics are usually described with adjectives (e.g., eager, quiet, sincere, etc.) or adverbs (e.g., quickly, carefully, etc.) that describe the manner in which people do things. It often identifies people's uniqueness. For example, anyone can cook but their styles may be very different.

• **Values, meaning**

Values express what is important to people, what gives a sense of meaning to them, and/or what guides their behavior. Often values are expressed in the negative, when people complain about values that have been violated. In psychological counselling, counsellors are often discouraged from asking people the question *"Why?"* because it is seen as threatening. But in self-assessment, it is an important question that points to values.

• **Balance**

This looks at the life balance people experience or wish to experience and at how work fits into it. We have added this to the circle in order to increase focus on identifying those things which people need in life to be whole and healthy. Different people need different life balances to be healthy; different jobs reflect different life balances. *How do we match these more effectively?* Listen for life balance issues through people's comments such as *"I need time to …"* or *"I like to get away because …"*

- **Learning**

We use the word "learning" because the word "education" can be intimidating to people without a positive school experience. There is value in all learning whether formal or informal; but, though everyone has learning, not everyone has formal education. If you ask about people's learning, those who have had formal education will probably talk about it; so nothing is lost. If you ask someone without formal education about their learning, they won't raise their defenses because they will have learning to share. Life/career counselling can learn from the work being done in the Prior Learning Assessment field. In addition to content, learning can also refer to the way people learn (e.g., verbally, visually, manually, etc.).

- **Life/Work roles**

This refers to the roles people have had in life, whether paid or not. If people have a hard time understanding the concept of roles, illustrate possible areas in which they might have taken on responsibilities, such as work titles (carpenter, cook, driver, etc.), relationship titles (husband, wife, mother, father, child, brother, sister, friend, etc.), community relationships (coach of local hockey team, community volunteer, etc.), or task relationships (listener, story teller, helper, initiator, etc.).

Often the roles people play in their families and communities come naturally and reflect much about who they are and what they are capable of doing. Even if people have never had a formal paid job, they will have had many life roles and most life roles have a corresponding paid job somewhere. People may take their dog for a walk and there are paid dog walkers. People cook their meals and there are paid cooks. People drive and there are paid drivers. Therefore, when you examine life roles, you can discover many of the same things as if you were examining paid jobs.

- **Work connections**

Even if they don't realize it, people have connections with the world of work, both formal and informal (e.g., their knowledge about the world of work, potential careers, understanding of the labour market, etc.) or the people they know or the needs in their community.

Two Rings

Usually life/career counselling is done with individuals alone. In self-assessment, individuals may be looking at themselves only from their own perspective. But the themes of holistic life/career counselling, interconnectedness, and the career conversation suggest the need for the perspectives of others.

The two main rings of the Career Circle are for recording insight gained from two perspectives. The inner circle is for people's self-reflections and the outer circle is for insight from others. Others may see what we don't see and say what we don't feel free to say.

The Centre

The centre is for career possibilities that the eight components point to. The aim is to set career goals that are consistent and in harmony with the different components in the circle. People will need to prioritize and balance the different components. The greater the harmony, the greater the likelihood of people being successful and finding career satisfaction.

Using the Career Circle Effectively

People can often be impatient, wanting you to provide them with a career goal or a job immediately. The Career Circle emphasizes the need to start well in order to finish well. People will be more effective if some time is taken at the beginning to discover who they are and what they are capable of doing. Sometimes people don't look at all the components and so make incomplete assessments of themselves; this leads to ineffective, incomplete career decisions. This is very noticeable when people take new jobs and talk of them as if they were the best jobs ever, only to complain of them as the worst jobs imaginable in just a short time. Listen carefully and you'll hear that often they took the jobs for one reason (one component of the circle) and now hate the jobs for another (other components of the circle). If they had done a more thorough self-assessment, this might have been avoided.

Take time to find the right starting points to enter the circle; inappropriate starting points may raise barriers. Use holistic approaches such as storytelling to discover these components in a holistic context. Develop a diverse toolkit of activities for each of the different components to supplement what has been found through storytelling.

Keep a balanced perspective; not everything in the Career Circle will necessarily be fulfilled through any particular job. The question is whether or not it is being fulfilled in some area of people's lives. Without this perspective, people may have unrealistic expectations regarding what work may accomplish in their lives and be disappointed.

Remind people that not all the components will carry the same weight. One person may give more weight to balance, while another gives more weight to interests. Each person's circle will be unique.

Remind people that their Career Circles are dynamic and will change with time. As they go through life, they will perform different work/life roles, learn new things, develop new skills and interests, and so forth. People are more than their past and present; they have a future full of possibilities. So they may wish to come back to their Career Circles from time to time and update them as necessary.

Uses of the Career Circle

The Career Circle can be of value not just for self-awareness and self-assessment but also for many different aspects of crafting a career. In fact, the use of a consistent approach and framework throughout all the different processes of crafting a career (self-assessment and career exploration, career decision making, life-long learning, work search, and work maintenance, Figure 5) will be more effective in helping people understand what they are doing in each phase.

Throughout *Hope-Filled Engagement*, we will present different activities that can be used to assist people to discover insights about themselves that can be placed into their personal career circles.

The Connections Circle

The goal in self-assessment is to facilitate people's self-discovery of who they are. The Career Circle sets forth many of the key components for self-assessment. But as interconnectedness implies, people are more than their skills, interests, values, personal style, balance, learning, life/work roles, and work connections. Their identity is interrelated with all their connections to their larger world. The Connections Circle (Figure 13), originally used by our colleague Dr. Rod McCormick (1997) in Aboriginal healing contexts, is an effective framework to use when facilitating people's discovery of these connections.

Figure 13: Connections Circle

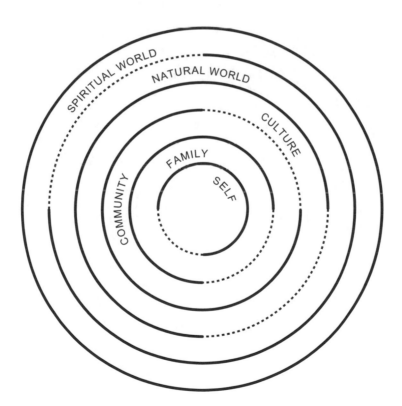

It is based on a collective orientation rather than the individualistic one often seen in counselling. This orientation reflects the worldview of many peoples. As ripples formed when a stone is dropped into a pond, so each person is connected to a series of relationships that start with self and move out to family, community, culture, the natural world and, ultimately, the spiritual world. It is in the context of these relationships that people negotiate their identity and their life/career journeys.

These connections are an essential aspect of the life/career journey. Identity must be centred in relationships if it is to have meaning. The Connections Circle complements the Career Circle. Both are needed if people are going to have a sense of identity in context, identity with meaning (Figure 14). People may identify many characteristics in their

*Figure 14: **Identity in Context***

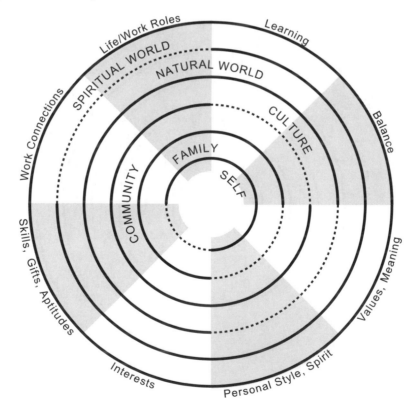

Career Circle; but if they feel disconnected from their world, they can still reflect a hopeless attitude. You hear it in comments such as, *"So I'm good at teaching. So what?" "What's the point?" "Who cares?" "What difference does it make?"* These are usually statements of disconnection. When people are stuck in perceived disconnection, it is easy for them to feel isolated and depressed or even look for connection in destructive contexts such as abusive relationships or gangs.

When explaining the Connections Circle, it is important to be open and flexible in explaining each of the spheres. These connections overlap and so different people may understand them differently. What is important is not that people meet some sort of formal definition in each of these spheres but that they are able to connect or reconnect with them.

- **Self** refers to anything about a person that is not connected to someone or something external (e.g., personal characteristics, memories, dreams, self-talk, etc.).

- **Family** refers to biological family or even other groups, such as peer groups or social groups that people view as family.

- **Community** can refer to a physical community (e.g., country, city, town, neighbourhood, etc.) or a relationship community (e.g., sports community, arts community, etc.).

- **Culture** is a very broad concept referring to shared beliefs, customs, social forms, activities, and so forth of any group (racial, religious, social); it can refer to anything from language to clothing, from social mores to arts and crafts.

- The **Natural World** refers to the physical world that we can connect with through senses such as sight, hearing, smell, or touch.

- The **Spiritual World** may be understood in a very formal sense (formal religions or philosophies of life) or very informally (a sense of oneness with the world); it refers to that which is metaphysical in some way. Some people may reject the concept of a spiritual world and may not wish to consider this sphere; others will find it an essential component.

There are many reciprocal facets to these diverse connections. People have been created as part of the larger whole. This implies, on one hand, that people have been gifted with all that is in their Career Circles in order to enable them to fulfill all the roles they will play in their world. This provides a context of meaning and purpose to all that they are. On the other hand, it is in the context of these various relationships that people ought to be able to find the support they need to fulfill these roles. The Connections Circle, therefore, can be used to identify the roles people have in their world and then to identify and be encouraged to access potential sources of support and meaning.

This understanding of connections can be applied in all the processes of crafting a career. For example, the roles in each of these spheres can be illuminating during career exploration. During decision making, it can give needed perspective into the possible influences upon people and into the possible ways in which others may be affected by people's decisions. During work search, it can provide an important network of people for discovering employment opportunities.

Activity: Connections Circle

There are many ways in which the Connections Circle could be used; in this activity, we will be focusing only on the connections that provide "support" for people. Support is something that is essential throughout life/career journeys. Unfortunately many people don't know how to access all the support that they have in their lives. Discovering and intentionally re-connecting with this support engages people with dynamic hope. The activity below can be easily adapted for individual counselling.

As with many of the activities in *Hope-Filled Engagement*, we recommend using a multi-step approach. We don't start by asking people directly to identify their connections. People who feel disconnected may find it challenging to think about their connections directly. Without any sense of connections, people will often just talk about their disconnections. It may just remind them that their lives don't have any meaning or that they have no support or that they don't fit anywhere. And once people move into this problem orientation, they often get stuck in it and just focus on what they don't have in their life.

So how can you approach it? Zander and Zander's (2000) concept of starting with possibilities rather than problems points to a solution. Rather than asking for a specific answer, start by asking: *"What are the possible connections people may have in life?"* People may not feel connected themselves but they still know possible connections. Once people have creatively brainstormed about possible connections, use these possible connections to identify the connections they actually have. We have found that people often begin to recognize connections that were right before them but they had not been conscious of before. They can make a fundamental shift from reacting to what they don't have to celebrating and embracing what they do have. Seeing all the possibilities for connections may be a major first step in reconnecting to their world and generating a sense of hope.

Introduction

Explain the Connections Circle. Emphasize an important aspect of discovering who they are and what they can do with their life is understanding the connections they have. It is these connections that provide a context for all that they have been gifted with in their lives. As well, these connections can be sources of real meaning and personal strength that can help support them through their challenging life/career journeys.

Arrange people into small groups (3-6 people each). Give each small group a flip chart and markers. They will list their findings on the flip charts which will be posted on the wall for further reflection.

Brainstorming Ideas

Using the "possibilities" approach, ask them to brainstorm on possible sources of meaning, purpose, or support in each of the six spheres of the Connections Circle and listing their ideas on flipcharts. Each group could brainstorm on all of the spheres or six groups could each brainstorm on one of the specific spheres. If you are working with people with low literacy, instead of writing ideas down, they could draw their ideas or make a collage of pictures. You may wish to have an individual or group generate a large collage of the Connections Circle using pictures. This could be posted and referred to in the future.

Review the rules of brainstorming, especially that there are no right or wrong answers. Allow people to place connections where they see them on the circle. If someone wants to put something under "family" and someone else wants to put it under the "spiritual world," then put it under both.

Emphasize that at this time they will not be focusing on their own personal connections but rather on possible connections that people generally could potentially draw support from in life. The starting point is not the support they think they have or don't have but what is possible. This objectifies the activity and makes it easier for people to discuss support connections without getting sidetracked by personal problems. However, once people get going, they may suggest their own personal connections.

Encourage people to use their imaginations to answer the question: *"Who or what do you think can give people a sense of support, strength, meaning, or the like?"* For example in the "self" ring, they can brainstorm about those things that people draw from within themselves to keep themselves going through the ups and downs of life's journey. In order to stimulate thinking in the outer five rings, ask people to brainstorm by asking five questions for each of the rings:

- *What people?* (individuals or groups)

- *What activities?* (things that people do alone or with others)

- *What places?* (locations, buildings, etc.)

- *What things?* (think of things that people connect with through the senses: sight, smell, touch, etc.; things may be animal, vegetable or mineral: animate or inanimate)

- *What concepts or ideas?* (formal or informal; e.g., a formalized moral code or a general sense of belonging)

Circulate among the groups to encourage and give assistance as needed. Sometimes it helps to have them ask themselves some other questions such as *"When people are down, what helps?"* or *"What gets people through hard times?"* or *"What keeps people going?"* Keep positive. Encourage the group to focus on what is possible and not what they don't have. The Sample Connections Circle (Figure 15) provides several examples of ideas that have been generated in hundreds of workshops with life/career practitioners.

You may wish to keep a photographic record of the various circles that groups or individuals create. When counselling individuals, you don't have the benefit of the group brainstorming dynamic, so you can show them these sample charts, after they have generated some ideas on their own. Let them know that these ideas have been generated by people like themselves. Ask them if they think of any other ideas after looking at the ones others have generated.

Figure 15: Sample Connections Circle

Debriefing the Possible Connections

Allow 30-60 minutes if each group is brainstorming on all six spheres; 15-20 minutes if they are only brainstorming on one of the six. Post each of the flip charts on a wall. Ask the whole group to gather around the charts and to read what people have written. If there is time, you may ask each group to read out what they have written; this can be helpful for auditory learners.

Facilitate an initial discussion of their findings by asking questions about what they see and think and feel, as they review all the posted support connections. People usually respond with comments such as how surprised they are by how much support there is around them, how much longer these lists could be if they had more time, how interconnected all the ideas are (e.g., so many ideas could appear under several spheres), and how simple and accessible many of these support connections are.

Personalizing the Possible Connections

Up to this point, the group has been dealing with general possibilities. In order to personalize their findings, pick a volunteer and ask him/her to go to the flip charts and circle some of the connections he/she has access to at that time. We ask for "some" rather than "all" because it is less threatening. Others can mentally circle the connections that they have while the person is drawing circles on the charts. Usually people are surprised at how many they circle for themselves. Ask the group how all of these connections make them feel. People often speak of feeling encouraged, inspired, and more connected. They often talk about having pride in their lives and communities when they reflect upon the richness of the connections available to them.

If there is time and it seems appropriate, you could ask them to identify those connections which they believe they have lost. Disconnections are part of life for all of us. But these disconnections can now be seen in the context of all the connections we still have. For most people there are many more connections than there are disconnections. Next ask the group to reflect on whether any of the connections they still have in their lives address the ones they have lost. For example, someone may have lost a loving parent but may still feel connected to them through memories, heirlooms, lessons learned, favourite activities, or locations.

Working with this aspect of people's identity may also prove to be helpful in a very common situation that many people, especially Aboriginal people, face. People who live in remote communities often have to leave those communities in order to obtain further schooling or to find work. It is unfortunate that far too many of these don't survive when they go to the urban communities. Many return home because they couldn't make the adjustment and a few get involved in harmful pursuits. This is a complicated issue with no simple answers. But one aspect is that when people leave these communities, they are encouraged to take care of themselves, do their best, and not get into trouble. This is right and proper. But from the perspective of the Connections Circle, one must ask what disconnections will occur when these people leave their communities. There are disconnects in most, if not all of the spheres. If that is so, what happens to people who face such disconnection? Clearly they become disoriented and may struggle finding support they can relate to. It may be helpful after having done the Connections Activity on possible support, to identify what disconnections may take place and then to strategize what connections remain and how they may fill in the void created by the loss of the other supports. Perhaps if people were better prepared to cope with these disconnections, their success rate would be much higher.

Closing

Review the activity and encourage people to continue to reflect on possible connections in their lives. Ask them how much more they would see if they were to take the Connections Circle and, over the next week or so, continue to brainstorm additional ideas. Remind the group that tragically too many people live as if they were impoverished, when in fact their lives may be full of rich connections that they have lost sight of. Sometimes the only time we become conscious of how many connections we have is when we lose them. It is important to acknowledge these connections on a regular basis.

Activity: Resolving Conflicting Values

Values are essential to our life/work journeys. But learning to sort out values conflicts is a challenging life skill, because they are often unrecognized, inconsistent, conflicting, and unrealized. As a result, many people struggle with life/career choices and live very fragmented lives. Because values are an increasingly difficult area to process, it is important that life/career practitioners be able to equip people with tools and strategies to assist them in resolving conflicting values.

Ineffective Ways to Deal with Conflicting Values

As people talk of their situations, you can often hear struggles with conflicting values and ineffective strategies being used to resolve them. At such times, it is important to stop and unpack the conflicts and then examine alternative strategies.

Over the last several years, one of the authors, Gray, has facilitated a number of *Guiding Circles* discussion groups on this topic. Through this process, the following metaphors have been identified as typical ineffective strategies for resolving conflicting values:

1. **The warrior**: values become a battle ground; resolving conflicting values may be confusing; some find clarity labelling things as black or white, claiming a position, and fighting all others.

2. **The ostrich**: head in the sand; unaware; *"I don't know why I do it!"*

3. **The juggler**: performing; but feeling guilty and stressed because one can't keep all the balls in the air at the same time.

4. **The marketer**: trying to sell values to oneself: *"I know this should be important to me."*

5. **The hypocrite**: saying one thing but doing another.

6. **The chameleon**: interacting with surroundings and blending in rather than choosing one's own values.

7. **The victim**: feeling defeated and out of control; *"I can't do anything?"*

8. **The guilty**: feeling guilty because one can't live consistently.

Steps to Resolving Conflicting Values:

There is no simple answer to the challenge of resolving conflicting values. We would suggest five steps to resolving conflicting values:

Step One: Recognize and acknowledge values conflict

The first step in dealing with values conflict is to recognize and acknowledge that such a conflict exists (Cochran, 1995). This is a big step for people who don't like conflict and would rather ignore it, deny it, and/or avoid it. Unfortunately unacknowledged conflict doesn't go away. It is important for people to be personally self-aware and identify spheres in which there is indecision, confusion, uncertainty, inertia, or angst. These may point to values conflicts. Encourage people to normalize their experience by understanding that such conflicts are a normal part of today's world.

Step Two: Gain perspective

Second, it is essential to gain perspective on the values that are in conflict. People need to identify what is really motivating their life and career choices by asking themselves a number of questions. Sometimes simple questions such as *"Why do I do this?"* or *"What is important to me in this experience?"* can reveal core values that affect attitudes and actions. The unpacking process is stimulated by looking from different perspectives, such as the following:

- **Past and Future**: *"Have I every faced a similar conflict in the past? How did I resolve it?" "Would my future self really want this?"*

- **Others**: the values choices we make are influenced by others and will in turn affect others. *"Who will be affected by my choice?" "How do the significant people around me view this conflict?"*

- **Core values**: It is helpful to probe for the value behind the value. *"Why am I doing this?" "Why do I want to do this?" "Why is this important to me?"* As with the peeling of the layers of an onion, so there is often a need to ask these questions several times to arrive at the inner core values. It may be that two apparently different values have the same core values underneath. At the level of core values, the conflict can be resolved.

- **Source**: Values are influenced by many factors, both internal and external. We usually assimilate unconsciously different values systems through family, community, cultural, and spiritual influences. Therefore, it is helpful to identify the source of the values we hold. *"Where did this come from? Connections? Role models?" "How has this value developed over time?" "If I knew where it came from, would I still want it?"*

- **End/Intention**: Since values influence attitudes and actions, it is important to consider the consequence of accepting any particular value or set of values. Ask some basic questions: *"Where does this value lead?" "What will happen if I choose to follow this path?"* Then ask if the probable result matches people's intentions: *"Is this going where I want to go?"*

- **Cost/Risk**: Value implies cost. Whatever values we choose, they will cost something, whether it be time, money, energy, prestige, or the like. *"What will this value cost me?" "Is it worth it?" "What will the cost be if I don't fulfill this value?" "Can I live without this?"*

- **Expression**: We can confuse the way in which a value may be expressed with the value itself. The seeming conflict may not actually be between different values but between different ways of fulfilling the values. There may be no real values conflict at all. *"How do I think I have to express this value?" "Why?" "Is this the only way to express this value?" "What alternatives are there?"*

- **Hope**: No matter how important a particular value may be, we will make choices based on our sense of hope. If we don't think something is possible, then we will tend not to try. *"Do I really believe this is possible?" "Why?"* or *"Why not?"*

Step Three: Release or modify values

Once values conflicts are unpacked, the next step is to release or modify values that are no longer relevant. For example, knowing the source, end, or cost of values may help us see that we don't really want them at all. If we don't want them, we must choose to say *"no"* to them. This can be challenging, especially in situations where values have been "pounded into" us through abusive situations; sometimes the tragedy is that the abused unconsciously assimilates the values of the abuser with the end result that the abused person becomes the abuser. Forgiveness often becomes the best path to release such values.

Step Four: Negotiate conflict resolution

Once unnecessary conflicts are dealt with, there may still be situations in which there are conflicting values. There are several strategies which could be employed alone or in combination. The following list is not exhaustive but it does contain several common strategies that people use.

- **Questions**: It can be helpful just to stop and ask some questions, such as those in Step 2 on gaining perspective.

- **Priorities**: Not all values are equal; and, therefore, it is possible to group them based on relative importance.

- **Plumblines**: Sometimes people can identify some values which are clearly most important. These can become the standard against which unclear or conflicting values can be evaluated. If people decide that family is a core value, they can examine other values in terms of their influence upon family.

- **Intuition**: Sometimes people's "gut" feelings can communicate deep values even before the conscious mind can sort things out.

- **Times and Seasons**: Not all values need to be fulfilled at the same time; some can be fulfilled at a later time.

- **Deal Breakers**: Sometimes what is really most important becomes clear when we lose or think we will lose it. *"What will happen if I don't have this in my life?" "Could I live without this?"*

- **Negotiation and Compromise**: Some level of give and take can result in a solution which is the best possible in a situation.

- **Role Models**: Role models are people who have already travelled along a life journey and made choices to fulfill their goals. They are especially helpful to young people who haven't had enough life experience yet to really judge what is important and what isn't. If they wish to be like their role model, then they will probably need to make similar choices. *"What would he/she do?"*

- **Spiritual Exercises**: Clarity can sometimes come through the review of core spiritual beliefs and the peace of mind that comes through activities such as prayer and meditation.

Step Five: Embrace life balance; learn to cope with dissonance

Some conflicts may not be conflicts at all and can be dealt with by releasing unnecessary values or ways of expressing values. Some conflicts are real and may be resolved through negotiation with oneself or with others. There may still be others where, because of the complexity of life's circumstances, it is difficult to find a clear solution. At such points people must be encouraged to accept that part of life balance it to learn to cope with a measure of dissonance with the hope that a clear path may become apparent at some time in the future.

This segment has focused on the dynamics of resolving values conflicts. The process of enacting change can be done at an individual level but, in many cases, this is a time to involve others. Life/career practitioners or discussion groups can play an important role in helping people to identify and resolve their values conflicts.

Activity: Balance

Life balance is an essential theme of the *Hope-Filled Engagement* approach because it is an essential aspect of a holistic life/career journey.

This activity uses a Balance Circle (Figure 16), adapted from a traditional Medicine Wheel that Rod McCormick (1995) uses in Aboriginal healing. It enables people to examine their own life balance, to reflect on its impact on their current life/work situation, and finally to encourage them to consider ways to come into healthier life balance where necessary. It is presented as a group activity but may be adapted for use with individuals.

Introducing the Activity

Some people may see no point in doing the activity. They may protest that they can't afford the luxury of life balance when all they are trying to do is to survive. The goal is not just the next job, but a healthy life balance as they follow their life/career journeys. At a very pragmatic level, once work is found, the better the life balance, the better are the chances for people to be able to maintain a job successfully.

Life balance looks at all of life, not just work. If possible, use this activity after other self-assessment activities (Chapter 6), such as storytelling which help people to reflect on their life experiences more holistically. For example, in the Favourite Things activity people answer a series of questions about some of their favourite things in life. The last question in that activity asks about the place of the mental, emotional, spiritual, or physical in each of their favourite things. This can be a starting point as they move to thinking about their life balance more specifically.

This is not a formal in-depth examination of life balance, but a general reflection of how people perceive their current life balance. As with the

Figure 16: Balance Circle

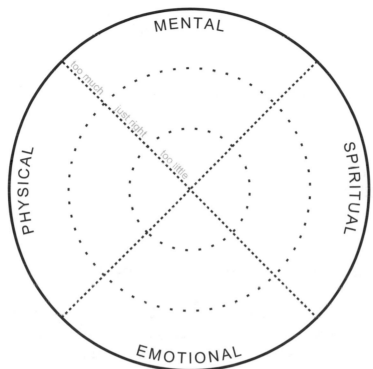

Favourite Things activity, we usually avoid giving a detailed explanation of these areas, but provide simple explanations/illustrations, such as:

- **Physical**: anything related to the body, such as exercise, eating, grooming, energy and physical stamina.

- **Mental**: anything related to thinking (formal or informal), such as self-reflection, self-talk, learning, planning, or decision making.

- **Emotional**: recognizing and expressing emotions appropriately.

- **Spiritual**: metaphysical perspectives (formal or informal); being inspired by concepts and activities, such as meaning, hope, faith, forgiveness, or prayer.

If people are still unsure, encourage them to think of concrete life experiences and to reflect on how these four areas were present in these experiences. Any one activity may reflect one or more of the four areas.

After the four spheres of life are introduced, direct people to the three levels of balance. Ask them to fill in for each sphere whether they think that they have "too little," "just right," or "too much" of it in their life as a whole. Remember that answers will be subjective; they will refer to peoples' sense of whether or not this area of their life is in balance or not. You should illustrate by filling out a sample balance circle (Figure 17). In this example, the mental is too high, the emotional too low, and the physical is too inconsistent; the spiritual is closest to being in balance.

Balance in Evaluating Life Balance

It is important to be sensitive and realistic when exploring life balance. It is easy for people to fall into the trap of being judgmental. The following thoughts will help in keeping the discussion positive and hopeful.

- Life balance is very much a personal matter. There is no set right or wrong. Each person's balance will be unique.

- Life balance doesn't mean that everything will be perfect but whether people have a balance they believe is appropriate for them at this point in life.

- Life balance may be looked at globally or specifically. Even though people may feel like their entire life is out of balance, there may be some areas in which they have a reasonable balance. These areas may reveal balance strategies that work for them.

- Life balance is dynamic not static. What may be an appropriate life balance today may not be tomorrow or next week or next year. What may work in one situation may not work in another. For

Figure 17: Sample Balance Circle

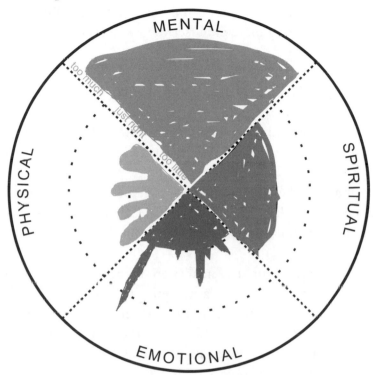

example, we often hear new mothers frustrated with being out of balance: physically exhausted, emotionally all over the map, lacking mentally stimulation, and spiritually confused. But are they out of balance or do they reflect the normal life balance for new mothers with newborn babies. People need to be realistic in their balance expectations and avoid unnecessary judgmentalism.

- Life balance is a daily choice. Balance is dynamic, so people will not find balance by standing still but by "walking the tightrope of life."

- Life balance is more a process of integrating the various aspects of life than merely juggling them. While juggling is a component of balance, it can imply that you do one thing by putting aside others. This can lead to a competition between aspects of life rather than a harmony. We can't do everything at once, so we need to make choices between different activities. But it may be possible to bring more of ourselves to whatever we choose to do.

Reflecting on the Balance Circle

Once people have filled in their balance circles, debrief their perceptions of their life balance. Ask people to identify the sphere which they think is "closest" to being just right. Some people may not perceive any of their areas as being in balance but everyone will have something that is closest. If they have more than one that they think is close to just right, ask them to choose the one they feel is the closest.

Divide the larger group into smaller groups according to the sphere they see as their strongest. This is a strength-based approach. We will explore the impact of balance in the context of employment or unemployment. The question is *"How?"* Ask them to share within each group how they think the sphere they are discussing impacts people when at work or when unemployed if it is "too little", "just right" or "too much." Ask each group to share what they have discussed. Affirm their observations and add thoughts as necessary. If you are working with an individual, you can ask similar questions.

Once each group has shared, ask the whole group what they learned. People often talk about their surprise at how each sphere affects employment and unemployment and how interconnected these four spheres are. They realize that what happens in one sphere affects all the others. For example if people feel their physical sphere is too low, they can lose energy (physical), become discouraged and stressed (emotional), lose the ability to concentrate (mental), and lose a sense of identity and hope (spiritual). This emphasizes the importance of all four areas and not just a few.

As you debrief the Balance Circle, remember not to be judgmental. Allow people to draw their own conclusions. If you sense that they are missing something significant, use questions to dig deeper and assist them to gain greater insight.

"Why do you think that you spend too little or too much time and energy in this area?" "What do you think is missing?" "What do you do to maintain balance in this area?" "Can you think of specific activities that put this sphere in or out of balance for you?" "Have you always felt that this area has been in or out of balance? If not, when did it start to change and why?" "As you reflect on this activity, do you still feel that your life is in or out of balance?" "Do you have a sense of wholeness? To what degree?"

If you are working in an individual context, you can ask more personal questions. In a group context you may wish to follow-up with individual interviews with people as seems appropriate.

Growing in Life Balance

Once you have discussed the Balance Circle, explore possible actions that could be taken to improve life balance. Ask questions to help people evaluate their current situation: *"As you look at your Balance Circle, how do you feel about the balance you now have in your life?" "Is this the balance you would like to have?" "What would you like to change?" "How do you think you could do that?"* To ensure the activity is not lost in generalities, encourage people to be specific in listing things to do to attain better balance.

If people are unsure how to gain or maintain balance in a certain sphere, there are several strategies to help them find answers. Often people don't recognize things in their lives that could bring greater life balance.

First, ask people to reflect on the spheres that are closest to being just right for them. *How have they been able to maintain balance in those areas?* If they have found an answer in one sphere, they may be able to apply it to others.

Second, if people overlay the Connections Circle (Figure 13) over the Balance Circle, as in Figure 18, they can draw on many of the supports (people, activities, places, concepts, and things) they have already identified to assist them in working towards better life balance. For example, they don't have to work out life balance alone; there may be people who can help them. Supportive activities may be used to find a better balance. Special places may be more conducive to developing balance. Meditating on meanifingful concepts may give insight or perspective. Specific things may helpful; for example, a warm bath can do wonders for helping someone relax physically and emotionally.

As you conclude this activity, Encourage people to be focused and realistic in working toward life balance. Emphasize that working on life balance will help them during all stages of their life/work journeys.

Figure 18: Balance and Connections

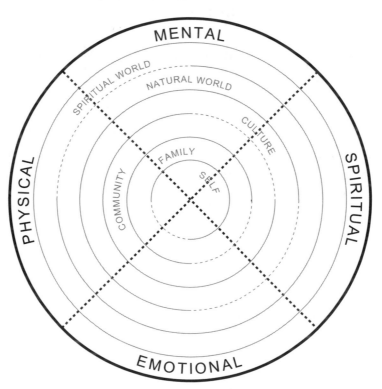

Insight from Others

Self-assessment doesn't have to imply only self-perception. The Career Circle calls for self-assessment from two perspectives: people's own self-reflections and insight from others. These perspectives are recorded in the two main rings of the Career Circle (Figure 12). We suggest that others might see what we don't see and say what we don't feel free to say. This concept is also related to the themes of Interconnectedness and the Career Conversation (Chapter 3). In this segment, we will explore this in more detail as well as look at some strategies for getting meaningful insight from others.

The Need for Others' Perspectives

Three significant questions show that the perspectives of others are really needed for a full and realistic self-assessment.

1. *"How much do you know about yourself?" "Do you know 100% of all there is to know about yourself?"* People usually quickly answer *"No!" Why don't they know everything about themselves?* Many reasons are given, such as blind spots, still learning, or life changes.

2. *"How much of what you know about yourself is 100% accurate?"* Everyone usually answers *"Not everything." Why not?* Again people recognize their own subjectivity and blind spots. This question often arouses the most laughter.

3. *"How much of what you know about yourself do you feel comfortable talking about?" "Can you easily talk about your personal strengths?"* Many answer, *"No!"*, because of issues such as enculturated humility.

Honest answers to questions like these suggest that what people know of themselves is at best somewhat incomplete and somewhat inaccurate.

Add to that people's reluctance to talk about themselves, and the value of expanding the Career Circle to include others becomes very clear.

Tragically, for multi-barriered people this reality is usually accentuated. When self-esteem goes down; self-knowledge tends to go down. When self-esteem goes down; accuracy of self-perception tends to go down. Often what does go up is the sense of enculturated humility and the sense of freedom to share only what they think is wrong in their lives. It is not hard to realize then that working with people in isolation may have negative effects upon the process of self-assessment.

The Benefits from Others' Perspectives

This multi-perspective approach has many benefits. First, it can provide a needed completeness and greater accuracy to self-assessment. Second, it helps people strengthen their connections with others. Third, it gives others permission and a workable process to express their support for people and helps people to be aware of this support. Finally, it incorporates the themes of holistic life/career counselling, interconnectedness, and the career conversation (Chapter 3).

One of the most common responses we receive from those who get feedback from people close to them is surprise at how positive the feedback is. Youth have commented that they didn't know their parents had such positive views of them. Often even spouses express this same surprise. How can this be? Sometimes when people are close, they don't share because they think others know what they think of them. Unfortunately, people often don't know what others are thinking if it isn't stated explicitly. Sometimes it is simply that people don't have a safe framework for sharing such insight. Providing such a framework can have a powerful effect as people find new hope by connecting at new levels.

One additional benefit is the potential impact on a community in which such insight is sought and given. In an indirect way, people in the community are learning more about the self-assessment process as they help others. This can help increase the capacity not only of individuals but also of communities to be more effective in their own life/career journeys.

Identifying the People to Ask

Once we recognize the benefits of gaining insight from others, the first task is to identify individuals from family, friends, or community who people believe could provide relevant insight to assist in the self-assessment.

People can complete an activity such as the Connections Circle (Figure 13) to identify those people with whom they already feel connected. These would be the logical people to look to for insight. If they have not already identified such people, it is important to help them identify some.

Once people have been identified, discuss briefly the relationships with those being assessed. First, gaining insight from a variety of relationships ensures a broad range of perspectives. Second, it is important to watch for relationships which are toxic and to guard people from those who would use this as an opportunity to abuse them. This can be very damaging, especially when someone has chosen to be vulnerable and requested input. Check such factors as their knowledge of those being assessed and the level of trust in the relationship.

Strategies for Obtaining Insight from Others

Feedback may be obtained using several effective strategies from simple to more complex. They can be used alone or in combination.

1. Ask people what others have said about them

When pushed to share some of their strengths, sometimes people who have been hesitant to share do so, by prefacing their comments with

"People say I'm ... " They do not feel free to state something directly but they can say something that others have said. People often know what others think of them and so this knowledge may be explored.

2. A talking circle

A more complex approach is that of the talking circle. Talking circles have long been a cultural practice within Aboriginal communities across Canada. They can also be effectively adapted into other contexts.

Identify significant others that people feel comfortable with and that have insight to share. Invite them to participate in the talking circle and give a simple explanation of what will take place.

When the circle is called together, set forth the expectations and norms of the group. It will be important to facilitate this in a positive affirming manner; the talking circle should be a place of safety for those involved. Emphasize that the purpose of this circle is not to identify shortcomings of anyone but to identify the positive things. Each person around the circle will be given an opportunity to speak in turn. While one person is speaking, the others in the group are to respectfully listen.

The Career Circle (Figure 12) can be an effective framework for gathering the insight from the group. Prepare a circle large enough for all to see. Explain the purpose of the circle and the meaning of the different sections of the circle. With the person for whom the talking circle has been called, briefly present the insights that have been discovered so far. Invite each person around the circle to add what they see in the person's life and record the insights into the appropriate sections of the circle.

Once everyone in the circle has shared their insight, review the insights gained and ask the people in the circle what career possibilities they think would fit all that has been revealed about the person's personal characteristics.

3. A simple questionnaire

A third strategy is a simple questionnaire to collect insight from family, friends, and community. We have used this in several of our workbooks and have found them to be easy to use and very effective.

There are times when the direct involvement of family and community in something such as a talking circle is not feasible and yet you still would like some direct feedback. Questionnaires allow for feedback from others even though they cannot be there physically.

Our one-page questionnaires provides a simple introduction to the questionnaire and then six simple questions. For example, Figure 19 reflects questionnaires used in our workbooks:

Explain the use of the questionnaires to the people you are working with. Ask them to identify at least three people whom they would like to send the questionnaires to. If you identify actual names when they are with you, people are more likely to use the questionnaires. Provide a copy of the questionnaire for each person they have identified. Encourage them to give out the questionnaires as soon as possible and to give their connections a specific time period to fill out the questionnaires. If any people are unable to read, the questions may be asked verbally and recorded by someone else. Once the questionnaires have been returned, people can summarize the answers onto a summary form.

Debrief the Insights of Others

No matter what strategy you use, it is important to debrief the insights given by others. Encourage people to interact with what others have said through questions, such as the following: *"What have others said?" "Do you agree with what they have stated?" "Have you ever seen these things in your own life? When? If not, why not?" "What new insights have they provided?" "How does it make you feel?"*

You can complete the debriefing by adding these insights to their Career Circles. Discuss with people, where each of the insights provided would fit best on the Career Circle.

Encourage people to continue to listen for positive insight from others in their regular contact with them. When they hear something new, they can add it to their Career Circle.

Figure 19: Insight from Others Questionnaire

Please answer the following questions briefly and return to me when completed. I am seeking to learn more about myself in order to make good life and career choices. Your input is important in getting a complete look at myself from many different perspectives. Therefore, your honesty is greatly appreciated. If you need more space, please write on the back of this form.

1. What are the things you have seen me do? What do you see as my strengths?

2. What do you think are my major interests?

3. How would you describe my personal characteristics?

4. What positive changes have you noticed in my life over time?

5. What do you see as areas I should be seeking to develop in the future?

6. What specific career suggestions would you have for me at this time?

chapter six

STORYTELLING

<u>*Storytelling: A Craft*</u>

Storytelling is a traditional activity with broad appeal across most peoples and cultures. It can be a very simple yet profound means of discovery within the self-assessment process. Just as storytelling has helped generations of people to discover their world and their imaginations, so too storytelling can open up people's eyes and hearts to see their own lives in new and fresh ways.

Some life/career practitioners may be wary of trying storytelling either because they feel unsure of the approach or because they have found some people to be unresponsive to other types of activities. Hopefully the next few chapters will help you feel more comfortable with storytelling. As to unresponsive people, these are the ones that storytelling can have the most dramatic affect upon. It is surprising how people can open up when they realize someone is actually interested in their life stories.

We have discussed barriers that make it difficult for people to see new things in their lives. There has been much written about teaching people to draw by teaching them to see with the innocent eye, the eye of a child who naturally asks and asks and then asks again with an insatiable curiosity to learn. The barriers that books such as *Drawing on the Right Side of the Brain* (Edwards, 1989) address not only apply to art but also to self-discovery and self-assessment, as do their suggestions for overcoming these barriers.

Far too many people seem to lose their natural curiosity as they get older. Their images of themselves and of the world around them become frozen in time, when they begin to become critical of what they draw (often in the pre-teen years). People have selective sight and habit focus; they begin to see only what they have been conditioned to see.

Frederick Frank (1973, pp. 3-4) writes in *The Zen of Seeing* about people doing a lot of looking, but seeing less and less:

Never has it been more urgent to speak of SEEING.
Ever more gadgets, from cameras to computers, from art
books to video tapes, conspire to take over our thinking,
our feeling, our experiencing, our seeing. Onlookers we
are, spectators… "Subjects" we are, that look at "objects."
Quickly we stick labels on all that is, labels that stick once
– and for all. By these labels we recognize every thing but
no longer SEE anything."

The same can be said of the way that people look at their own lives.
They may spend considerable time looking at themselves but not seeing
what is really there. It is as if they have been blinded to the riches in their
lives. Whatever the reason (enculturated humility, life experiences or lack
of them, real or perceived feedback from others, or just not knowing
what to do), people can become stuck with negative self-images, crippling
labels that hinder a free life/career journey of discovery and hope.

Just as people can learn to see and, therefore, learn to draw, people
can also learn to see what is in their lives and, therefore, learn to draw
new conclusions about who they are and what they are capable of. If the
ways of seeing that people know are too narrow, then new ways of seeing
can be learned with time and attention. All that is needed is an accessible
approach that teaches people what to see and how to see. Storytelling is
such an approach. In storytelling, people learn to see and then to draw
their own lives with words and story.

In Chapter Four we set forth CareerCraft as a metaphor to supplement
the metaphor of career management. Any craft, including storytelling, can
be understood from three perspectives: function, skill, and creativity.

Function

As a craft, storytelling should be very practical, purposeful, and hands-
on. There are many different styles of storytelling or narrative which

reflect different priorities, goals, and approaches. What is the purpose of storytelling in the context of self-assessment? We will be exploring storytelling for the primary purpose of facilitating people's self-discovery of who they are and of the personal assets they have in their lives. The goal is for people to discover their "psychological DNA" (Amundson, 2003), that is the patterns in their life which make them who they are.

Engaging people in storytelling engages them with hope. Such self-discovery encourages them to value and take ownership of what they discover. Though people's views of themselves may have been stunted, discovering such incredible riches within their lives can have a positive effect on their self-esteem. As people begin to value themselves, they can then be helped to see that they have things in their everyday lives that could also be of value in the world of education or employment.

Skill

There is skill involved in storytelling, but it can be learned in the doing. It is a natural ability that can be as simple as toddlers talking about themselves or as deep as an autobiography by a master writer. Every craft involves skill in three areas: materials, tools, and processes.

- **Materials**

What are the materials of storytelling? Obviously it is the stories that make up people's lives. Since people's lives are full of stories, there is no shortage of material for storytelling.

- **Tools**

There are several tools which can enhance the storytelling experience. The Career Circle (chapter 12) provides a framework for what

We ask to know the will of God without guessing that his will is written into our very beings.
- Elizabeth O'Connor

to look for in people's lives and for organizing the findings in a way appropriate for self-assessment and career exploration. As well, questions are the tools of discovery. In upcoming segments on questioning, we will explore the wealth of information that can be found within any life story.

- **Process**

Every craft, including storytelling, has its own processes; a practical understanding of these processes is essential to being skillful in that craft.

There are many different approaches to storytelling in self-assessment. Over the years, the Pattern Identification Exercise presented in *Active Engagement* (Amundson, 2009) has proven to be very effective in helping people discover who they are. It is an approach that engages people where they are engaged in life and that is culturally appropriate and accessible to most people. It is not our goal to repeat what has already been presented, but to examine storytelling from the perspective of craft and expand on its use, especially as it applies to *Hope-Filled Engagement*.

Whatever storytelling structure is used, the structure must address realistic and accessible starting points, mutually-agreed-upon goals, and clear steps for facilitating people's telling their own stories, for facilitating people's self-discovery (versus our telling them), and for facilitating people's ownership of the findings and growth in self-esteem and hope.

Creativity

Effective facilitating of storytelling involves a balance between art and science; therefore, creativity is essential.

The science of storytelling is seen in the focused tools and structure used to examine stories. When people are first starting, they can follow simple steps and specific goals which are both logically sequential and organically interrelated. But without creativity such a process could be cold, impersonal, and mechanical. Storytelling as art suggests the process ought to be creative, organic, fluid, engaging, open, curious, accessible, and non-threatening. It must not only follow a focused structure but also be always open to the unexpected and allow the story to guide the process.

Creative elements are evident throughout the storytelling process. For example, storytelling enables people to look at themselves from different perspectives with the innocent eye and to discover new possibilities. Creativity emphasizes beauty, Storytelling also looks at the unique stories of unique people. Many people do not think that they or their stories are interesting or that they will discover anything in them. But the storytelling process brings out the riches and the beauty in the stories and in the people. Storytelling balances the right and left brains as it holistically examines people within the context of actual life experiences. The use of a flip chart to list discoveries provides a visual depiction of the story to stimulate further discovery and reflection.

You may find it helpful to re-read the chapter on CareerCraft from the perspective of storytelling. Many other aspects of it are very applicable to the storytelling approach we are suggesting.

Remember that you don't have to be perfect in order to start. Craft is something you learn by doing. If this storytelling approach is new to you, start simple. Practise with someone you feel comfortable with, such as a family member, friend, or someone you are working with that you know would be open to the activity.

Storytelling: Starting Points

Choosing Starting Points

If you have decided to try storytelling, you may be wondering: *"Where do I start?" "What stories should I have people share?" "Which will be most helpful for this process?" "How do I find these stories?"*

At one level the answer is very simple: you have to find the stories that people are willing to talk about. But this just raises another question: *"What are people willing to talk about?"*

It is important to start where people are engaged in life. It is at these points that people often find their voice. To start by asking questions about stories in which people aren't engaged is to potentially raise barriers and invite resistance. This is especially true when people are asked about areas of life which they know little about or which contain negative associations. People don't like to talk about situations which they feel reveals only their failures, weaknesses, and problems; they already know these.

Fortunately there is no shortage of stories in people's lives to choose from. People may not have had meaningful education or work experiences, but they probably will have had many other life experiences which can be rich sources for stories. The riches are not so much in the activity itself as in the person in the story. When people are engaged in things they choose to do, it is there that they will most clearly reveal themselves and their uniqueness. For example, both Gray and his wife are good cooks but both have vastly different cooking styles. Gray's style is much more detailed and meticulous and naturally reflects his scientific background, while his wife's is more carefree. His collection of cookbooks point to his love of research. His pantry is full of cooking utensils and points to his interest in always having the right tool for the job.

Finding Starting Points Generated from Life

So where does one find such stories, such starting points? The answer is as diverse as the people we work with. When the usual areas of schooling and jobs don't prove to be too helpful, practitioners often turn to other areas for secondary possibilities. But this order (always starting with school or work) may have the unfortunate effect of raising barriers and of unintentionally devaluing other life experiences. This subtly implies that these other areas of life aren't quite as good.

Many people already tend to discount many of their life experiences as so normal or boring that they can't imagine anything of value in them for the world of school and jobs. If they have been enculturated to believe that only the worlds of school and jobs are relevant, they may be blind to the wonderful things these other areas reveal.

By asking, first, about areas in which people are engaged, the process is more accessible. If people are really engaged in school or work, they will naturally bring these up. If people aren't engaged in them, these won't be raised as a barrier to the process.

Some of effective starting points may be found by exploring areas such as:

- Leisure activities
- Social activities
- Volunteer activities
- Family activities
- Spiritual activities
- Life/work roles
- Interests
- Hobbies
- Accomplishments
- Sports
- Learning experiences
- Reading

- Role models
- Fond memories

- Dreams of the future
- Portfolio artifacts

Such an approach reflects the fundamental principle that people learn by connecting the unknown to the known. When people tell stories about aspects of their lives in which they are engaged, they are usually talking about things they know something about. Such stories often reflect areas of people's lives where things are actually working for them; this enables them to see that their lives are more than problems. This in turn cultivates hope.

Focusing on "ordinary" life experiences is also more likely to create a sense of commonality between practitioners and the people they work with. There may be little in common in the worlds of formal education and work, but they may share an interest in some hobby or leisure activity.

Another aspect to consider when finding stories has to do with the time of life the story is taken from. Sometimes people discount stories because they are not current. Yet in helping people identify stories to share, it is surprising how often we hear stories from when people were very young. For example, one practitioner in a training session, shared a story of playing in the snow with a parent at the age of six. After the story was finished, all of the person's coworkers were surprised how much the story reflected the person's current work practices. Looking into the past may be especially helpful if people are struggling with dysfunctionality in their current life. The past may be the best place for them to see themselves before their lives became distorted with problems.

Accepting that stories may come from diverse life experiences at different times of life still leaves the practical question of where to start the search. Instead of trying to guess where to start, why not ask people themselves. They know where their lives are engaged; they are the experts in their own lives. The Favourite Things activity in the next segment can be a simple yet effective way to identify important starting points for storytelling. Asking people to list their favourite things in life is a very accessible, non-threatening way to identify where people are engaged in life.

Once people are committed and engaged in the process, it may be easier to address other life experiences such as schooling or jobs.

Need for Specific Stories

Finally, it is important to find specific stories. Being specific and concrete helps people be reflective; general thoughts lend themselves to generalized answers. The more general the story, the more likely people will share thoughts that may have been filtered through their mental screens, which may be negative and self-depreciating. When people are telling specific stories, they can draw more on remembering than on reflecting. It is often easier for people to remember the details of actual life incidents than it is to be reflective about who they are. Once the details have been remembered, people can then reflect on the specifics of the stories and unpack them for relevant patterns.

Storytelling Activity:
Favourite Things

Activity Overview

Favourite Things (Amundson, 2009) focuses on the things that people enjoy. These favourite things are a rich source of positive concrete life experiences which provide excellent starting points for storytelling.

Favourite Things is a short, simple activity which engages people with hope in many ways. Because it focuses on people's joys, it engages them where they are engaged in life. When passed through the filter of the challenges discussed earlier, this activity is clearly very accessible to a wide spectrum of people.

It is not culturally dependent; whatever people's background, all people have things they enjoy. It is not dependent on connections with the world of formal education or employment; if people view these as favorite things, they can put them down; if people don't like these, they can look at other things. Rather than assuming that people can do positive focused self-reflection, it leads people through a step-by-step process that helps them focus and reflect on positive things in their lives. Finally, enculturated humility doesn't tend to be an issue because it is usually culturally appropriate for people to talk about things they enjoy. There is a big difference to many people's ears between *"I am a good cook"* and *"I enjoy cooking."*

The Favourite Things activity, when used early in counselling, can be a means to gently encourage participants to open up and begin talking. Rather than putting up barriers and shutting down in the counselling process because they are faced with questions that they don't have good answers for, people find it easy to talk about the things they enjoy and, therefore, themselves. Once talking, it is easier for people to keep talking.

Another wonderful outcome of this activity is that it is effective not only in assisting people to discover things about themselves but also for developing meaningful working relationships between practitioners and the people they are working with. People often recognize commonalities when they share their favorite things.

Finally, this can also be used to prepare people to reflect upon life balance issues, one of the major themes of *Hope-Filled Engagement*.

For the sake of simplicity, we will describe this activity for use in a group setting. It can be adapted for use in individual counselling sessions.

Orienting People to the Activity

Introduce the activity as one that has been effective in helping many other people get to know themselves better.

Explain that in the first part of the activity, they will be asked six questions one at a time in a specific order. For the sake of the activity, ask them to answer these questions in the order given and not to move on to the next question before the next question is given. This activity is not a race; but a time to pause and think about life. If they finish a question before the rest of the group, encourage them to use the extra time to reflect on the answers they've already put down. Explain that it is ok not to answer each question fully, either because of time or because they cannot think of any more answers.

Encourage them to answer each question as honestly as they can. Remind them that in this activity, there are no right or wrong answers. They should keep their answers short and simple. If possible, give personal examples for each of the questions as you ask them. This not only illustrates the process but also helps develop relationships with the people. Figure 20: Sample Favourite Things is an example of a partially completed circle relating to some of Gray's favorite things.

Figure 20: Sample Favourite Things

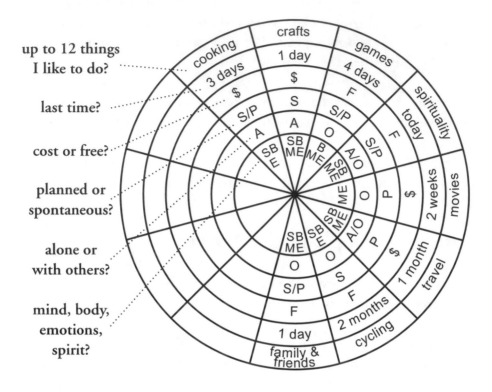

If you use this circle, explain that there are 12 sections, like 12 pieces of a pie. Each piece of the pie has space for answers to each of the six questions. As you ask each question, indicate the appropriate ring of the circle.

Facilitating the Activity

Ask the following six questions in order.

1. *What are up to 12 things you like to do?*

The favorite things can come from any area of their lives past or present. The important thing is that they think of things they enjoy doing.

Notice that the question doesn't ask them to write down *"12"* things but *"up to 12"* things. If we ask for 12 things and people cannot think of 12, they may feel as if they have failed the activity. This may seem like a little thing, but it is important to avoiding wording that may trigger feelings of failure in those who are accustomed to seeing themselves as failures. We want to assure people that what is important is identifying only the favorite things that they can think of.

2. *How long since you last did each of these 12 things?*

Clarify for people that it may be today, yesterday, a week, a month, a year, or longer. If they have time, ask them to try to visualize that last time.

3. *Does it usually cost money ($) or is it free (F)?*

A key word in this question is "usually." Which is the most common? If people find that it is evenly split between the two answers, they can put both down. Someone may even have a favorite thing that makes money.

4. *Is it usually planned (P) or spontaneous (S)?*

If people hesitate because they're not sure of this, ask them to think back to some of the times they did this favourite thing and ask them if they did anything to prepare for it or if they just did it.

5. *Do I usually do it alone (A)? with others (O)?*

You may ask them to think about who these people are. *Is it the same people for all the favourite things?*

6. *Does it involve mind (M), body (B), spirit (S), emotion (E), or a combination?*

This is the most subjective of all the questions. Keep this simple. This is not a formal in-depth examination of life balance, but a general reflection of how they perceive these spheres of life at this time. We usually try not to give formal explanations for these areas unless asked. This activity is intended to identify their perspectives on these areas. If we define them too much, we run the risk of biasing their answers. So, if necessary, we give illustrations rather than definitions. The segment on Life Balance contains discussion and illustrations of these four areas.

As you ask the questions, move around the room to ensure that everyone understands what is being asked of them. If people are having some difficulty, take the time to help them and assure them that it's okay.

Reflection

Once people have recorded their answers, ask them to review their answers and look for any patterns. Patterns may be seen in each question; for example, *"Have you done things recently or has it been awhile?"* or *"Do you tend to have most things free or do they cost money?"* Patterns may also be seen across questions; for example, someone may see that the things they do alone tend to be free and the things they do with others tend to cost money.

As they review their answers, ask them to note those things they already knew about themselves and the things that surprised them. Remind them that there are no right or wrong answers. The answers are meant only to help them think about their lives and who they are.

Group Discussion

Give people two or three minutes to reflect on their answers. If working with a group, ask them to turn to the person beside them and share some of the activities on their list (they only need to share things they feel comfortable sharing). As they share the lists ask them to also reflect upon any patterns or surprises.

Debriefing the Activity

After five minutes or so, call the group together again in order to debrief the activity together.

First, it is always interesting to ask if anyone found anything that surprised them and, if so, would they be willing to share it with the group. Allow a few minutes for people to share things that they found surprising. Try to help them reflect on why they found the answers surprising.

For example, some may be surprised that they did many things with other people. They may have thought that they were loners, that they were not social people. But when they thought of their favorite things, they realized that they did most of them with other people. Why would this be so? It could be that when they were younger, they were loners for various reasons; but now their lives have changed and they've become much more social. However, while their lives may have changed, often their perceptions of their lives have not.

This is a good illustration of one goal of *Hope-Filled Engagement*, that people will be surprised as they discover things about themselves before habit focus kicks in or before they have a chance to put up any defenses. Because they are looking at themselves from different perspectives than they are used to, they don't have predetermined answers and they are often able to see things about themselves that they've never seen before.

After the sharing of some of their surprising discoveries, ask the group to discuss what they learned about themselves through the activity. Be sure to affirm their discoveries.

Their findings at this point could be recorded directly into the "Interests" section of the Career Circle (Figure 12). If you intend to use the Favourite Things activity as a source for stories, inform the group that you will be coming back to this activity at a future time.

This activity has proven to be one of the favourite activities of the Guiding Circles workbooks both for people and for practitioners. Practitioners have found several elements of the activity to be helpful:

- It's simple, short, and inexpensive.

- It builds relationships.

- It is accessible to virtually all people no matter their background. Rather than asking specific questions people may have no answers to (such as *"What work experience have you had?"*), it directs people to things they know and enjoy; things easy to talk about.

- It is very concrete. Rather than starting with general requests (such as *"Tell me about yourself"*) that require a high degree of prior self-reflection, this activity starts with concrete memories and then moves at the end to greater reflection. This provides a step-by-step approach to facilitating positive focused self-reflection.

- Another step-by-step aspect is that they are first asked to answer the questions on their own, then asked to share with a peer, and then asked to share with the group and the facilitator. This is easier for many people than just asking them to share with the larger group right away.

- Finally, this is an activity that can be adapted for those who are not literate. For example, people could answer the questions orally and someone else could record the answers for them. Or people could bring pictures of their favourite things.

Storytelling: Cultivating Ownership

Importance of Taking Ownership

The entire process of storytelling should be one that assists people in discovering for themselves the riches with which they have been gifted. There are many ways to state it—taking ownership, the light turns on, someone clues in, fitting the pieces of the puzzle together—but they all refer to that "AHA" moment, when people see something that they haven't seen before and make it their own. Such self-discovery is effective in assisting people to take ownership of what they learn, to value themselves, to find hope for the future.

A fundamental principle to remember in the midst of storytelling is that for people to take ownership of the results, they must take ownership of the process. At the end of the day, people must know that it is their stories, their personal reflections, and their connections. This is easy to affirm but challenging to actually accomplish.

The challenge is that it is often easier to tell people what we see than it is to facilitate their seeing what they can see for themselves. The corollary is that many people find it easier to let others do the work for them than to do it for themselves. The answer to this challenge is to develop more effective facilitating skills in storytelling. Specifically, focus more on the role of coach rather than that of expert and lecturer in order to:

- facilitate people's telling their own story,

- facilitate people's self-discovery as opposed to telling them, and

- facilitate people's ownership of findings and growth in self-esteem.

Challenge for Life/Career Practitioners

When people aren't fully engaged, they are often passive and will let the practitioner take over. While there may be value to what the practitioner shares, it may not be as effective as possible. The reason for this becomes clear when we consider the "Taking Ownership Window" (Figure 21). This window charts typical responses of people to feedback they receive from others based on their level of self-esteem.

Figure 21: Taking Ownership Window

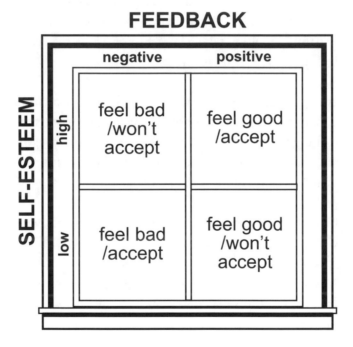

When people have high self-esteem and someone says something positive about them, they usually feel good about it and will accept the feedback, because it fits with their image of themselves. When someone says something negative about them, they will usually feel bad (no one likes being told negative things) but will likely reject the feedback. They may think about what was shared and later decide that there may be some element of truth; but if the feedback doesn't match their self-image, they won't accept it uncritically.

But what happens to people with low self-esteem? When people share something negative about themselves, they will feel bad and will probably accept it. Because they have a low view of themselves, they assume that anything negative said about them must be true in some way. When others share something positive about them, they will probably feel good. But the question is whether or not they will accept it. Unfortunately they usually don't, because they can't relate it to their poor self-image.

Obviously this poses a challenge for practitioners. They become experienced at seeing wonderful things in people's stories. They are committed to helping people see these things. So when people don't seem to see what they have, it is natural for practitioners to tell them directly and to stress the significance of the insight. For example, during a story in which someone shares about organizing an outing for a group of friends, the practitioner excitedly shares, *"As I listen to your story, I can really see that you are a natural leader. Have you ever thought of developing your leadership skills? I think you could do really well in some sort of management position."* The practitioner also moves quickly from details of the story to reflection to implications for career choices. What the practitioner has shared is probably true, but is it the most effective way to bring it to light?

It may not be. Such a process may be deceptively ineffective, especially if the person is struggling with low self-esteem. Such people may feel good because of the positive feedback. They may leave encouraged; but because they don't take ownership of the insight, it may soon be lost. The next time they come in to see the practitioner, they may be back where they started from, discouraged and defeated. No matter what the practitioner shares with them, they just have a hard time believing it.

The problem is that the practitioner has taken over. The process starts with people sharing their story but what happens then? If the practitioner begins to do the talking and to make observations and reflections on the story, who is identifying the detail in the story? The practitioner. Who is reflecting on the story? The practitioner. Who is connecting the insight to the world of work? The practitioner. Who takes ownership of the insight? The practitioner. Depending on people's self-esteem, they may or may not accept what the practitioner has shared, no matter how true it may be.

The goal should be to use a process that facilitates people's self-discovery. As they take ownership of their discoveries, their self-esteem will more likely rise as well. As their self-esteem rises, they will be better able to accept the insight shared by practitioners.

The Alternative to Directing and Taking Over

So what are practitioners supposed to do? If being directive isn't effective, what alternative is there? Should they ignore their experience and insight? Certainly not! It is not that they don't use the experience and wisdom they possess; it is that they should express it in a more effective way—through questioning. Rather than stating, *"I can see that you are a natural leader"*, this insight could be turned into a question such as, *"What kind of people are good at organizing such events?"* or *"Have you ever thought that you might have some leadership ability?"* When the insight is turned into a question, it engages people in finding the answer. So the person may reply, *"I guess I do lead sometimes; I'd never thought of it that way."* The practitioner may then respond, *"I'm glad you see that, I was thinking the same thing."*

So instead of a statement which may be lost because of low self-esteem, practitioners can use a question and an affirmation to give a double punch so to speak. People then think about the question and their story; they see the answer; they state the answer; their conclusion is affirmed; they take ownership of the answer. Why? Because the answer is theirs not someone else's. Then as people's self-esteem is raised, they are more open to accepting positive feedback and it may be more appropriate for practitioners to share their insights more directly.

When we are training storytelling during our workshops, many life/career practitioners, once they are aware of this challenge, are surprised by how frequently they are directing rather than facilitating and also by the difficulty they have in shifting approaches. Being aware of this is an important step to changing.

Objections to Facilitating Storytelling

Life/career practitioners often share that directing people becomes the easy thing to do in many counselling situations because of several factors: the challenges some people have reflecting and then expressing their reflections, the insight and expertise of life/career practitioners at reflection, and the challenge of time restraints. Let us examine these in more detail.

First, people may come across as reluctant and quiet at different times. Don't jump to conclusions as to the reason for this reluctance. It may be true that some just aren't willing to be cooperative or that they lack the ability to do such mental reflection. But as we discussed in Chapter Two on challenges that some people face, not all reluctance is the same.

It may be simply that people are not ready for storytelling, that there are life issues that need to be addressed first. You may need to refer such people to more appropriate counselling resources. Some may feel intimidated by the career counselling process. They may not understand the process or the language or the values or other aspects of the counselling. In this case, you may wish to do activities such as Favourite Things, so that they can feel more comfortable talking about something they know and so that there is a better working relationship. Reassure people by encouraging them and setting clear goals and objectives so that they know where the counselling is going. Encourage them that you will be working with them to discover wonderful things in their lives.

Second, another issue that makes facilitating difficult is the cultural expectations on practitioners. In our culture the "expert" is, all too often, expected to have all the answers and to express them. This is one reason why it is usually easier to give answers than ask questions. People may defer to the "expert" when meeting with them, but that doesn't mean that they will automatically take ownership of the "expert" advice.

Such an approach sometimes limits new discoveries and true insight. When we ask questions, we acknowledge that we don't know everything. It is people, not others, who are the experts in their lives. Rather than basing our counselling on our assumptions about their lives, it is more effective to assume an attitude of genuine curiosity and openness. When we have that urge to tell people our profound insights, it may be wiser to hold back until we have ensured that they have first had the chance to discover for themselves the patterns underlying their behavior. Through insight, questions, and affirmation, we can become the "experts" at equipping and motivating people to do the work for themselves, to tell and reflect on their own stories, and to take ownership of their own discoveries.

A final objection to facilitating storytelling is that some practitioners believe they just don't have the time to do it. They need to get results in very limited time periods. But it must be asked, *"What results are we wanting to achieve?" "If people don't accept the results, what has been achieved?" "How often have you talked with someone for an hour or so and got nowhere?"* The answer to the time dilemma isn't to shortcut the process but to be more effective in facilitating a process that has the potential to work even in the typical time frames in which practitioners must work. In a sense, the reality is that we don't have the time not to use effective strategies such as storytelling. In the next few segments, we will outline a more effective process.

Developing Facilitating Skills

So how do we become more effective at facilitating rather than directing. First, it is important to recognize the difference. Learn to listen to what is being said during storytelling activities with people and to ask yourself some basic questions: *"Who is talking and for how long?"*

*"Am I talking more than the storyteller?" "Who is saying what?" "What types
of things am I saying?" "Am I making lots of declarations or am I asking lots
of questions?"*

Second, if people are not talking much, we must ask ourselves, *"Why
not?"* It may be because they just are not talkers or it may be that the
process in some way is shutting them down. In the next few chapters, we
will outline a hope-filled approach that we have found to be effective in
facilitating storytelling and creating better interactions with people.

It may be a touch simplistic, but the old saying, *"Give people a fish,
and you feed them for a day; teach people to fish and you feed them for a
lifetime"* is still relevant. One of the goals in *Hope-Filled Engagement* is to
equip people with the attitudes, perspectives, and skills to help them learn
to fish in their own lives and discover some of the wonder that makes
them who they are. If they can learn to do this on their own, the process
will be worth it.

Storytelling: The Spiral
of Curiosity and Discovery

In the previous segment, we presented the need for a facilitating approach that equips people to self-discover through storytelling and then to take ownership of their discoveries. The Patterns activity has proven to be such an approach. Before we go into detail on the Patterns activity, we must first prepare for it by exploring the effective use of questions. As we equip people to discover the riches of their lives through their stories, we must also teach them what to look for and how to look for it. Over the years, one of the most common questions raised when we are training practitioners in the Patterns activity, is, *"What questions do I ask?"* The next three segments will answer this question.

Questions are powerful tools that have the potential to change lives. "Questions open our minds, our eyes, and our hearts. With them, we learn, connect, and create. And with them, we can create better futures and better results." (Adams, 2009, p. 8). They are powerful because they are the key to observation and, therefore, to discovery. The essential connection between the questions we ask and the things we see and learn can be clearly seen in all aspects of life/career counselling when we look at the concept of the Spiral of Curiosity and Discovery (Figure 22).

We can see this spiral in action in everyday life. Learning by questioning and observing and by observing and questioning utilizes an innate ability that everyone has. It is evident in every child who drives adults "crazy" by asking a seemingly unending stream of questions. If you listen to two friends as one friend asks the other about a recent trip, you'll recognize this spiral in the back and forth of questions and answers. This innate ability has been highly developed in many spheres of learning (for example, it is clearly seen both in the scientific method and in the arts), but it is important not to lose the simplicity of the process.

Figure 22: The Spiral of Curiosity and Discovery

Though it is a natural ability, sometimes, as adults, we do lose confidence in our ability to question. Therefore, we may need to re-learn the craft of asking questions.

Questions and observations feed off each other. Each stimulates the other. The more we see, the more questions are raised. The more questions we ask, the more observations we make. For example, suppose several people tell you that they enjoy the outdoors. You could record this as an interest for each one; but at this point you don't fully see the uniqueness of them

Great results begin with great questions.

A question not asked is a door not opened.
- Adams (2009, p. 9, 133)

as individuals. However, if you were to ask them another question such as, *"What is it about the outdoors that you like?"*, what would you learn? In response to this question, people have answered in many different ways, such as the fresh air, the colours, the smells, the activity, being close to nature, solitude, exercise, adventure, flowers, birds, animals, camping, hiking, and so on. It is at this point that you find differences.

As well, you can follow the spiral with an individual to find many of their interconnected characteristics. For example, notice how the learning increases in the sequence of questions and answers in Figure 23: Sample Question and Answer Spiral.

If facilitators were to have stopped at the first question, so much may never have been learned. This asking and asking and asking is just a natural form of the curiosity that continually says *"tell me more."* Part of the art of facilitating storytelling is discerning when to focus on breadth and when to focus on depth, while balancing issues of time and importance.

This natural process may be enhanced. If we know what we are looking for, we are more likely to see things and ask natural questions. If we know what can be asked, we are more likely to see things and ask natural questions. Therefore, before getting deeper into storytelling, it will be helpful to review what kind of observations we are looking for and the kinds of questions that can be asked to help people see them.

The Patterns activity is a positive focused questioning approach to storytelling that reflects this spiral of curiosity and discovery. Practitioners uses simple questions to facilitate people seeing the patterns in their lives in the details of their stories. The goal is to help people discover the riches in their lives that can be useful as they seek to craft their careers. What kind of riches may be discovered within people's life stories? What kind of riches should we be asking questions about? Since we are working towards people filling in the various sections of their Career Circle, it is the logical place to identify what to look for and some of the questions to ask.

Figure 23: Sample Question and Answer Spiral

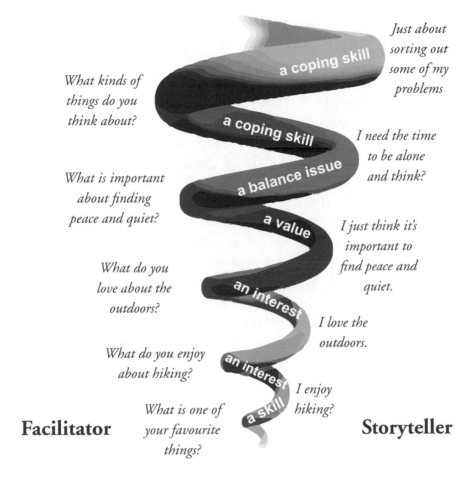

Facilitator   **Storyteller**

The Career Circle (Figure 12) suggests the sort of information that may be found within any life story. Any life story will yield information about what people have done (skills), what they enjoy (interests) and what they think is important (values) and how they go about doing things (personal style). Stories often reveal something about balance in their lives, things they have learned and how they learned it. Within each story, people are usually fulfilling some life roles. The story may even tell something of people's understanding of the world of work or of possible contacts with the work world. If the Career Circle calls for certain information about people, it can also indicate the logical questions that should be asked. If we want people to discover their skills, interests, personal style, values, balance, learning, life/work roles, and connections, than it makes sense to ask the questions that will help people to see these things in their lives.

So what questions will do this? It is helpful to learn more about the various types of questions generally and then specifically the types of focused questions which could be asked for each of the eight components of the Career Circle. Different types of questions can be used for different purposes. The segment on Storytelling: Question Possibilities will discuss possible questions that could be asked during storytelling and what each one helps people to see.

But just knowing the different types of questions isn't enough. In order to avoid using them as if they were some sort of interrogation list, it is also important to learn how to use them dynamically so that people are engaged in the spiral of curiosity and discovery. The next segment on The Penny presents an activity which can be used to illustrate and teach the use of observation and questioning in a spiral of curiosity and discovery.

Storytelling Activity: The Penny

The Penny activity is a short simple activity that Gray has used for years to introduce questioning to people. It uses a focused questioning approach that engages people in the spiral of curiosity and discovery introduced in the previous segment. This is a good backswing activity because it equips people with the skills and perspectives that they need to do the storytelling and reflecting effectively. Many life/career practitioners have found this to be especially useful, and teachers report that their students love it. This group activity can be easily adapted for use with individuals.

Introduce the Activity

Give each person a coin. We use a Canadian penny because it is inexpensive and it is something that Canadians use all the time so they are especially surprised when they actually observe the details.

Ask the group what they see when they look at the penny. Usually there are a few general observations; for example with the Canadian penny, people usually notice the maple leaves, the Queen, the shape and colour of the coin. Then ask how many observations they think are possible about the penny. The typical answer usually is quite low (10 to 30 or so). Suggest that there are over 200 possible observations when people learn how to observe and ask questions. At first people often express their unbelief; but once they get going, their eyes begin to open and they find themselves actually seeing way more than they ever thought possible.

Illustrate the Activity

Start the activity by illustrating how to observe and question using just one part of the coin, for example the Queen's cameo. Start with general questions and then more specific questions. Explain simply the spiral of curiosity and observation. As they see things, they can ask questions about what they see. As they answer those questions, they will see new things. They can then ask questions about those things. And so on. The activity draws in elements of brainstorming and mind mapping. Figure 24: Questions on a Penny illustrates some initial questions about the cameo as well as other features of the penny. If they get stuck making observations, suggest a few questions to get them going again. You may wish to attempt your own observations and questions before checking out the example.

Ask the group what parts of the Queen's cameo they see. They will begin to see parts such as face, hair, clothing, and jewellery. If they miss any part, ask them to think of what parts make up a person's cameo. Write their observations down on a flip chart. Then draw their attention to each part of the cameo. Ask what they see when they look at the Queen's face. They should be able to recognize things such as the forehead, the nose, the lips, the cheeks, and the neck. Then draw their attention to each of these parts. If they ask themselves what they see when they look at the nose, they should see the bridge of the nose and the nostril. Continue this process as you have time for illustrating the process.

Ask the group how many things they see just on the cameo. The answer is usually *"lots!"* Then ask if they can see so many things just in the cameo, how many things should they be able to see if they used the observing and questioning techniques in the spiral of curiosity and discovery to really look at the rest of the penny. The answer again is usually *"lots!"*

Small group activity

If there is time, the group could be divided into triads and given the opportunity to discover what else they can see in the penny. It could be set up as a competition to see who can make the most observations. Ask them to use this approach to examine the penny and to write down everything

Figure 24: Questions on a Penny

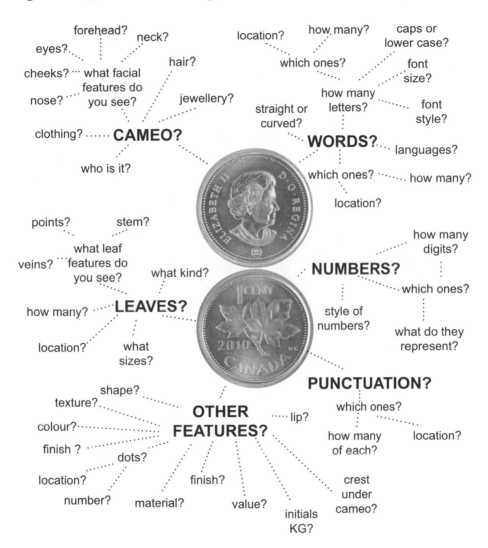

they see. Remind them of the process: observe, question, observe, question, and so on. For each of the observations they make, ask questions about the details they see just in that part. Visit the different triads to assist as needed. Ask each triad how many observations they have found. As time allows, review some of the observations with the whole group.

Debriefing the Activity

Debrief the activity by asking what they can learn from the Penny activity. Affirm their answers and, when necessary, supplement them. Encourage them regarding what they have discovered both in their observations of the penny and in their observations about the process. It clearly teaches that there are many more details than we are consciously aware of. As we learn to ask questions and look for details, we learn to see more. *If so many observations can be made about something as simple as a penny, how many more observations could be made about the incredible details in our own lives, as we look at our stories?* Just as people can learn to use questions and observations using the spiral of curiosity and discovery concept, so too they can learn questions which will help them observe new things in their own lives.

Storytelling: Question Possibilities

The previous two segments presented a focused questioning approach reflecting the spiral of curiosity and discovery. This segment will present some sample questions that could be used in the upcoming Patterns activity while facilitating people's telling and reflecting on their life stories.

This is not an exhaustive list. It is essential to avoid an interrogation mode in which the questions drive the process. If people feel like they are being interrogated, they often put up defenses. The process is more like an informal yet guided conversation, not an interrogation. The different types of questions should be mastered to the point that they may be used flexibly, organically, and almost transparently. People and their stories are the starting points; the questions are just tools to facilitate the storytelling in order to assist people to discover meaningful things about themselves.

The different types of questions have been divided into several groups. The first group contains foundational questions which can be used in any activity involving questioning. The second group contains focused questions specifically related to the eight components of the Career Circle.

A. Foundational Questions:

1. The 6 Ws

The 6 Ws (7 if you include How?) are the most basic and versatile questions. Their simplicity sometimes belies the breadth and depth of the information that they can call forth.

- *Who?* : people and their relationships

- *What?* : actions, events, experiences

- ***Why?*** : motives, values, reasons, purposes

- ***When?*** : time, sequences, duration (how long?)

- ***Where?*** : locations, places, relationships, journeys

- ***So What?*** : implications, results, meanings

- ***How?*** : means, manner, methods

2. **Questions for different levels of depth of reflection**

The Art of Focused Conversation (Stanfield, 2000, p. 17) presents a model of a focused "collaborative dialogue of discovery" that helps people process their experiences through different phases of reflection. Stanfield suggests the use of questions at four levels of reflection.

- **objective**: facts, external reality (e.g., *"What happened?"*)

- **reflective**: internal personal responses (emotions, feelings, or associations) to external realities (e.g., *"How do you feel about this?"*)

- **interpretive**: draw out meanings, values, implications (e.g., *"What does this mean to you?" "Is this important to you? Why?"*)

- **decisional**: elicit response (e.g., *"What are you going to do now?" "In light of this, what choices do you think you should be making?"*)

3. **Solution-focused questions**

Instead of a psychological type of questioning that focuses on problems, solution-focused questions identify strengths or coping strategies. Identifying where things are working in people's lives or where they are doing things right can point to possible solutions in other areas (Amundson, 2009). For example, when people have worked through some difficulty, this can help them see that they can overcome other problems (e.g., *"How did you manage to work through this challenge?" "Do you think that you could work through other challenges in your life in the same way?"*).

4. Exception-finding questions

People often speak in generalities. Sometimes those generalities just focus on the negative. Exception-finding questions (Amundson, 2009) are a type of solution-focused questions that shift from generalities to exceptions (e.g., *"Are there times when this is not so?" "Describe how you have worked through something similar to this in other circumstances?"*).

5. Theory-testing questions

When people have a distorted view of themselves or the world, you can test such theories with questions that foster a broader perspective. *Active Engagement* (Amundson, 2009) sets forth a three-fold questioning strategy:

- **evidence** (*"Why do you think this is so?" "Is there any area in your life where this doesn't happen?"*)

- **development** (*"Has it always been like this?" "When did this first happen?" "How long ago?" "Has it changed over time?"*)

- **perspectives of others** (*"What do others say about this?" "If someone watched you doing this, what do you think they might say about you?"*)

6. Connecting/linking questions:

Such questions help avoid any sense of interrogation. Linking back to previous things that people have already said creates the feeling that the new questions are naturally unfolding the details of the story rather than intruding into it (e.g., *"Is this related to what you said back here?" "You mentioned that you prepared all the stuff for the dinner, how did you actually go about doing that?"*). This can also help when people go off on tangents.

Such questions can also help people see that the discoveries they make in a story are not just isolated to that particular story but are in fact patterns of psychological DNA that are throughout many other aspects of their lives (e.g., *"Do you do this at other times? In other ways? Where?" "How have you seen or experienced this in other parts of your life? Where?"*). This is important when people are not transferring some of their strengths from one aspect of their life to another (e.g., *"If you were to do the same types of things in this other area of your life, what do you think would happen?"*).

B. Focused Questions Based on the Career Circle:

Once you have a general picture of the story, shift to more focused questions designed to help people discover the specific details of the story. Since you are seeking to help people understand themselves from a career perspective, you want to ask the kind of questions that will lead to the type of information needed in a career context. We have already suggested that the Career Circle can be an effective framework to collect relevant information in self-assessment. Therefore, it makes sense to develop a series of questions for yourself that are based on the Career Circle. This does not mean asking questions using career language; rather, develop questions that are in the language of the people you are working with. For example, instead of asking *"What skills did you use in order to arrange this party for your friends?"*, it may be more effective to ask, *"What exactly did you do as you arranged this party?"* As people tell their stories, listen for details related to each of the section of the career circle. Mentally go around the circle and ensure that all points have been touched on. If some section has not been touched on adequately, you may ask questions related to that section. Remember the use of the spiral of curiosity and discovery to keep the story flowing.

1. Skills, gifts, aptitudes:

Skills are identified by asking people what they did. If they did something, then there is some level of skill there.

"What did you actually do when you…? Think step-by-step through everything that happened and don't leave anything out."

"You said you did [action], how exactly did you do it?"

"If I were to do this, what would I have to do?" "What does a person have to be able to do to accomplish what you did?"

"Did you do anything else? What did you do before/after this?"

2. **Interests:**

"What did you enjoy about this experience? What exactly did you like?"

"Why did you enjoy/like this?"

"Was there anything else you enjoyed?"

"What did it feel like? How did you show your enjoyment?"

3. **Personal style:**

"Not everyone does things in the same way; could you tell me more about how you went about this?"

"What kind of a [hiker, dancer, runner, baker, etc.] were you?"

"How else would you describe yourself during this activity?"

"What kind of personal characteristics helped you in this activity?"

Sometimes because of shyness or enculturated humility or lack of previous reflection, people have a hard time answering this type of question. At such times, people usually have an easier time saying what others would say; it objectifies the observation and frees them to see and state more than they usually would. For example, *"You mentioned that your friends were with you while you were doing this. If I were to ask them what kind of a skateboarder you were, what do you think they would tell me?"* If they were alone in the experience, introduce the possibility of someone else. *"If others (other people or even a 'fly on the wall') were watching you, what would they see? How would they describe you as you did this? What would they say about you?"*

"Is this any different from how you would describe yourself. If so, why do you think there is a difference? Would you agree with them?"

4. Values:

Review the segment on Values in Chapter Three and think about questions which help people discover what is important to them. You may need to ask the same question several times to get to core values.

"Why did you do this? What was important to you when you did this?"

"You say that [something] was important to you; why was this important to you?"

"Was there anything else important to you?"

5. Balance:

Review the segment on Balance in Chapter Three. Listen for clues that point to people doing something in order to balance other areas of life.

"You mentioned that you take the dog out to get away from a hectic life. What is it about your life that you need time from? Why did you do this? How does this activity or experience help you cope with these things?"

"How does this fit in your life? Is this a relief from something else?"

"What does this activity add to your life that is missing in the other parts?"

"What would happen if you didn't have experiences like this in your life?"

6. Learning:

Whenever people say that they did something or know something, they have to have learned about it either informally or formally.

"What things did you have to learn to do this?"

"How did you learn to do this?" "When?" "Where?"

"Did you learn this from anyone? Who?" "How did they teach you?"

"Is there anything you'd like to learn more about?"

"If you were to teach me to do this, what would you have to teach me?" "How would you go about teaching me?"

7. Life/Work roles:

Usually in any story, people are manifesting life roles (formal or informal), especially if they were with other people. These questions help people see the roles they take on in different contexts.

"As you think through your story, what part or parts did you play in it?"

"Were others with you? Who? What relationship do you have with them? How did you fit in the group? What role did you play in the group?"

"Do you find yourself in this role in other areas of your life?"

8. **Work connections:**

This part of the Circle may need to be explored separately. It may be too early to bring out connections to the world of work if talking about the world of work is too threatening.

"What jobs do you know of in this area? Is any of this work available in your area?"

"Who did you meet in this story? Who else was involved in this story" "What jobs did they have?"

"Did you meet with anyone who could help you in anyway in discovering yourself or exploring career possibilities?"

"You seemed to enjoy this a lot. Have you every thought of doing something in this area as a job? Could you see yourself doing this kind of activity or something related as a job?"

C. Directed Questions Based on Observations:

During the telling of the story, these questions may be used over and over again in different ways. But what do you do when you ask a question and people can't seem to see the obvious answer?

As people tell their stories, you may notice some detail(s) that people have overlooked. Use your expertise at this point to facilitate their discovering what you see. Let them self-discover and then affirm their discoveries, as we discussed in the segment on Storytelling: Cultivating Ownership.

You can take any detail you have observed and turn it into a question to help direct people to possible observations that you have seen. People have freedom to answer the question as they wish. If they don't agree with your observation, it is easier to clarify the point by answering the question than by trying to say that you are wrong.

"*As I hear about your challenging experiences on this hike, I wonder if you would see yourself as a risk-taker?*" If the response is "*yes,*" you could affirm their response and ask further questions. "*Great. You know I thought the same thing. Have you ever thought of this before? Can you tell me a little bit more about this?*" If the response is "*no,*" ask questions like, "*Why not*" or "*How else would you describe yourself?*"

"*You've talked a lot about the other people around you. Do you like having other people around?*"

"*You know you've talked a lot about doing this art project. It sounds as if you did a great job. But I notice that you've never referred to yourself as artistic. Do you think you are artistic?*"

"*Earlier you said that you like to do things spontaneously: but I notice several times in this story, you've talked about planning out the details. Can you plan as well as do things spontaneously? How do these two fit in what you do?*"

Conclusion

These questions are not all the questions that could be or should be asked, but they reflect the types of questions to consider asking. The on-going dynamic dialogue between you and the storyteller should determine the questions you ask with any story. An understanding of these questions and the type of information they direct people to should stimulate people to experience the spiral of curiosity and discovery in their stories.

Work on developing a large "toolkit" of questions you feel comfortable with. Make these different types questions your own and learn to use them creatively.

Storytelling Activity: Patterns Overview

The Patterns activity is one of the primary tools for facilitating people's self-discovery in the *Hope-Filled Engagement* approach. It is an adaptation of the Pattern Identification Exercise (Amundson, 2009).

Starting with stories that are non-threatening to people is an important aspect of providing a safe environment for people as they tell their stories. The Patterns activity does this by engaging people where they are engaged with life. Stories, such as those from the Favourite Things activity, are usually easier for people to talk about because it starts with areas of strength rather than areas of perceived weakness and failure.

Tips for Facilitating the Patterns Activity

The Patterns activity, at one level, is a very simple activity, but it can also be very challenging until practitioners practise it and make it their own. The following are some practical tips for facilitating the Patterns activity.

Review the previous chapters on storytelling and take note of the need for facilitating rather than directing; genuine curiosity; a dynamic process rather than interrogation; a "toolkit" full of a wide-range of questions; following a spiral of questions and observations to discover a greater depth of insights; and a "natural" flow, linking new questions to what people have already said.

Keep your questions simple. It is often better to have many short questions rather than long questions that people can't follow along. Use simple "natural" questions as much as possible in the language of the people you are working with. Be careful of translating rather than paraphrasing as you respond to peoples' comments. If you are always translating their comments into more technical language, people struggling with esteem issues may begin to feel as if they are being corrected all the time and that they can't even tell their story properly. If people say they like being around other people, note that rather than translating it into the more formal concept of being "social." Don't bring the formal technical language of career in until it is really needed.

Being specific and concrete with questioning is easier for many people to reflect upon. As well, general thoughts lend themselves to generalized answers. Such generalized answers may be highly influenced, even distorted by the self-perceptions and self-esteem of people. It is often easier for people to accurately remember the details of actual life incidents than it is to be reflective about the more general question of who they are. Once details have been remembered and shared, the next step is to help people reflect on them to discover their life patterns.

Listen for people talking about others rather than themselves. Sometimes, when their story involves being with others, people start talking about what the others did rather than what they actually did. When you hear "*we*" too often, gently bring them back to their own involvement. "*You've been mentioning what the group was doing. What about you? What were you specifically doing?*"

Don't get sidetracked. It is easy to end up talking about the activity highlighted in people's stories because they are so interesting. Keep the focus on the person not the activity itself. The goal is to discover what the story says about the person's life/career, not to learn about the activity.

No one story will tell you everything about the people telling the story. If possible, have people tell and unpack several stories from several areas.

Keep the Career Circle in the back of your mind. It will remind you what to look for and the types of questions to ask.

As the story unfolds, record the details of the story on a list; this list becomes a crucial tool for both the facilitator and storyteller. The list is a visual prompt that helps you and the storyteller to keep track of the details of the story, to link new details to previous elements of the story, to identify details to reflect upon when looking for patterns, and to provide something to take home as a reminder of the session. Without such a list it is very difficult to remember all of the details which are an essential part of discovering life patterns.

It is best to use a large flip chart because it provides lots of room to write. If that is not available, use a regular sheet of paper. Whatever you use, make sure that both you and the storyteller can clearly see it. If you are using a sheet of paper, you should sit beside people with the paper between you and them to ensure that they can see. If the storytellers can't see it, they may be unsure of what you are writing and might feel threatened. More importantly, if the list is to be a tool to help them with their storytelling, reflecting, and connecting, they must be able to see it.

If there are concerns about propriety or safety issues which prevent you from sitting beside someone, the flip chart can provide some separation. If you do not have a flip chart, you could attach paper to a wall. If you have to sit beside someone, you can sit across the corner of a desk so that it provides some separation.

Finally, don't forget to relax and enjoy getting to know the people you are working with.

Storytelling Activity: Patterns

The Patterns activity can be divided into five steps that have proven to be effective with a wide range of people: choosing the story, telling the story, reflecting on the story, connecting the story, debriefing the story. Clear steps are helpful in equipping people to do more of their own self-assessment. They learn a process and a framework for positive focused storytelling and self-reflection that gives them confidence that they can discover more of who they are on their own. Some school boards in Canada have been using the Patterns activity with students as early as Grade 5 and younger. The students tell stories to each other rather than teachers, and it has been amazing to see how much they discover about themselves and how much they enjoy this process. It is important to equip children with this skill as early as possible; if they can learn to see themselves and develop a strong sense of identity and self-esteem before the challenges of the teen years, everyone benefits.

Step 1: Choosing the Story

Introduce this activity by explaining the concept of psychological DNA: who we are will come out in how we do what we do. Therefore, by telling their life stories and reflecting on the details of their story, they can learn much about who they are by seeing the patterns in their lives.

First, if they have not already done the Favourite Things activity, ask people what some of their favourite things in life are. Remember to ask for several favourite things rather than just one; this prevents people from getting stuck trying to think of the best one when asked only for one thing.

List the activities mentioned. Quickly review in your mind the different activities and try to identify which ones might be good ones to start with. It is possible to discover things about people in any activity but some are easier than others. For example, if someone likes to sit and watch

TV and also is involved in a local hockey team, it might be better to start with stories focusing on the hockey experience since it will be more active and involves others. However, don't forget about the TV watching as well. Everyone has a unique style in watching TV (e.g., which shows do they watch, are they alone or with others, which characters do they identify with, how has TV watching changed for them over time, and so on).

Some practitioners find it difficult when people put down favourite things like sex or drugs. If you ask for several favourite things, you have a choice and do not have to choose any potentially awkward stories. You can identify several activities to start and ask, *"These ones sound like good ones to start with; which one would you like to look at in more detail?"* or *"Which one of these sticks out to you?"* This approach allows you to screen the activities while also allowing some choice on the part of the storyteller. Don't get bogged down trying to get the perfect story. It is amazing how sometimes the most unlikely story reveals the most interesting insights.

Once you have selected a specific activity, it is time to identify a specific experience *"Can you think of one experience in which you had a particularly good time with this activity? Or one you really enjoyed? Or one that was especially special?"* If people have difficulty identifying one specific instance that was better than others, you can ask, *"What about the first or last time you did this? Can you tell me about that?"* During our training workshops, this is one point that some practitioners often forget and then, as a result, they have a hard time finding specifics in the storytelling and in the reflection. Finding a specific story is important because if people start talking in generalities, they are not really telling a story so much as reflecting upon the activity (outside of the story). As a result, you learn about the activity rather than the person. When people tell a specific story, they are drawing upon their memory of the specific details of the experience. It is by unpacking the specific details of the story that the patterns of people's lives are seen.

In *Active Engagement* (Amundson, 2009), there is also the suggestion that people talk about a positive experience and a negative experience of the same activity. This results in two stories to unpack. The process of facilitating the telling of the negative experience is basically the same as the positive. The only difference would be that you would want to use some solution-focused questions to discover how people cope with negative experiences. If you are short on time or if you are working with people struggling with dysfunctionality, it may be better to focus only on positive stories. In our earlier discussion on the "art of possibilities" in Chapter Four, we suggested that some people get stuck talking about the problems in their lives; once they are in that rut, it can be challenging to get them out. If you know that someone is prone to this, it may be better to look only at a positive experience to avoid this trap.

Some career practitioners are wary of storytelling, because they don't want to deal with the messiness that often comes with the stories of people with challenges. But this very selection process makes this very unlikely. This is storytelling that focuses on a double positive. A favourite thing in life is probably going to be positive and asking for a good experience of this positive thing is really asking for a positive of a positive. Even if you chose to look at a negative experience, it can still be very positive. People react differently to negative experiences that are part of their favourite things than when they are talking of the parts of life in which they don't feel engaged.

It has been our experience that rarely do these positive stories lead to difficult emotional situations. Such stories usually evoke very positive emotional memories. Sometimes, however, such positive stories do touch upon something that is now painful for people. For example, people may tell a story in which a loved one is mentioned; the experience with the loved one was positive; but if the loved one has recently passed away, the mention of the person evokes painful emotions. If this does happen, it is important to ask them if they wish to continue or to stop. If they wish to stop, the story must be stopped immediately. Another story could be examined at that time or later.

Step 2: Telling the Story

Once a specific story has been chosen, the next step is to facilitate the storyteller's remembering and telling of the story. Ask people for permission to record the details of the story for future reflection. Write the name of the activity at the top of the paper and below it write the specific experience that the story is about. As people tell their stories, capture the details in a list format. Don't write sentences; it is harder to write neatly and it takes too long. This may also make it harder for some to read what you have written. Just write key words as reminders. If someone, while telling a story about a hike, says, "I *really enjoyed the fresh air while I was on the walk*", only the words "*fresh air*" need to be recorded. This is enough to jog memory about the rest. Put down as many details as possible at this point because you don't know until you reflect on them what will be most significant. If you spend time trying to decide what to write, you will never keep up.

The actual facilitation of the storytelling should reflect the spiral of curiosity and discovery: question—observation—question—observation, and so on. It is helpful to ask three styles of questions as needed to help the story keep going and focused on the storyteller: general questions, focused questions, and directed questions.

1. General questions

When starting to explore a specific story or portion of a story, it is helpful to start with general questions to get a general picture of what the story is about. These questions bring out a few observations to help ignite the spiral of curiosity and discovery, establish the context for the story, and provide the points to which to link more focused questions. For example:

- *"Why did you choose this particular experience?" "What stands out in your mind about this experience?"*

- *"What happened in this experience? Tell me a little bit about it."*

- *"What made this experience good for you? What else made it good?"*

- *"When did this happen?" "Where?"*

- *"Was anyone with you? Who?"*

- *"Can you remember anything else about it?"*

2. Focused questions

Once you have the general picture, shift to more specific focused questions as set forth in the segment on Storytelling: Question Possibilities. Link questions to things they have already said so they feel as if you are helping them unfold their story rather than following an agenda. As people are telling the details of their story and you are listing them, think about where the details might fit around the Career Circle (Figure 12). Think about what hasn't been said. Are there sections of the circle that are missing? Are there details that need to be fleshed out more?

You will need to use your insight and experience to determine how deep to go in exploring any particular aspect of the story. Pace yourself; you will want time at the end for the reflecting and connecting steps. Practitioners often ask how long the Patterns activity should take. There is no simple answer; each situation is different. But Patterns can be viewed as an "accordion" activity; that is, it is adaptable to almost any length. If you have lots of time, you can keep asking questions for observations of greater breadth and depth. If you have little time, ask a few strategic questions.

3. Directed questions

Sometimes during the storytelling, you see things that the storytellers don't. It is at these points, that instead of stating what you see, you can turn the observation into another question. The segment on Storytelling: Question Possibilities illustrates this type of questioning.

Step 3: Reflecting on the Story

In the telling stage, the goal is for people to remember the details of their stories. In this stage, the goal is to facilitate people's self-discovery of themselves by reflecting on the details of the stories they've just shared.

First, thank people for sharing their stories. Remind them that these stories tell many things about who they are and it would be worthwhile to take a few minutes to discover some of these things.

You can use the same types of questions mentioned in Step 2, the telling stage, to facilitate reflection and discovery. The three styles of questions—general, focused, and directed—are helpful in this step as well. Continue to use the flip chart or paper to record the observations that are made.

Begin with the general question, *"What does this story say about you as a person?"* This will help focus the reflection. Allow people to list as many things as they can. Affirm people as they make observations.

Usually after a few observations, people begin to slow down; sometimes as few as only 3 or 4 are made. This is because reflection is much more difficult than storytelling. In storytelling, people rely on memory to recall details. In this step, they are called upon to use a different part of their brain, the reflective part. As noted in our discussion on the lack of positive focused self-reflection, many people have not developed this part of their thinking. Usually it is easier to reflect on others' stories than your own. They may only see a few things, but you will probably see many things. Resist the urge to immediately tell them what you see. Here again, it is important to facilitate rather than direct. The list of details recorded during Step 2, the telling stage, is the key to this. Look over the list and note which details were not commented upon. Each one of these can become a focused point for reflection. One by one, point to them and ask, *"What do you think this point says about you?"* Often this is all people need to see things. Be patient and allow them time to answer the question for themselves. Again, as people reflect, affirm their observations.

This has a double benefit; you are affirming not just what they discover about themselves but also their ability to reflect and see things for themselves. When possible, try to link ideas as they are noted.

If after pointing to a specific item on the list and asking questions about it, you think that something important may be being missed, you can ask directed questions, such as "*You haven't said it directly but you certainly get excited as you talk about this. Is it fair to say that this is something you really enjoy?*" or "*I notice here that you mentioned that you were showing others how to do this. Have you ever thought that you might have the ability to teach? or Do you find yourself teaching others very often?*"

Step 4: Connecting the Story

Once you have listed people's reflections on the details that came out during the storytelling, the next step is to facilitate their connecting what they have discovered in the stories to their lives, first to other life situations more broadly and then specifically to the world of education or employment.

Sometimes people see things in some parts of their lives but don't connect them to other parts. Ask them to review the list of things they have discovered about themselves in the reflection step. Then ask if they see any of these personal characteristics in other parts of their lives. If they do, you can ask for examples. This will help people take ownership of what they discover in the story. These characteristics aren't just something that come out in the activity they were talking about; but they will come out throughout their lives because these characteristics are part of who they are.

You could ask people to think about what would happen if they were to apply these characteristics to other areas of their lives, such as the world of learning or work. For example, mention that all they have discovered may have real relevance to the world of work. Invite them to see how each point will actually fit in one or more of the sections of their Career Circle.

Look at each of the personal characteristics discovered in Step 3: Reflecting on the Story and discuss where it might fit in the Career Circle and then record in the appropriate section(s). Inform them that they will be able to use their discoveries in the Career Circle to help them to discover career possibilities for themselves.

Step 5: Debriefing the Story

Ask people what they think they have discovered through the Patterns activity. Usually people are surprised at how much comes out of just one story. Encourage them to consider that if they discovered so much in just one story, how much more would they discover if they did the same thing with several stories.

If you have time, you could arrange for another storytelling session. Whether you have time or not, remember that one of your goals is for them to be able to do this for themselves. This is a tool people can use by themselves in the future. Ask if they have someone else they could talk with, family or friends. Who would they be? Suggest that they ask these people to do this activity with them. Review the process and encourage them to do the best they can. They could give these people a list of basic questions to ask in order to help see more details. After they have told their stories, they could talk with the person or persons interviewing them about the life patterns they see in the stories. If possible, arrange for them to return for a follow-up visit in which they share what they discover in these other storytelling sessions. They may not find as many things as they would if they were to do it with you, but they will be making their own discoveries.

Conclusion

As you practice the Patterns activity and make it your own, our hope is that you, as many others before you, will find this to be an effective tool for self-assessment. This self-discovery process generates hope because it engages people where they are engaged in life, facilitates their own insight, and equips them with a process for positive focused self-reflection. People will discover the riches that are in their lives, which have only been waiting to be discovered and owned. Other activities focusing on specific areas, such as skills, interests, personality, or values, may also be used to focus more specifically in these areas. Such activities will be enriched, if they are grounded in people's real life stories.

Note:

For a description of the Patterns activity being field tested with clients in a community context, read "Career Counselling First Nations Youth: Applying the First Nations Career-Life Planning Model" (Neumann, Amundson, & McLean, 2000) and "First Nations Career/Life Planning Model: Guidelines for Practitioners" (McCormick, Neumann, Amundson, & McLean, 1999).

To view the Pattern Identification Exercise in action you may want to view some of the segments from the "Active Engagement in Action" DVDs (available through Ergon Communications). These DVDs highlight in a number of places how the Pattern Identification Exercise can be used with a wide range of people.

Storytelling Activity:
Circle of Strengths

One of the main challenges in working with stories is the inability of many people to acknowledge the many strengths that are imbedded in the stories they are telling. The Patterns activity (or the Pattern Identification Exercise) illustrates one way of helping people to draw out the patterns from their stories. In this concluding section we would like to introduce another method, the Circle of Strengths, that makes good use of the input from others (Amundson, 2009).

The Circle of Strengths is particularly useful in situations where people are describing specific accomplishments. As with the Patterns activity, it is important to draw out as many details as possible. These details can be recorded on a flip chart, or you can just focus all your attention on really listening to the story that you are hearing.

Once the story has been told, the focus shifts to interpretation. On the flip chart draw a large "S" in the center of the page and indicate that this reflects the story that has been told. Now it is time to try to understand how these stories tell us something about strengths, interests, personality, and values. People will usually give three or four illustrations and then state "*that is about it.*. With each of these illustrations draw a line out from the "S" in the center (like spokes in a bicycle wheel) and write down a descriptive word(s). For example, if people talked about organizing an event, they might indicate that they were good planners, they enjoyed meeting people, and they liked to help others.

As a next step, it is important to acknowledge the points that have been made and then suggest that the story actually leaves a great many other impressions. This is your opportunity to now indicate how many other things were imbedded in the story. The lines from the center show people how this story captured many more strengths. Continuing with the above example, the practitioner may note that in addition to the three qualities mentioned, the story also highlighted many other skills, interest, values, personal style characteristics, and so forth. The picture is transformed from a "story" to a Circle of Strengths (Figure 25).

Figure 25: Sample Circle of Strengths

This Circle of Strengths is particularly powerful in a group context where peers indicate the strengths and the facilitator writes them down on the page. In some situations it can be even more powerful to have everyone who contributed a statement of strength to sign their name afterwards.

As has been mentioned earlier, many people have a tendency to want to deny their strengths. The Circle of Strengths is built on the evidence of the story; and, thus, it is hard to deny or set aside the circle that emerges. If people say that "*it was only in this one instance*" that is fine. But the point to be stressed is that even if it only was on this one occasion, all the strengths that were expressed in this activity could possibly be expressed in other areas of life. People often want to take their Circle of Strength diagram with them, since it is such an empowering activity.

Using the Circle of Strengths

People who do well in job interviews are often good storytellers. When they are asked questions, they know how to use stories in framing their responses. Stories are the evidence that assures interviewers that the people in front of them have the capacity to handle the job. Of course, educational or learning qualifications and work experience also play an important part, but there are many aspects of the interview that depend on the telling of a good story.

The story mentioned above highlights a wide variety of strengths. Depending on the question asked in the interview, the story could be modified slightly to answer the question that is being asked. With a few good stories people are prepared to answer a multitude of questions.

Of course, the story under observation may only be one illustration of strengths. The practitioner should help people to identify their "best" stories and then show them how to adapt the stories to answer some of the questions they can be asked in interviews. With this additional preparation, people gain greater self-confidence and they are also better prepared to handle job interviews.

chapter seven

CAREER EXPLORATION

Potential and Possibilities:
Career Exploration

Career exploration naturally follows from self-assessment as possibilities naturally follow potential. Through self-assessment, people engage in the lifelong journey of discovering who they are and the potential that they have been created with. Through career exploration, people engage in the lifelong journey of discovering what they can do with all they have in their lives and the possibilities that all their potential points towards.

Self-assessment & Career Exploration

The dynamic interconnection between these two foundational processes of the life/career journey points to the impact self-assessment, or lack there of, can have upon career exploration. Before people can meaningfully begin to generate career alternatives, they must first learn about themselves through self-assessment. People take what they have discovered in the process of self-assessment and use that information to generate and explore realistic career possibilities and then make effective career decisions.

> *The greatest barrier to someone achieving their potential is their denial of it.*
> - Author unknown

Hope-Filled Engagement is as necessary for career exploration as it was for self-assessment. When people take ownership of who they are and of the potential they have, there is a solid basis of hope as they approach career exploration. If they have been gifted with something in their life then it is possible to find some way to express it in their lives. On the other hand, if people don't take ownership of their potential, it can be a challenge to maintain any sense of hope as they look towards the world of work.

All the challenges addressed earlier also apply to career exploration. People can experience hopelessness as they look toward a world of education and work that they don't relate to, without knowing how to see their possibilities and struggling with enculturated humility.

Just as many have a very limited knowledge of themselves and all the potential they have, they also may have a very limited knowledge of the world of work and all their possibilities. But just as they have far more personal assets than they ever imagined, so too people often have far more possibilities than they ever imagined.

A *Hope-Filled Engagement* approach to career exploration also addresses the issues of Career Integrity (Chapter Three). It may be necessary to balance the concept of many possibilities with the realities in which people find themselves. The myth that you can be anything you want to be may be untrue but that doesn't mean that people don't have many more possibilities than they think they have. However the number of these possibilities may be severely restricted by life's realities. Even so, it is important to identify all the possibilities that are open to people.

Challenge of Career Exploration

It is important to understand some fundamental challenges people face in understanding the career exploration process itself. When thinking of career exploration, practitioners should ask themselves three questions:

1. *How many different occupations are you personally aware of?*

2. *How many different occupations are those you work with aware of?*

3. *How many different occupations are actually out there?*

Though practitioners may be aware that there are thousands of jobs, many state that they really only know a few hundred. And the people they work with know even fewer—often not many more than ten or twenty. Yet the actual number of jobs is much higher. The *National Occupational Classification* or NOC (Human Resources and Skills Development Canada, 2006) which categorizes all the known occupations in Canada, describes over 900 distinct occupations with over 25,000 job titles.

This obviously is a serious barrier to effective career exploration. Suppose people knew of 100 or 1000 jobs. What are the chances that the best career for anyone of them would be one of these 100 or 1000 occupations or one of the other 24,900 other jobs out there?

What's the answer? You could just ask people to read the NOC. This would give them access to all the available jobs. This is overstating the case somewhat, since the NOC does classify occupations according to criteria, such as aptitudes, interests, education, and physical activities. But with such numbers, for most people, looking for the right occupation may still seem like looking for the proverbial needle in a haystack. The sheer number of occupations in such tools is overwhelming, and for many people the jobs listed may also seem meaningless.

Nature of Career Exploration

Another challenge is implied in the question *"What is the fundamental nature of career exploration?"* In training workshops, we introduce this question by asking life/career practitioners a series of questions:

- *What is your current job?*

- *What was the very first work that you were paid for?*

- *How many jobs have you had between that very first job and your current one?*

Practitioners state their current job titles, such as career development officer, guidance counsellor, employment assistance worker, or teacher. Their first jobs often took place some time as a child or teen and display an astonishing variety from the more common babysitters, paper deliverers, or grass cutters to the more exotic such as herding goats or collecting mistletoe. There may be a great deal of variety in the actual work people have done, but they all share one thing in common—most have had many jobs in their lives. It is common for many to have had ten, twenty, thirty, or more jobs.

Two further questions inform this issue: *"How many of you are doing what you thought you'd be doing when you left high school?"* and *"How many of you are doing what you thought you'd be doing when you left college or university or tech school?"* A few years ago, Gray asked this to a group of 450 Career and Education Transition workers in New Zealand schools during their national convention. Only ten said they were doing what they thought they'd be doing when they left high school and only about 25 what they thought when they left college. This is very typical. People's life/career journeys are often marked by change as a result of intentionality and/or happenstance.

What do these typical answers to such questions tell us about careers and career exploration? The answer is clear: **career exploration is a journey, a path, not just a destination**. Most people today will have multiple occupations and jobs throughout their lifetime. Therefore, it is logical to approach career exploration from the perspective that we must prepare people not so much for "the one lifelong job" but for "a lifelong journey."

This concept in itself is a real challenge, because many people see career exploration as finding that one "perfect" job that will fulfill them somehow. For example, those who work in high school guidance find that many parents focus on what their children are going to do with their life after graduation and understand this in terms of a single career path. It is clear that many people are still thinking in the older paradigm of the "one" job.

It is important to remember that self-assessment and career exploration are both dynamic lifelong processes. At any particular moment in their life journeys, people need to be able to grasp their own potential and unlock their sense of possibilities. Therefore, tools and processes are needed that will equip people not only to understand self-assessment but also to understand the ongoing life skill of understanding the labour market and learning to relate to it in the most effective manner in whatever situation they find themselves in.

As with self-assessment, people need to know two things: what to look for and how to look for it. In *Hope-Filled Engagement*, we will explore the use of the same fundamental frameworks and tools (such as the Career Circle and Connections, Figures 12 and 13) used in self-assessment for career exploration. Such consistency will make career exploration more accessible to people.

Career Exploration Processes

There are five basic steps in the career exploration process. These five are logically linear but are often dynamically worked out in real life.

- **Generating career possibilities**

- **Researching career possibilities**

- **Evaluating career possibilities**

- **Decision making**

- **Planning**

We will explore the first two (generating and researching career possibilities) in this chapter and the next three (evaluating career possibilities, decision making, and planning) in the next.

Activity: The Pencil -
Equipping for Career Exploration

Earlier we demonstrated the value of equipping people with a creativity perspective that stimulates questioning and observation. The right stimuli are also important for generating career possibilities. Rather than asking people immediately what they want to do with their lives or to go to resources listing the various career options out there, try some backswing activities. Creativity activities not only stimulate people's brainstorming abilities in preparation for generating career possibilities but also provide them with a hopeful perspective on the nature of the world of work.

One of the most effective stimuli for introducing the concept of career and career exploration is a common wooden pencil. The following three "pencil" activities prepare people for career exploration by introducing them to key concepts and processes in a fun and non-threatening way. They may be used alone or in conjunction with one another.

Each activity asks a different question about a common object to stimulate creativity and imagination on the nature of careers and career exploration. Once stimulated, this creativity and imagination may then be applied to people's own lives and career exploration. But instead of a pencil, stimuli will be drawn from people's own lives.

If possible, flip chart the responses. As with similar activities in this book, these may be easily adapted for use with only one person.

1. *What does this pencil "teach" about the concept of "career"?*

Tom Wujec (1995) presented this activity to stimulate people's thinking by using a familiar object for inspiration. Ask the question and allow people to brainstorm. If they get stuck, draw attention to the individual parts of a pencil and ask what each part says about "career". Figure 26 mindmaps some of the career concepts that can be seen in a pencil.

Figure 26: Career Insights from a Pencil

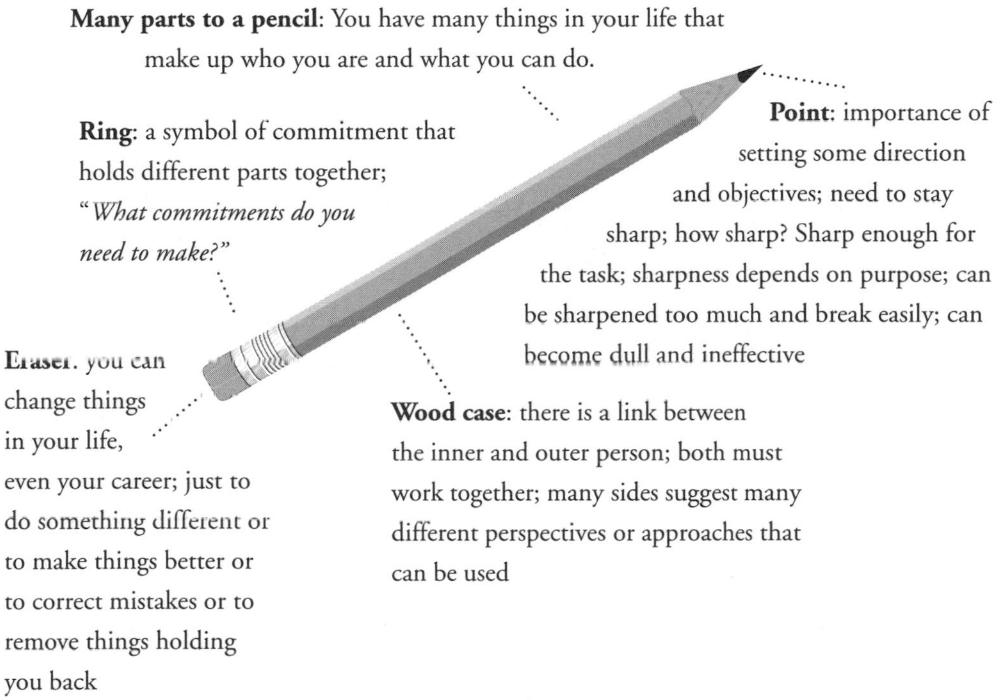

Many parts to a pencil: You have many things in your life that make up who you are and what you can do.

Ring: a symbol of commitment that holds different parts together; *"What commitments do you need to make?"*

Point: importance of setting some direction and objectives; need to stay sharp; how sharp? Sharp enough for the task; sharpness depends on purpose; can be sharpened too much and break easily; can become dull and ineffective

Eraser. you can change things in your life, even your career; just to do something different or to make things better or to correct mistakes or to remove things holding you back

Wood case: there is a link between the inner and outer person; both must work together; many sides suggest many different perspectives or approaches that can be used

2. *What could I do with this pencil?*

A key observation about a pencil is that it can be used in many different ways. This second activity asks people to be creative in thinking of possible uses. Figure 27 mindmaps some of the many uses for a pencil.

Once the group has identified a large number of uses, ask them what this says about the number of career possibilities people may have. *"If something as relatively simply as a pencil, could have so many possibilities, what about you? If you could do all these things with a pencil, how much*

Figure 27: Uses for a Pencil

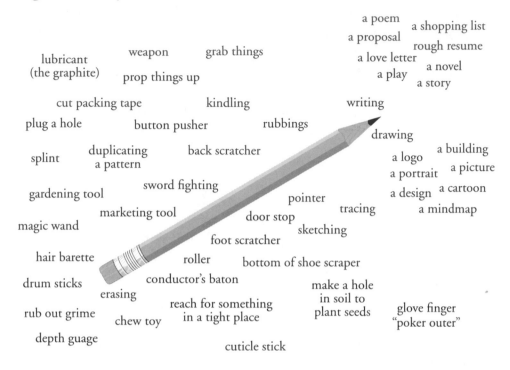

do you think you could do with all you have in your life?" People have incredibly more potential in them than a pencil, so it is clear that they also would have incredibly more possibilities. What is more, the same pencil could potentially be used in all these ways in its lifetime. In a similar way, people may express themselves through many different occupations and jobs throughout their life/career journey.

This activity may be closed by asking the question, *"What makes the difference between the pencil being used in any of these ways and it just gathering dust in a drawer?"* The answer is simple: *"Someone making a choice to pick it up and do something with it."* In the same way, often the difference between people's potential being used or just left dormant and forgotten is dependent upon people choosing to take a hold of what they have been gifted with and using it.

3. ***What is the work history of this pencil? What jobs had to occur in order for me to have this pencil?***

This final activity is designed to open up people's minds to the world of career possibilities that exist. Ask the group to brainstorm on the work history of a pencil. A pencil just doesn't come into existence; it is the product of a succession of jobs held by ordinary people. Identifying and reflecting on this succession of jobs always surprises people with a new way of understanding the world of work.

The process is very similar to the observe-question process presented in Chapter Six. The different parts of the pencil suggest different industries. For example, people see the wood and think of loggers. Expand this to the forestry industry and keep asking about what other jobs will be needed: *"OK, we need the forestry industry. What other jobs had to occur in the forestry industry in order to obtain the wood necessary for the pencil?"* Once there are a few jobs listed under forestry ask, *"What jobs are needed for the other parts of the pencil?"* When people mention a job related to another field, such as mining, ask what mining jobs will be needed. Keep brainstorming through the different parts of the pencil.

As people make new connections, they will begin to list jobs that are related to the obvious industries such as forestry or mining; usually these are important in all the other industries. For example all industries will depend to some extent upon the finance industry. List these to the side. Ask questions such as

- *What other related jobs are needed for these jobs to be possible?*

- *You mentioned a logging camp? What jobs are needed to create and maintain a logging camp?*

- *How are people going to get around?*

- *What are people going to wear while they work?*

Figure 28: Work History of a Pencil

WHAT JOBS HAD TO OCCUR FOR SOMEONE TO HAVE THIS PENCIL?

heavy machinary operators

environmentalists   skaters   shipping &
                                                                                 receiving
surveyors   chokers   technicians
   tree planters   colour specialists   type specialists   forklift drivers
loggers   fallers   chemists   designers   inventory control

FORESTRY   **CHEMICAL**   **DESIGN**   **WHOLESALE &**
                                                                          WAREHOUSING

MINING   **AGRICULTURE**   **MILLING &**   **RETAIL**
                                               MANUFACTURING

      miners   rubber farmers   green-chain operators   sales people
drillers   explosives   machinists   stock control
   exploration   graders   display
                                              millwrights
testing   quality control   assembly workers
      sorters   tool & dye workers   packaging
                                                 forklift drivers

Figure 28: Work History of a Pencil shows some of the usual jobs listed in our workshops. Obviously this list could be quite long so you will limit the jobs listed under each industry. In a half hour or so, the group should be able to come up with dozens of jobs. The goal is not an exhaustive list but enough of a list to expand people's thinking. Some teachers have had classes do this on long sheets of newsprint to ensure lots of writing space; this could also be set up as a competition between groups.

Ask the group to reflect on the work history of the pencil and then discuss what it implies about careers and the world of work.

People are often surprised at the jobs that come to mind that they wouldn't have normally thought of. There are lots of jobs and people

WHAT OTHER JOBS HAD TO OCCUR FOR THESE JOBS TO OCCUR?

TRANSPORTATION:
trucks, cars, boats & barges,
drivers, mechanics, dispatchers,
roads builders ...

MANAGERS:
managers, supervisors,
human resources,
admin support ...

**RESEARCH &
DEVELOPMENT:**
scientists, technicians ...

COMMUNICATIONS:
phones, phone towers ...

PAPER & CARDBOARD:
pulp and paper ...

**MARKETING &
ADVERTISING:**
graphic designers,
colour experts,
research ...

LEGAL:
lawyers, notary publics ...

UNION:
leaders, shop stewards,
admin ...

COMMUNICATIONS:
phones, phone towers,
line workers,
installers ...

**INFORMATION
TECHKNOWLOGY:**
computers, programmers,
analysts, technicians...

GOVERNMENT JOBS:
policy makers, department of
forestry, wildlife services,
environmental, licensing,
enforcement ...

PLASTICS:
chemists, technicians,
form makers ...

know more than they thought they knew. The jobs are obviously in their minds but they needed a stimulus to bring them to mind.

World-Wide Web of Work

As they review the list of occupations, people see that there are many specific jobs directly related to each industry but there are also many jobs in common with all the different industries. Often when people are doing career exploration, they are thinking in terms of lists of unrelated career fields. It is more effective to recognize that there is a "world wide web of work." Recognizing this interconnectedness of work can be a real eye opener for people. Rather than being separate and isolated, occupations and jobs are actually interconnected in this web. If you place yourself at any point in this web, there are numerous jobs connected to it. This concept of a web of work in which jobs are "hyper-linked" to one another is one that ought to be easily understood by anyone who is computer and internet savvy. It is especially accessible to most youth today.

This activity could be done with almost anything. In fact, if people were to look at the things around them from this perspective, they would see that they all have a similar work history to the pencil. For example, a young person's skateboard also has wood, metal, rubber, paint, design, on it. Opening people's eyes to this web of work can be very powerful in changing the way they see career possibilities.

The task then is to help people find their initial places in this web of work and to help them see what is possible from those places. There are many forms in which such jobs may manifest themselves. A person can be an accountant or administrative support or cleaner in the banking industry, but also in forestry, mining, manufacturing, milling, wholesale and distributing, retail, government, and so forth. People may miss career possibilities because they are thinking too narrowly about a particular occupation. For example, someone may reject being a photographer because they wouldn't want to do weddings, but fail to realize that there are many photographers who never take wedding photos. They don't realize that every picture they see in magazines, newspapers, journals, newsletters, and websites are taken by photographers, many of whom were paid.

The question then becomes, *"How do we help people find their initial starting points in this web of work?"* Answer: find the right stimuli. In the next few segments, we will explore some different stimuli that can be effective for this approach to career exploration.

Generating Career Possibilities

The first logical step of career exploration is generating career possibilities. We will emphasize an approach that is not only creative but also progressive, balanced, person-centred, and hope-filled.

There is always the temptation to minimize the generating step and move quickly on to the other four, yet this may short-circuit the process. Generating career possibilities lays the foundations for the other stages. During work search, people access the hidden job market by checking every possible place where the work may be found. This is the only way to ensure that nothing will be missed. In a similar way, taking time to generate all possible career possibilities is an effective strategy in career exploration to ensure that nothing will be missed. Though some may resist, thinking they will never consider many of the occupations generated, people shouldn't limit themselves at this stage.

In later activities, such as researching and evaluating their possibilities, people will learn how to focus on the most appropriate ones.

Progressive Approach

Rather than generating all the career possibilities all at once, people will have the opportunity to generate them step by step. The next four activities illustrate different ways to generate career possibilities. These activities build upon one another and so are most effective if used in sequence but could be used flexibly. People will generate career possibilities, first, from their own lives, then expand these using available labour market information, then expand further by exploring career fields of interest, and finally expand even more by looking at what work possibilities could be created through entrepreneurship.

Balanced Approach

Two metaphors have been used to describe the process of generating career possibilities. The "funnel" approach suggests that people need to narrow down their options. This is often seen when parents are concerned about what their children are going to do after high school. The "lampshade" approach, on the other hand, suggests that rather than bringing the focus down to a few options, it is important to generate many possibilities. This way, if one or more of the possibilities proves to be unreachable, there are always others to consider.

These two approaches are not mutually exclusive. In fact, effective career exploration requires a balance of both the "funnel" and the "lampshade." Throughout the career exploration process, people should be going back and forth between the two; the wisdom is knowing when to use each one most effectively. For example, when starting to generate career possibilities, one should be using the "lampshade" to generate many possibilities. When moving to the research phase, one will need to narrow down the possibilities to a few key ones (the "funnel"). When researching career possibilities, people will want to use the "lampshade" approach to find as much information as possible in order to identify the relevant information through a "funnel" approach.

Person-centered Approach

This section will emphasize a person-centered approach to the initial generation of career possibilities. We will explore several different strategies to creatively generate new career possibilities but the starting point will ultimately be people's lives. People's lives will serve as the "pencil," as the initial stimuli to generate possibilities. Once they have generated possibilities from their own lives, other tools will be used to expand the initial possibilities.

Hope-filled Approach

This progressive, balanced, person-centred approach can bring hope to the career exploration process. Just being surprised that there are many more career possibilities than imagined can be a great source of encouragement and hope for people. These new possibilities will be more meaningful because they are based upon their lives. As well, because they will be generating these possibilities themselves, it is easier for them to take ownership of them. Our goal is that the very process of generating career possibilities will generate hope from the first step through the last.

Activity: Generating Possibilities from a Life

As the Pencil activity demonstrated, one key to effective generating of career possibilities is to find the right stimuli, the right starting points. The starting points should be where people are engaged in life. At these points, people will find their natural points of connection into the world-wide web of work. Once starting points have been found, a second key is the use of questions that will stimulate people's brainstorming of possibilities, using the spiral of curiosity and discovery.

People can start with many different aspects of their lives, such as their favourite things (Favourite Things activity, Chapter Six), past experiences, dreams, suggestions from others, meaningful connections (the Connections activity, Chapter Five), even things they possess (e.g., the Pencil Activity, Chapter Seven).

Another effective starting point is the Career Circles (Figure 12) people generate during the self-assessment phase. The Career Circle summarizes who people are; this is a natural starting point for exploring what they could do. This has the advantage of starting with a framework that people are familiar with and building on a process that has already helped them discover that they have many more personal assets than they had ever realized. We wish to open their thinking even further; these points of self-discovery can now be points of career discovery as well. With the Career Circle, they are ready to discover that, though they may think they have few career possibilities, they may have many more career possibilities than they had ever realized.

We would like to illustrate this process with a real life example. A few years ago, the salmon fishing fleet on the British Columbia coast was drastically reduced because of overfishing. A group of 25 people (average age 55) who had lost their livelihood because of this had been attending a government-sponsored program for several months to assist them in finding other work possibilities. But they just wanted to fish; unfortunately this was no longer an option for them. Gray was asked to do a session with them and help them see new options. The challenge was very apparent; they didn't really want to see any other possibilities and were not particularly open to a "so-called expert" telling them what to do.

Gray assumed the position of a learner and facilitated a session of self-assessment and career exploration for them using the Career Circle. He started with a large copy of the Career Circle, wrote the word "Fisherman" in the centre and asked a series of questions touching on each section the circle:

- Skills: *What do fishermen do? What else do they do?*

- Interests: *What do fishermen usually like or enjoy?*

- Personal Style: *What kind of workers are fishermen?*

- Values: *What is important to fishermen?*

- Balance: *What do fishermen need to stay balanced?*

- Learning: *What do fishermen know? What do they usually learn?*

- Work/Life Roles: *What roles do fishermen fulfill on the boat or off?*

- Work Connections: *What other areas of work do you come in contact with as fisherman?*

None of these were difficult questions for them to answer. Why? Because this is where they were all engaged. Once they got going, they proudly talked of their lives as fishermen and a large list of key points were listed on the Career Circle. Though there were some differences, they shared many characteristics in common.

After this was completed, Gray affirmed all that these fishermen had in their lives and suggested all of these things could help them see alternatives to fishing. At this point, it would not have helped to direct them to books that listed career possibilities because they weren't interested in them. The alternative was to start with their own lives and connect them to the world wide web of work. Two simple questions were key to this process:

- *Are you the only ones who…?*

- *Who else?*

Gray went around the Career Circle and asked these two questions for every point listed on it. For example, under skill they put down that they work with boats. In response to the questions, *"Are you the only ones who work with boats? Who else works with boats?"*, they were able to generate many ideas. Other questions were used to stimulate their thinking when things started to slow down (e.g., *"What kinds of boats are there?" "Where do you find boats?" "What do you find on a boat?" "Who uses boats?"*).

The following is a list similar to the one they generated:

"Who else works with boats? People who work in the following areas:"

- Tugs, sailboats, yachts, ferries, navy, coast guard, police boats, fireboats, water taxis, leisure craft, row boats, dinghies, canoes, kayaks, long boats, windsurfing, freighters, houseboats, racing boats, cruise boats, research vessels, submersibles, float planes, barges, skiffs, rafts, boom boats, etc.

- Longshoremen, port authority, boat pilots, etc.

- Design, build, maintain, clean boats, etc.

- Carpenters, upholsterers, electricians, plumbers, painters, mechanics, sail makers, window makers, etc.

- Boat builders, boat shows, dry docks, marinas, security, etc.

- Ecotourism, sport fishing, whale watching, scuba divers, snorkelers, movie & TV media, whitewater rafting, etc.

- Design, make, and sell specialized clothing and equipment for boats (shoes, pants, coats, hats, safety equipment, binoculars, paddles, outboard motors, flags), etc.

- Computers, electronics, radios, radar, sonar devices, GPS, etc.

- Government regulators, fish and wildlife personnel, etc.

- Models and toy boats, etc.

- Publishing, boating magazines, journals, newsletters; writers, photographers, illustrators, etc.

- Trainers and teachers about boating and boating safety, etc.

- People who track marine weather, tides, etc.

After asking such questions on all the various things they had identified in the Career Circle as characterizing fishermen, they were able to generate scores of ideas around the Career Circle. Again, they had no problem generating ideas such as these because this was the world they knew and were involved in. Figure 29: Sample Possibilities from a Career Circle shows a simplified example of the mind map of career possibilities generated by this activity.

Once this brainstorming was finished, it was a simple matter to ask the group what all these areas that flowed from who they were told them about their career possibilities. There was an "AHA" moment. Their eyes were opened to the web of work that they lived and worked within as fishermen. From where they stood in this web, there were many possible directions they could move. This possibilities perspective brought new hope to the group, and they were able to move on from that point.

At this point, some people may not generate many possibilities, but they usually generate far more than they every imagined. What is most important is not the number they generate but that people are generating possibilities themselves from their own lives. What they generate in this manner can then become starting points for further activities.

Figure 29: Sample Possibilities from a Career Circle

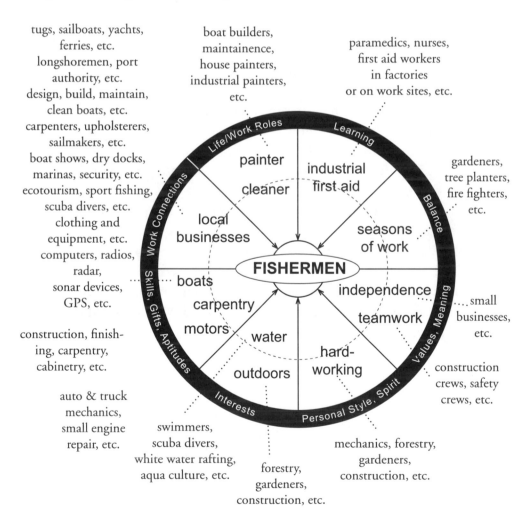

Activity: Generating Possibilities from Labour Market Information

Once people have generated lists of career possibilities from their lives, it could be helpful to generate more possibilities by looking at relevant labour market resources.

The order of activities is significant. A basic rule of learning is to move from the known to the unknown. Once personal mental connections have been stimulated, available information about career possibilities will make more sense. Curiosity will be engaged and people will naturally be looking for possibilities they missed and will be looking to connect the new possibilities to those they have already generated. Once people have generated possibilities from their own life, they will get more out of looking at the various sources of career possibilities that are available. Such information may be available in many forms:

Labour market trends: for example, the increasing number of seniors suggests that there will be an increase of jobs working with seniors. *"What kind of work will need to be done with seniors?"*

New construction or the opening of new businesses may suggest new possibilities. For example, in one small town, a new hospital was to be opened in five years. The local career office was encouraged to organize a trip to a similar sized hospital in another community to meet with the human resources department to hear about the wide diversity of jobs in such a hospital. This could help people prepare for the new possibilities that might open up.

Lists of occupations, such as you might find in career books or websites. Once people have generated their own possibilities from their own life, lists will look different. For example, consider the following list of occupations taken from the More Possibilities activity in *Guiding Circles 2* (pp. 12-13):

Accountant/Bookkeeper	Animator
Actor/Actress	Arborist
Administrator	Archeologist
Advertising, Sales/Production	Architect
Agriculturalist	Archivist
Aircraft Pilot	Artist
Aircraft Mechanic	Assembly Worker
Ambulance Attendant	

If Gray were to have started by showing this list to the group of fishermen referred to earlier, they may have seen it as irrelevant to them as fishermen. But after generating possibilities from the fisherman Career Circle (Figure 29), they would look at it differently and probably make associations they would never have noticed previously. For example, just consider the first few occupations on the list. Most of these could be connected to the possibilities generated. In the labour market of boats, there is certainly a need for accountants, administrators, mechanics, and assembly workers. There are TV and movies that involve boats. There is certainly advertising, sales, and production. There are floating planes and water ambulances. There are architects who design houseboats, and archivists who keep track of the boating history and records. There are artists who draw, paint, and photograph boats. There may be arborists who look a trees beside water and there are certainly marine biologists who study water plants. In other words, the list starts to make sense because it is no longer a random list but part of the world-wide web of work.

Activity: Generating Possibilities from an Occupational Field

One of the subtle challenges that some people face when generating career possibilities is that they stop too soon, often with a goal such as being a "nurse" or a "teacher." What is the problem with career goals like "nurse" or "teacher"? These may be too general, because they are actually identifying occupational fields in which there are countless distinct jobs, many of which can vary quite radically from each other. For example, someone may love to teach and, therefore, set a goal to become a high school teacher. This may be a very realistic goal. But if this specific goal has been arrived at because that is the only type of teacher the person knows, the person may become a high school teacher but in fact hate the job once in it. Why? One reason could be that, though they do have the ability to teach, there are many other factors than that one skill which must be taken into account. People may be natural teachers but that doesn't mean they are suited to teach in every context. They may do well with adults but not relate well to children. They may thrive in small workshops but cringe in a large lecture hall.

It is important to go beyond the generalities of career fields to the specifics associated with the diverse jobs within that field. People want to be teachers. Great! *"But what kind? Who should they teach? What should they teach? Where should they be teaching?"* And so on. People ultimately will be making specific occupational decisions, and it is difficult to make specific decisions from generalities. As people need to look for details as they work on self-assessment, so too they need to look for details in career exploration.

When people go beyond general career titles to mind mapping career fields, they are able to more finely tune the career possibilities which most closely match their unique combination of personal characteristics as presented in their Career Circle.

Even more career possibilities can be generated by using a simple brainstorming technique. The occupational field is the stimulus into the web of work instead of the "pencil" used earlier. As people do this activity, take pictures of the mind maps they generate and keep them on file for future reference. If you are working with people having difficulty with the brainstorming, you could show them examples that could stimulate them. If you have a mind map of a career field people are interested in, you could give them a printout and ask them to add to it. Showing them something that people, like themselves, have already generated may be more readily accepted. The following sets forth the process of generating possibilities from an occupational field:

Divide the group into smaller groups of three or four people and hand out one flip chart sheet of paper for each person in the group along with flip chart markers. The group will work with one person at a time; allow 10-15 minutes per person (or longer if time allows).

Each person is asked to write the name of a career they are interested in exploring in the centre of the page. The group is then to brainstorm all the forms of that career that they are aware of and write them on the flip chart. Once they have listed all the forms they can think of, they are to list all of the related jobs they can think of. Start with jobs closest to the initial career possibility and work out from there. Figure 30 provides a simplified example of a mind map relating to the job "nurse."

This is brainstorming; there is no right or wrong. They should write down all the jobs that are mentioned. They never know when one job might link to another job that could be a great fit for the person. It helps to have people other than the person whose mind map is being generated to do the writing; they are less likely to be evaluating and rejecting too soon.

Encourage the groups to use questions to stimulate their thinking. For example, the following questions could be helpful when mind mapping the career field of nursing:

Figure 30: Mindmap of "Nurse" Possibilities

- *"What types of nurses are there?"*: surgery nurses, registered nurses, licensed practical nurses, etc.

- *"What jobs are related to nurses?"*: doctors, technicians, therapists, dentists, dental hygienists, etc.

- *"Who gets nursed?"*: infants, children, teens, women, men, seniors, etc.

- *"Where is nursing provided?"*: hospitals, doctor's offices, camps, industry, clinics, Third World, cruise ships or retreat centers, etc.

- *"Who supports nurses as they do their job?"*: administrators, unions, trainers, cleaners, food services, etc.

- *"What else is nursed beside people?"*: animals (e.g., vets, vet assistants), plants (e.g., plant doctors).

As with the mind map of the work history of a pencil, the list is almost endless. The career field is only a starting point from which to move around the world wide-web of work.

Once everyone in the group has generated a mind map, post them around the training room. Give people markers and ask them to read all the different mind maps and add any jobs they think others may have missed. Many times seeing the other mind maps will stimulate new ideas.

Debrief the activity by asking the group what these mind maps tell them about generating career possibilities. Groups normally are shocked at how much they have generated and how much fun they had doing it. No one usually expects to have fun while doing career exploration but fun is an effective strategy for engaging people.

Demonstrate some of the ways they might use such a mind map. For example, suppose people want to be nurses but say they couldn't do it because they can't stand the shift work. You could point out all the related jobs that don't involve shift work, such as nurses in doctor's offices or clinics. If they don't like people, they could consider being a vet assistant or a technician. If they like to travel, they could consider being a nurse on cruise ships or in the Third World. If they only have a certain amount of formal education, identity the possibilities that require only that level.

You can show how such mind maps can contain entry points and potential career paths. You can use these mind maps to help people get the closest possible job to their ideal. For example, someone may really enjoy working around college students but lack the academic requirements for many faculty or administrative jobs. But what about the janitor or custodian? Sometimes in small colleges these are the very people whom students most remember. This can also be helpful with immigrants who are trying to get local credentials. While working on certification, it may help to find them a survival job related to the area they are looking into. For example, finding an immigrant nurse a job as a janitor in a care facility rather than a warehouse or office would help him/her learn the local world of nursing, including the technical English that he/she may lack. This could also assist them in establishing a network of contacts.

In other words, assist people to begin to think in terms of who they are and what they would like to do, not just in generalities but in specifics, in terms of the world-wide web of work. If they look at a field only in terms of their limited generalized outlook, they may prematurely reject it. But if they are able to see the broader view of a career field, it may generate a much greater sense of hope that they can find something that will actually fit for them.

Activity: Generating Possibilities through Entrepreneurship

Most life/career practitioners acknowledge that entrepreneurship is a serious option in today's world of work. If so, how do we assist people to explore entrepreneurship as a career possibility in the first place. This raises some basic questions: *"What makes an entrepreneur an entrepreneur?" "How do you tell what an entrepreneur looks like?"* These two questions are inter-related; the way you answer the first question to a large extent will influence how you answer the second and vice versa.

It is common to test entrepreneurial potential through some sort of quiz that tests whether or not people meet a list of entrepreneur characteristics. This implies that there is some sort of "standard" by which you can recognize an entrepreneur. But such an approach can create a sense of hopelessness with people when they "fail" the quiz with the result that they wouldn't even consider entrepreneurship as an option to explore.

Let us explore the entrepreneur quiz approach more closely. The kinds of questions in such quizzes usually revolve around a pre-determined list of personal characteristics assumed to be essential for someone to be a successful entrepreneur. Such quizzes typically ask questions such as…

- *Do you know who you are?*

- *Do you know what you are capable of?*

- *Are you a self-starter?*

- *Do you enjoy setting goals and accomplishing them?*

- *Are you a hard worker? Organized?*

- *Are you persistent? Self-confident? Competitive?*

- *How do you handle challenges?*

- *Are you a risk-taker?*

- *Are you an active lifelong learner? Creative?*

- *Do you work well with others? Are you a team builder?*

- *Are you good at decision making, problem solving, managing time, communicating, budgeting?*

These are all meaningful questions, but practitioners should evaluate the use of such quizzes with three questions:

1. *How many of the people you work with would say "yes" to most of these?*

2. *How would most people relate to these questions?*

3. *What do these questions ultimately say to many people?*

Practitioners often acknowledge that many of their clients or students would answer "*no!*" to most of these, because they can't relate to them in their life situations. And for those with low self-esteem, these questions ultimately say to them that they have failed again and so there is no point in even trying. This is hopeless. But is it?

The problem is that many of these quizzes are not really asking if people are potential entrepreneurs; they are actually asking if people have mainstream business personalities and can start a business. This presupposes that an entrepreneurial personality is a business personality and that entrepreneurship always involves starting a business. What happens then if you don't have a business personality?

The flaw in this approach is clear. Not all entrepreneurs start or run their own businesses. Not all have business personalities. They come in all sizes and shapes. For example, Gray has been self-employed in the career field for over 20 years and would define himself as a "reluctant" entrepreneur who doesn't have a business personality at all.

Therefore, such an approach to exploring entrepreneurship may be ineffective with many people and may be producing the opposite effect from the intended one: namely encouraging people to consider entrepreneurship. Jeff Cornwall states this in *The Entrepreneurial Mind* (2005), "For years we got stuck thinking about entrepreneurship as a type of person or even type of personality. But this really got us nowhere, because in reality entrepreneurs come in all types, particularly when we start to look at them around the world."

How can we make entrepreneurship more accessible to people? How can we expand people's perspectives on entrepreneurship and help them think about this as a realistic option?

First, we must expand our definition of entrepreneurship. Though many entrepreneurs are business people, it does not automatically mean that all entrepreneurs are business people. If we go back to the French root of the word, entrepreneurship means "to undertake, to attempt, to try in hand, to contract for or to adventure" (Cornwall, 2005). One helpful definition is that an entrepreneur is "one who recognizes opportunities and organizes resources to take advantage of the opportunity" (Businessknowledgesource.com, n.d.). In other words, entrepreneurs are people who see that there is work to be done, who see that they have the potential to do that work, and who try to find some way to make that happen. Such people seek to create their own work opportunities. This bringing together of people with opportunity is at the heart of entrepreneurship.

This basic entrepreneur perspective is evident, when a teenager, wanting money to buy a new skateboard, sees a need (sees sidewalks and driveways covered in snow after an overnight snowfall), takes his resources (his father's shovel), and proceeds to meet the need (by going down the block, knocking on doors, and offering to shovel the snow for a fee).

With this perspective, the potential for entrepreneurship is as diverse as the opportunities for work that needs to be done and the people with the personal assets to do that work.

- It can be as informal as children setting up a lemonade stand on a hot day. It can be as formal as working through a formal business plan, raising funds, and opening a new business.

- It may be someone starting a business completely from scratch, someone purchasing a franchise, or someone working with an organization to create a new position (such as Bissonnette, 1994).

- It may be a "mom-and-pop" arrangement or a formal partnership.

- It may be someone setting up a business office or someone developing a home-based business.

- It may be full-time work or it may be part-time or seasonal.

Where do you start if you don't start at the usual starting points? As always, Hope-Filled Engagement starts by engaging people where they are engaged in life! The following activity will illustrate such an approach. If people decide this is a possibility they wish to pursue further, they can draw upon many of the already existing entrepreneurial tools available.

Even if people do not pursue entrepreneurship, this perspective will make them aware that there is a certain amount of entrepreneurial element in every work search. At the heart of work search, there is also the concept of matching work needs with people's assets. Though the goals may be different, the heart is the same; people recognize a need and then seek to meet that need with what they have in their life.

Activity: Discovering Uncharted Entrepreneur Potential

Introduce the concept of entrepreneurship by explaining to people that in today's labour market, especially in areas where there is a shortage of established jobs, more and more people find themselves having to consider the entrepreneurial path. Even if they have never considered themselves to be entrepreneurs, they can still benefit by taking the opportunity to evaluate their potential as entrepreneurs.

Explain the simplicity of the basic concept, as discussed in the previous segment. If they know who they are and what they have in their lives, they may consider creating their own work opportunities. Using the concepts in the last chapter, demonstrate that this may take many different forms.

Introduce the four sections of the Entrepreneur Circle: Spirit, Resources, Opportunity, and Plan (Figure 31, adapted from *Guiding Circles 2*, pp. 16-19). Ask people to review their personal assets recorded in their Career Circles (Figure 12) and then fill in the Entrepreneur Circle in the order indicated. Figure 32: Sample Entrepreneur Circle is a reconstruction of an actual circle completed by a small group of practitioners.

This activity may be done with individuals or small groups. Starting with small groups may be easier because people can learn from each other and encourage each other. After the small groups, those who are still interested in pursuing this further may wish to do their own personal circle.

1. The SPIRIT

SPIRIT refers to those personal characteristics which are more subjective in nature. In this section, ask people to review their personal assets found in four specific components of their Career Circles: interests

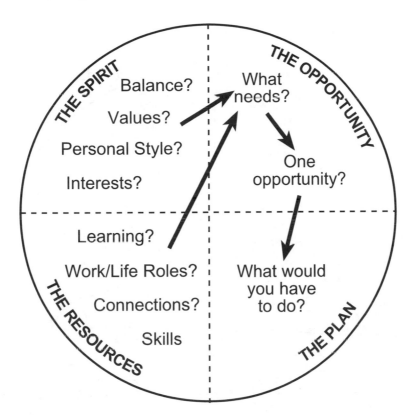

(including favourite things), personal style, values (and motivations), and balance. They should be selective and list the things they consider most important to them from each of these components. If working in small groups, suggest that each person contribute two things for each of the four components. This will keep the activity more manageable.

2. The RESOURCES

RESOURCES refer to those personal assets which are more objective. Ask people to review their personal assets in the remaining components of their Career Circles (e.g., skills, learning, work/life roles, and work connections, including people they know, possible sources of funding, etc.). They should be selective and list the things they consider most important to them from each of these components.

Figure 32: Sample Entrepreneur Circle

3. The OPPORTUNITY

The OPPORTUNITY section is for identifying what needs and opportunities they could meet with their personal assets. Once people have completed the Spirit and the Resources section, review what they have put down. Start with needs; ask the simple question, *"What needs could be met with these assets?"* Encourage people to brainstorm and list as many needs as they can think of. Remind them that, if they have something in their life, there is probably someone out there who could benefit from it. Ask questions, such as: *"What do you have in your life?"*, *"What needs are there in your area that could be met by what you have in your life?"*, *"How could you help meet them?"* For example, if someone can cook, there may be people who need someone to cook for them or someone to teach them to cook. If someone enjoys taking their dog for a walk, there may be those who don't have the time to take their dogs for walks and would be willing to pay for someone to do it.

Work opportunities happen when three things meet: people's potential, an identified need, an idea for bringing the two together. In other words, people are able to see a need for the type of work they can do and then are able to come up with an idea on how to make it happen. Once a list of needs has been generated, ask people to review the list and try to identify one of the needs (or a combination of needs) that they would focus on as an OPPORTUNITY to explore. Review what personal assets would help in meeting this opportunity.

4. The PLAN

The PLAN section is to list those things they think they might have to do to meet the identified opportunity. This is not a formal business plan but an initial brainstorming of the types of action steps that will need to be taken.

These should be based on the SPIRIT and RESOURCES they have in their life and the OPPORTUNITY they want to meet. Plans help in turning dreams into realities. They can benefit by asking questions, such as ...

- *Have we ever created our own work before or know anyone who has? What steps were followed? What did we or they do?*

- *Do we know anyone who could help us?*

- *What further information would we need to find? Where could we look for it?*

- *What are the different ways we could meet the need (e.g., A job proposal? Purchasing an existing business or franchise? Starting a business from scratch? Joining with others to start a business? etc.)*

- *What kind of funding and resources would we need? How could we find them?*

Once the Entrepreneur Circle has been completed, it can be posted on a wall and debriefed. Ask the person or group to review their thinking as they went through the activity. Ask what they feel they have learned. People are often surprised and encouraged by how much they have in their lives that could meet real needs in their communities If people are interested in pursuing this further, they can be encouraged to explore other entrepreneur tools and activities.

Activity: Career Information Circle

Once people generate career possibilities, what information do they need to get? How do they find it? People need to look for the information they need to make effective career decisions and plans. They need to compare their career research findings with their self-assessment findings.

This is where the Career Circle (Figure 12) can again be helpful. The Career Circle has been used for self assessment and for generating career possibilities. Now the same Circle, renamed the Career Information Circle, will be used to collect and organize information about specific career possibilities in preparation for career decision making. The use of a consistent framework for self-assessment and for career exploration makes this process accessible to people. People generate two circles: one containing the personal assets they discovered during self-assessment, the other containing the career information they discovered through career research. Any particular career possibility can then be evaluated by comparing and contrasting the two circles.

In Chapter 6, Storytelling, we introduced the Spiral of Curiosity and Discovery as a model for asking questions and making observations based on the Career Circle. The Career Circle suggests both the type of information being looked for and the kinds of questions which would naturally lead to finding that information. In career exploration, we will use exactly the same approach. We will use the Career Information Circle as a tool to generate the kinds of focused questions that will naturally lead to the kind of information that should be collected for any career possibility.

Set up one Career Information Circle for each career possibility that will be researched. Write the name of the career possibility in the centre of the circle. After reviewing their Career Circles, people should be creative in asking questions from as many perspectives as possible. The following are some sample questions:

- **Skills**: *What do people in this occupation do? What are the typical tasks they perform? What abilities are needed in order to do these things? What level of skill is needed for each task? How have people in this occupation developed these skills? Which skills are needed to get hired? Which can be learned on the job?*

- **Interests**: *What do people in this career tend to like or dislike in life? In their jobs? Why?*

- **Personal Style**: *What personal characteristics enable people to succeed in this occupation? What are employers looking for? What are others such as co-workers or customers looking for? To what degree? What types of personalities succeed in this career? What personal work habits are needed? How have people in the occupation developed these personal characteristics? What could be developed on the job?*

- **Values**: *What values are typically associated with this occupation? What are the values of the companies or organizations involved? The management? The workers? The people who come in contact with this career? Are they consistent with their values? How flexible are they?*

- **Balance**: *What kind of life balance typically comes with this career? What time commitments are asked for and how much time do people actually put in? What spiritual, emotional, mental, physical needs can be met through this career? Is there consistency between what is stated about life balance and what actually happens? Will this career enable or hinder you to do the things you wish to do outside your paid work life?*

- **Learning**: *What do you need to learn to be successful in this career? What do employers, co-workers, customers, and others expect you to know? How much flexibility is there? How do most people in this career get their learning? Where do people learn what they need to know for this career? How much formal education is needed to get started? (How long? Cost? etc.). What can be learned on the job?*

What alternative forms of learning are usually recognized? What kind of lifelong learning will be necessary?

- **Life/Work Roles**: *What are the typical roles someone in this career assumes? What work/life experiences are needed to enter this career? ... to progress in this career? Which ones did people currently in the career have when they started? Do employers want you to have had any community involvement? Where do people get their experience for this career? How do people usually get into this career? What are the typical career paths of people in this career?*

- **Work Connections**: *What businesses or organizations are associated with this career in your area? Who do you know that might have connections to this career or who might know someone who is connected? Who are the people that it would be good for you to contact personally? Are there any openings in your area? If not, where would you have to go for this work? Will there be any opening up in the future? If so, when? Are there any groups or associations you should be involved in?*

Some types of information are especially important to discover. Often there is a certain amount of flexibility and negotiation involved in people taking on a new career position. It is helpful to identify not only what is needed to succeed in a field but also the level of flexibility there is with these expectations. Also it is crucial to identify the deal-breakers, those things that either employers, educational institutions, or people themselves will not be flexible with. For example, if people know for sure that there are certain things they cannot live with or without, they must ask questions to ensure these points are clarified. If these matters are not clarified, they may step into a situation that they will quickly reject because something important to them has been violated.

The next chapter will explore strategies for researching and organizing the career information that needs to be obtained.

Activity: Career Research

Once career possibilities have been generated, the next stage in career exploration is to find out information about them.

Obviously it is unrealistic to explore all of them in depth. A simple way to reduce the number is to review the possibilities generated and ask people to take note of their responses to them. Levels of response may vary from high interest to actual rejection. Discuss with them why they responded as they did. Look for patterns as they talk about their responses for tentatively considering some possibilities, while definitely ruling out others. *Are there any patterns?* For example, people may be drawn to inside occupations while rejecting outside occupations. Such patterns may clarify those areas of most importance to people.

Through this initial discussion of subjective responses to the various career possibilities, seek to identify a few possibilities to explore in more depth. If necessary, more possibilities may be explored as needed.

Career Information Resources

In the last segment, we presented the types of information people need to find. Now they need to know where to find the information and how to find it. Figure 33: the Career Research Circle is a simple but useful tool for strategizing the best resources for researching a career possibility. There are three sections corresponding to the three primary sources of career information: paper, internet, and people.

One of the fundamental strengths and weaknesses of living in an information age is the amount of information people have available to them. People can learn much that is valuable; but people can also find out so much information that they get overloaded and it starts

Figure 33: Career Research Circle

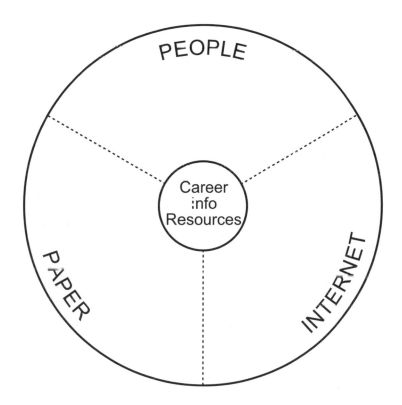

to become detrimental. This is certainly a danger when it comes to researching career information. The more people understand these three sources, the more effective they can be in strategically researching the relevant career information they need. The following are some questions to ask of each section:

- *What kind of information can you find through these sources?*

- *Where can you find these sources? How do you access them?*

- *What are the strengths and weaknesses of each?*

1. Print Resources:

There are many kinds of print literature that present helpful career information: books, magazines, journals, government reports and publications, business reports and marketing literature, newspapers, brochures, posters and postings, advertisements, to name just a few. Libraries and employment centers are good places to start; there are often librarians or life/career practitioners who can help. Other places to check include company offices (they often have promotional literature), educational institutions, chambers of commerce, professional and trade organizations and associations, conferences, trade fairs, career fairs, an so on.

Much of the basic information about career possibilities can be found in these resources: overviews of career fields, job postings, career demographics and trends, job descriptions, salary expectations, working conditions, educational requirements, work locations, and much more. Business and government trends and announcements may reveal upcoming employment opportunities. Professional or union associations have literature and conferences that can be a gold mine not only of career information but of potential contacts to network with. This type of literature may discuss the trends or issues in current career fields or personal stories of people working in the field.

It is also important to note some of the weakness in print literature so that it can be effectively evaluated. One fundamental issue is accessibility; finding print literature may be a challenge for some people, especially if they live in remote areas. It may be inaccessible to people with physical or mental disabilities. Another issue is language; in North America much is written only in English and often technical specialized English that makes it difficult for some to read. Two other issues are accuracy and relevance. These may be impacted by such issues as source, datedness, location, scope, perspective, and bias. Check for these issues with questions such as:

- *Who wrote or produced this information? Do they know what they are talking about?*

- *When was this produced?* If it is older, it may be out of date.

- *Where was it written?* Sometimes the information is only relevant to a very specific geographical area.

- *How much of the career field is being discussed?* If it is only a small part of the field, be careful not to generalize the findings. If it is very broad, realize that there may be exceptions in specific areas.

- *What is the perspective of the material? Is there any bias?* For example, often business and organizations (including educational institutions) are producing marketing literature which is only going to give their positive spin on things to the neglect of other issues.

2. Internet Resources:

Increasingly the internet is becoming an essential source of career information and actual job postings. The world-wide web of work is becoming increasingly visible through the world-wide web itself. Much of what is available in print form is also available online. Increasingly some information is only found online. This information may be more up to date.

Government career sites provide not only career information but also tools to assist in other areas such as self-assessment and work search. Career organizations, career centers (such as those at university or colleges) or online career companies such as www.monster.com can also be good starting points for broader career information. Other websites worth visiting include: private businesses, chambers of commerce, professional and educational associations, unions, and online newspapers.

One area to consider browsing is that of social media sites, such as discussion boards, chat rooms, and forums. For example, the postings dedicated to a specific career or job may be a rich source for finding people's perspectives on their jobs and the current issues revolving around them. As well, some of these may be a good place to network.

Accessibility can still be a major problem with the internet. Some people are not computer literate or don't have computer access. The accuracy and relevancy issues raised for print resources apply just as much to internet resources: source, datedness, location, scope, perspective, and bias. Anyone may write on the internet, even those who know nothing about what they are talking about. Sites may be outdated or relevant only in localized situations. Another obvious issue is information overload. It is easy to get lost in the seemingly endless maze that the web presents.

When possible, provide people with training on how to use the internet for meaningful career research. Summary sheets can be prepared for researching careers in general and specific career fields in particular.

3. People Resources:

Finally, people can be invaluable resources for career information. There is a sense in which people are interacting with other people when they read the available print or internet resources. After all, it is people who prepare these resources. Once people have a basic knowledge of a career through researching the literature and the internet, they should contact some people in the field. Paper and internet resources will provide a good deal of information that lay a foundation for meaningful discussions. But usually they won't provide the personal insight and practical advice that can be learned from people who have actual experience in a career field. Paper and internet resources focus on information chosen by others; in a personal interaction with someone, people can choose to ask for specific information that is important to them.

Talking with people shares the same weaknesses as paper and internet resources. Making contact with people may be a challenge. Issues of accuracy and relevancy (source, datedness, location, scope, perspective, and bias) are just as present. Therefore, it is wise to have interviews with several people. At the end of interviews, people should ask for the names of others that would be good to talk with. Talking with a diversity of people can help minimize any potential inaccuracies or irrelevancy.

Where can people find the people they should talk with? First, if they have completed the Connections activity (Chapter Five) during self-assessment, they will probably have identified people in their lives that they have found supportive. Or while they are doing their initial research to fill in the Career Information Circle, they may have identified people for the Work Connections section of the Circle. People may be named in the literature or online. Usually you only need to find a few people to start with and then things become easier. They may know something about the career field or they may know someone who does. The concept of "six degrees of separation" suggests that most of us are closer to meaningful network contacts than we realize. People may also be found by asking some simple questions: *"What do people in this field go to?" "Where do these people go?"* For example, some may be found at their workplace or at public events such as professional association meetings, chamber of commerce meetings, service club meetings, union meetings, conferences, or trade shows.

Asking information from people directly is usually referred to as informational interviewing. This may be very formal or quite informal in nature. There has been a lot of good material written about informational interviews and so we will only address some thoughts relating more directly to the Hope-Filled Engagement approach.

First, in terms of process, informational interviewing is often easier and less threatening than job interviews as a starting point for people. When trying to make contact with others about career possibilities, people are more likely to answer *"no"* if the starting point is *"Do you have a job opening?"* rather than *"I wonder if I could talk to you about this career field?"* Sometimes the first time people formally talk with people about specific career possibilities is when they go into the job interview. These situations can be very discouraging for some people. Informational interviewing not only provides helpful career information but also gives people the opportunity to develop their communication skills and become more comfortable talking about their career possibilities with others. Informational interviewing can also help create a network of people to access, if they choose to pursue the career in a formal work search.

Second, if the self-assessment and career exploration processes have been well done, it will be much easier for people to talk with people about career possibilities. They will have something practical to talk about and hopefully they will have a greater sense of confidence as they do it.

Third, the Career Circle can provide a practical framework for the types of questions that could be asked during the informational interview.

Fourth, talking with others through informational interviewing draws on the theme of personal connections which is central to self-assessment. If some people are particularly struggling with the idea of talking with employers and the like, then group informational interviews could be arranged. People could initially be sent out in small groups of two or three to do interviews together. This way they can support one another as they learn the process.

People can talk with life/career practitioners about the best resources in each of these areas and the most effective order to pursue them.

As people gather information from the various resources that have been identified, they can summarize their results on the various circles they have been using: new personal insights about themselves can go on the Career Circle (Figure 12); new information about career possibilities can go on the Career Information Circle (the Career Circle renamed); and any additional resources to check out can go on their Career Research Circle.

chapter eight

CREATIVE VISION/ DECISION/ ACTION

Turning Career Possibilities into Realities

In the previous chapter, we examined two of the five usual steps in career exploration/decision making: generating and researching career possibilities. Evaluating career possibilities, vision casting, decision making, and action planning logically follow generating and researching career possibilities.

A primary objective of life/career counselling is that people will actually take steps that make a positive difference as a result of the counselling they receive. In workshops with hundreds of life/career practitioners, we have found that many use action plans. But when asked whether they believe people will actually follow through on the plans, many hesitate and then express real uncertainty about that. This ought to alert us to the reality that the way action-planning is often done may not be as effective as hoped. If people aren't taking meaningful steps after counselling, then the process of action planning must be re-examined.

It may be that some people just don't want to be helped and stubbornly resist taking any positive steps. But could it also be related to the process itself? Can we find creative solutions to this which may be more effective with a greater number of people? If we desire people to actually move beyond potential and possibilities to reality, the vision/decision/action planning process must be realistic, adaptable, holistic, motivating, sustainable, consistent, and, above all else, hope-filled.

The process, first of all, must be realistic and be adaptable to a wide range of people who face many diverse challenges, such as those already discussed.

Such solutions must be holistic and build on the interconnectedness of vision, decision, and action. Though there are logical distinctions between these three, they are also interdependent. As people walk their life/career journey, it is helps to have a vision of the direction they wish to walk and then the decisions they will need to make and the actions they will need to take to move in that direction. Action follows decision which follows vision. They all motivate one another. Therefore, instead of just talking of action planning, we believe there is value in expanding the planning process to include both vision planning and decision planning.

Vision is clearly understood as that which is motivating. But the steps of decision and action must also continue to motivate people to express their potential in life. Unfortunately, vision can die out quickly when people don't take ownership of the decisions or actions needed for movement or if they feel the decisions and actions are beyond what they can do.

The vision/decision/action planning process must be sustainable. It must be a process that is applicable for the long journey; it must be a process that people can use to keep going through all the ups and downs of life.

We have emphasized the value of consistency in the life/career counselling process. We will approach vision/decision/action planning with the same concepts, paradigms, and frameworks that were used to bring hope to self-assessment and career exploration.

Vision is all about hope; decision is all about hope; action is all about hope. Moving from possibilities to reality is "hope in action." Hope sees things that are not yet and makes choices and actions as if they were. As in earlier sections, our hope is that, as people try creative forms of vision/decision/action planning, they will discover new levels of hope to motivate them and sustain them as they seek to walk their life/career journeys.

Challenges Going from Vision to Action

There are many challenges to overcome when people seek to move from vision to action in real life. People often get stuck at this point. In addition to issues already discussed—such as diversity, inadequate assumptions and conventions, and the changing and chaotic nature of today's world of work—there are other significant issues.

A Sense of Hopelessness

Hopelessness (conscious or unconscious) is the ultimate challenge. It can blind people into thinking that there is nothing they can do to move ahead. Nowhere to go! No choices! No actions! So what's the point.

Inadequate Information for a Decision

Effective vision/decision/action planning is dependent upon the right information. People may be working from incomplete or inaccurate knowledge about their potential or their possibilities. Inadequate self-assessment may leave people thinking they have nothing to offer their world. Inadequate career exploration may leave people thinking the world has nothing to offer them. As well, people may have too much information and lack an accessible framework to sort it all out.

Values Clutter and Confusion

People may have all the necessary information but still be ineffective in vision/decision/action planning. One major reason is that of values clutter and values confusion, discussed in Chapters Three and Five. These make it difficult for people to know what is most important to them and how to choose accordingly. This ability is foundational to effective vision casting, decision making, and action taking.

Inadequate Planning Models

Hopelessness thrives when people don't recognize their potential/ possibilities. But hopelessness may also be the result of inadequate approaches to vision/decision/action planning. Assumptions and conventions must be re-examined to ensure that the approaches being used address the challenges specific to vision/decision/action planning.

Usually this stage of the life/career counselling process is addressed through an action plan. But is traditional action planning adequate in the light of the challenges people face in today's chaotic and unpredictable world? Though traditional action planning has many strengths, it also has many weaknesses as well.

In this segment, we will examine some issues related to traditional vision casting, decision making, and action planning. In the next, we will suggest an expanded model of vision/decision/action planning.

1. Traditional Action Planning

Traditional action-planning (Figure 34), done well, has many strengths:

- It starts where people are at.

- It sets a clear goal or direction for people to follow.

- It sets clearly defined steps for people. The acronym SMART (Specific, Manageable, Achievable, Relevant, Time-related) provides excellent guidelines for evaluating potential steps.

Figure 34: Traditional Action Planning Model

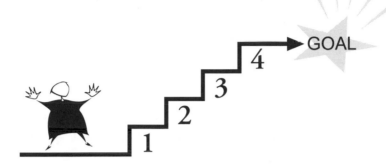

Done well, action planning can contribute greatly to people successfully reaching their goals. However, in light of the current chaotic world of work, the traditional action planning model has several weaknesses (which also affect vision casting and decision making):

- Linear Process

First, this model is very linear. This is not surprising considering it was developed at a time when the concept of career was very linear. However, today's world of work is anything but linear. People today follow life/career journeys with many twists and turns and with countless intersections where decisions are needed.

- Single Direction

The actions to be taken are usually presented as an arrow or a series of steps. In either case, the image is always one of proceeding "up" in some way (i.e., "climbing the ladder of success"). This can be a helpful image to represent growth but is "up" always the best direction? This assumption neglects the possibility that other directions may be better options for people. Kaye and Jordan-Evans (2002) expand the options for career movement to include not only vertical movement up but also the following:

- **Lateral**: horizontal movement across such as a change in job duties to increase breadth of experience

- **Enrichment**: creating a better job fit by staying in place and enriching the possibilities

- **Exploration**: temporary moves to explore other options

- **Realignment**: balancing work with other life priorities; perhaps even moving downward to relieve work stress or to open new opportunities

- **Relocation**: moving to another organization to find a better work fit

- Lack of barriers

This model usually never shows any barriers. There is no indication that there may be circumstances beyond people's control which will hinder or even prevent their reaching their goal. Yet such barriers, whether foreseeable or unforeseeable, will inevitably arise and people must be ready.

- Static Goal

Another weakness is that this model assumes that a person is able to see far enough to set the best goal. The challenge is that as people follow their career paths, they and their circumstances may change in such a way that their goals also may need to fundamentally change. Daniel Gilbert addresses the challenges of trying to look too far into the future in his book *Stumbling on Happiness* (2006, pp. 23-24).

> We insist on steering our boats because we think we have a pretty good idea of where we should go, but the truth is that much of our steering is in vain—not because the boat won't respond, and not because we can't find our

destination, but because the future is fundamentally
different than it appears through the prospectiscope. Just
as we experience illusions of eyesight ("Isn't it strange how
one line looks longer than the other even though it isn't?")
and illusion of hindsight ("Isn't it strange how I can't
remember taking out the garbage even though I did "), so
too do we experience illusions of foresight...

It is possible for us to set goals and work very hard to reach them. But
because of the powers and limits of foresight, it is also possible that once we
have reached our goals, we find ourselves regretting them. We wonder why
we even pursued them in the first place. Effective vision/decision/action
planning must, therefore, be flexible and dynamic in setting goals or risk
trapping people in life/career paths that become irrelevant as time goes on.

Another aspect of this is that the entire process is dynamic. Visions,
decisions, and actions must be evaluated and potentially revised, often
while life is still in motion. The static image of the metaphor *"stop the
world; I want to get off"* isn't always realistic in today's rapidly changing
world. A more accurate image is that of people paddling canoes down a
river; people must set direction (vision), make decisions, and take actions as
they go. Sometimes they may be able to go to shore for rest and reflection;
but more often than not, they have do what they can, while paddling, no
matter whether the river is slow moving or a rushing torrent. Dangers must
be avoided and opportunities must be taken as they arise, because it may be
too late if there is an inappropriate delay.

- Isolated Person

Finally, another fundamental weakness is that there is usually only
one person in the image. People are seen to be alone in setting the goal
and working through the steps to get there. This is not consistent with
the theme of connection, discussed throughout this book. People walk
their life/career journey in the midst of relationships that need to be
recognized and engaged.

Known or unknown influences are a reality. These impact how people see and cast vision, how people see the choices before them and then how they make them, how people step out and take actions. Unrecognized influences are often more controlling than recognized influences because they are never challenged.

2. Vision casting

One consistent challenge is that of confusing goals with vision. They are related but not the same. Vision answers the question: *"What do I want my future to look like?"* Goals answer the question: *"What must I do to realize my vision?"*

There is an advantage to starting with vision. People's perspectives change when they move from the place of problem to the place of solution. The "miracle question" (Amundson, 2009, pp. 116-7) is a strategy that encourages people to create a clear mental picture of what they would like their lives to be in the future, to describe the details of that future vision, to visualize themselves having reached this future, and finally to look back and see the steps they took in reaching their vision. Once people know where they want to go, they must accept that choices must be made if there is to be any movement. Once a choice is made, often the actions necessary to follow that choice become clearer.

It is clearly a temptation to move too quickly to goal setting before vision has been established. In a context of potential hopelessness, this order is very crucial. The goals may be the right ones, but without the inspiration and hope that vision stimulates, people may lack the motivation to take the steps they have set out for themselves.

3. Decision making

Decision making is often over simplified. People are encouraged to "just make a choice" as if this were an easy thing to do. But we cannot assume that people necessarily know how to make a good decision or, even if they do, that this or that decision is an easy one. While it is good to call for decisions to be made, this must be balanced with an understanding of the complexities involved in decision making.

People may use a combination of a wide diversity of decision making styles, such as impulsive, emotional, intuitive, hesitant, avoidant, fatalistic, compliant, rational, majority vote, reactionary, expert, or luck. As well, people may not use these consistently; they may have never examined how they are making decisions. They may even believe that they don't have any choices and fail to accept their responsibility to do so.

In mainstream life/career counselling, there is often the unrecognized assumption that people make decisions by themselves. Yet, we must recognize that some people have a collective decision making style rather than an individualistic one. Failure to recognize and acknowledge this can easily lead to problems for everyone involved. The upcoming activity on Collective Decision Making will explore this further.

Role of Practitioner

One of the issues in this process is that of the role of the life/career practitioner. Having evaluated numerous life/career counselling situations, we have observed a common tendency. Often under the pressure of time, practitioners have little time left at the end of a session for vision/decision/action planning. As a result, they may set the goals and action plans for people. People are then asked to commit to this plan: *"Do you think you can do this?"* People may meekly say they will, but they may not have taken ownership of the process or the resulting plan. Yet as we have already discussed, the role of the practitioner ought to be the same throughout the entire life/career counselling process, that of a facilitator.

Creative Vision/Decision/Action Planning Model

We propose that a Creative Vision/Decision/Action Planning Model (Figure 35) is needed to supplement the traditional model and to address the realities we have set forth in the previous three segments (Figure 36: Realities of Vision/Decision/Action Planning).

Figure 35: Creative Vision/Decision/Action Planning Model

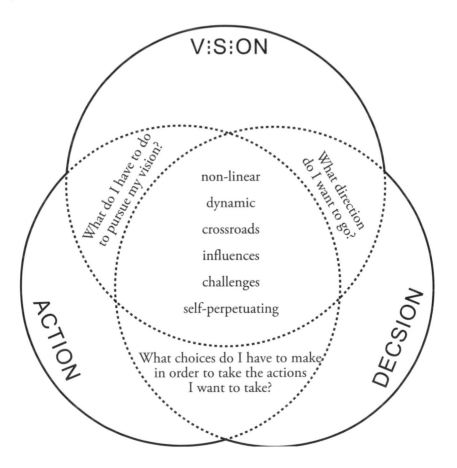

Figure 36: Realities of Vision/Decision/Action Planning

1. A Non-linear Path in a Chaotic World

First, instead of just a straight line or a flight of stairs, the image should look more like a clump of string with many twists and turns. This more accurately reflects the many twists and turns in the uncertain path of life. As well, the twists and turns acknowledge that "up" is not the only option. In order to move "ahead", people may have to go back or to the side or in some other direction.

2. A Dynamic Goal

At the end of the line instead of having a final goal, it might be more appropriate to have a tentative goal or vision. As people travel their life path, it is likely that they will be revising their goals as circumstances change. Changes may be intentional. For example people's values may change. When young, people may value traveling and seeing the world and choose jobs accordingly; but at a later stage in life, the same jobs may no longer be the best option if they start valuing staying close to home and family. Or changes may be imposed. For example, people often have to make major changes because of illness or labour market shifts.

3. Crossroads

Having a non-linear path to a dynamic goal is still not sufficient, for this pile of string is, in a sense, still linear. If you take the two ends of the string and pull, you would still have a straight line. In real life, people may be following a path and then come to a crossroads where they will have to choose the best path to follow from that point. And these crossroads often offer multiple paths. Such crossroads can be at each of the twists and turns. These crossroads emphasize the need to be intentional in choices and actions. If someone does not plan for these crossroads, they may, in the confusion of a moment, take a path that keeps them away from their intended goal.

4. Influences

Look carefully and you will see that there will be others walking with these people in their path. For example high school students will probably have parents or friends walking with them; later in life, they may have spouses or children or others. These others may take on different roles. Encouragers encourage people to follow the path that is best for them. Detractors put people down and make them feel they're not capable. Distracters just distract people as they try to follow their dreams. Gatekeepers hold the keys that open or close doors through which people need to go on their paths. For example, when people apply for university programs, there are often admissions committees that approve or disapprove people's application. If people don't plan for such gatekeepers, they may fail to identify the criteria by which the gatekeepers will open or close the gates. People need to be aware of such influences so that they are able to sort through the legitimate and helpful from those which are illegitimate and hindering.

5. Barriers

The model needs to include the concept of barriers. Challenges are a fact of life and any good planning will acknowledge them. People need to accept such challenges, whether foreseen or unforeseen, and be flexible enough to plan accordingly.

6. Self-perpetuating

Finally, the image must also picture the need for vision/decision/ action planning to be self-perpetuating. By placing people at some point in the line, the image is of those who have been journeying already and have come to a crossroads and will continue to journey. Instead of there being only one line with steps to a goal (as in the traditional model), each segment of the line, as it twists and turns, is a line with steps on it. As people continue on their journey, there will be many times when they will have to look at where they have come from, look at their current situation, look at the possible directions they could go, look at the choices they will have to make, and look at the actions that they will have to take. They will be continually asking themselves three questions: *"What direction do I want to go? What do I have to do to pursue my vision? What choices do I have to make in order to take the actions I want to take?"*

Such a creative vision/decision/action planning model will better equip people to handle the uncertainties of the labour market and of their own career journey. When presenting this model to people, we often ask, *"Which of these two models reflect your life journey to this point? The traditional straight line or the one with all the twists and turns?"* People invariably laugh and point to the non-linear model. They clearly understand and identify with the realities it portrays. Having a model that clearly addresses their life realities in itself can give people a sense of hope that they will be able to face and deal with whatever confusing twists and turns they encounter on their life path.

Activity: Connections - Influences and Affects

Earlier in this book, we introduced the theme of interconnectedness and the Connections Circle (Figure 13) as a model for understanding our connections with self, family, community, culture, the natural world, and the spiritual world. The Connections activity was introduced as a means of identifying and reconnecting with those connections that could be a source or means of support, purpose, or meaning in any way. In this activity, the same approach is used in the context of vision/decision/ action planning.

Rather than repeat the detailed instructions for the Connections activity (Chapter 5), we will discuss the use of the activity with the focus on influences and affects rather than roles and supports.

Review the Connections Circle. Explain that when people cast vision, make decisions, or take actions, they are being influenced in many ways, often unconsciously, from all six spheres. A personal failure in the past may cause people to avoid certain things in the future. Family pressures may weigh heavily on people as they step forward. Community resources will certainly influence directions people may take. Cultural perspectives on matters, such as gender, age, or status, often influence people. People may move in directions simply because they want to be close to nature; for example, many people working in Whistler, BC choose to do so because they want to ski. People often will pray and seek spiritual guidance as they move in new directions. Such influences are normal and to be expected. However, problems may arise when people are unaware of the influences in their lives. Unrecognized influences cannot be challenged. Someone may not realize that they keep avoiding certain career opportunities ideal for them because when they were a child, they were conditioned to believe they could never succeed in such careers.

But there is more than influences to be considered. When people set directions, make choices, and take actions, they will probably affect not just themselves but their world as well. In our individualistic society, some people have a hard time accepting and acknowledging this reality; they think they can act and it is no one's business but their own. But if people were to think more deeply, they would recognize that nothing could be further from the truth. For example, every time someone decides not to take advantage of an opportunity because of low self-esteem, they affect themselves as they further lower their self-esteem. When people take actions without regard to their families, it is often easy for people to be hurt. Whether people want to accept it or not, we are all role models in our families, communities, and cultures. If we make poor choices, it could encourage others to make the same mistakes. On the positive side, when we make good choices, it shows others what can be done. Environmentalism has demonstrated over the last years that the choices people make about how they live and work can impact the natural world around them.

Using the same group brainstorming approach as in the earlier Connections activity (Chapter 5), ask people to generate lists of possible influences. Emphasize that at this time they will not be focusing on their own influences but on what might influence people. This objectifies the activity and makes it easier for people to discuss influences without getting sidetracked by their own problems. Again, encourage people to focus on generating lots of ideas rather than getting sidetracked by belabouring any particular one.

Encourage people to use their imaginations to answer the question: *"Who or what do you think could influence people as they explore what directions to take in life or what decisions and actions they need to make to pursue those directions?"* As with the earlier Connections activity, people can stimulate their thinking by asking five questions for each of the circles:

- *What people?* (e.g., people are often influenced by family or friends or role models, etc.)

- *What activities?* (e.g., people may pursue careers because of what the career enables them to do either within or outside of their job)

- *What places?* (e.g., people may take a job because it is located where they want to live or because they are close to community resources)

- *What things?* (e.g., people may consider a career because of the things they work with or the things they might wear on the job)

- *What concepts or ideas?* (e.g., some people today are influenced regarding career choice by environmental issues)

Post the flip charts people generate and debrief. In order to help them personalize their findings, a volunteer can circle those influences they have experienced, while the others do it mentally. People are usually surprised by the large number of influences that are generated. They start to realize that people are influenced in many ways and that it is important to recognize these influences for themselves. Facilitate a discussion on the impact of these influences on their lives by using questions such as:

- *Which of these are my most significant influences? Why?*

- *How do they influence me? Do they influence positively or negatively?*

- *Are there any influences I don't want? Why? How could they be rejected?*

- *How could they help me as I try to set new career directions, make decisions, and take actions?*

If there is time, the Connections Circle could be used to explore who or what might be affected in this process. *"Who or what will be affected by the career decisions I make? In what ways will any possible future work I do affect them? What part will they play in my future work life?"*

Figure 37: Sample Connections Influences & Affects Circle illustrates some common influences that have been identified. These are only representative of the many ideas that could be put down.

Figure 37: Sample Connections Influences & Affects Circle

Activity: Evaluating Career Possibilities

Once people have collected relevant information about their career possibilities, the next step is for people to evaluate their career possibilities to see how realistic they are, to see what matches and what doesn't. In order to establish a vision, people need to know where they are and what it would look like if they followed potential paths. As people visualize the possible directions and destinations and evaluate them, they will be better equipped to make effective decisions and to take appropriate steps.

At the best of times, this stage of evaluating may be challenging simply because it could involve decision making with lots of possibilities and, as we have seen, this can be challenging for people for many reasons. A process is needed that is realistic and flexible enough to meet the diversity of situations that can arise.

First, the more effective the self-assessment and career exploration processes have been, the more effective the evaluation process will be. This is especially true if a consistent framework such as the Career Circle (Figure 12) has been used. If it has not already been done, people can summarize the personal aspects they wish to express in their next career on their personal Career Circles. For each career possibility researched, they can summarize the relevant career information they have gathered onto a separate Career Information Circle. Finally, people can place their personal Career Circle beside each Career Information Circle and then compare and contrast the two circles. When comparing and contrasting the two circles, two basic questions should be asked: *"What matches between the two circles?"* and *"What doesn't match? To what extent?"*

When answering these questions, remember that this evaluation is a process of reflection, not simply a "yes-no" matching. Even though not everything matches well, people shouldn't automatically give up on a career possibility; it may still be the best one to pursue. The best choice may involve compromise and negotiation on everyone's part. The goal at this point is just to process the information to get a clear picture

Questions should be asked for each section of the circle and for the circles as a whole. Reviewing the types of questions set forth for the Career Circle and for the Career Information Circle can be a good starting point.

The theme of the Life/Career Conversation (Chapter Three) suggests that the evaluation of people's suitableness for a career (or a job position) is a dialogue and not a monologue. As people evaluate their possibilities, it is helpful for them to do so not just from their own perspective but also that of potential employers. During the process of work search, potential employers will put people up beside the positions they wish to fill and evaluate how well they match or don't match. Therefore people need to ask themselves questions also from the perspective of potential employers. Angel and Harney (1997) emphasize the need for people to consider the employer's needs and concerns during work search. Work search, in a sense, is already under way when people are evaluating what type of career to pursue. Just as good evaluation for setting a vision is more effective when it builds on good self-assessment and career exploration, so too it is more effective when it is seen as preparation for work search.

The following are some sample questions from the two perspectives: that of the person considering a career or job and that of a potential employer:

The Entire Circle:

Person: *"What do I have in my life?"*

Employer: *"What does this career involve?"*

Skills:

Person: *"Can I do the necessary tasks? What can't I do?"*

Employer: *"Can he/she do what needs to be done? What can't he/she do? Does he/she bring skills beyond what we ask for"*

Interests:

Person: *"Which parts of this career will I like or dislike?"*

Employer: *"Will this person do the work with an appropriate level of interest or will he/she be disinterested?"*

Personal Style:

Person: *"Will I fit in? Will I get along with others?"*

Employer: *"Will this person fit in with our organization, with co-workers?"*

Values:

Person: *"Will I be able to express my values in this career? Will any of my values be violated? Are there any I can be flexible with?"*

Employer: *"Will this person see our company mission and goals as valuable? Will he/she support them?"*

Balance:

Person: *"What kind of a lifestyle comes with this career? Will I be able to stay healthy?"*

Employer: *"Is this person ready to put in the time, energy, and commitment we require?"*

Learning:

Person: *"Do I know what I need to know? Is there anything I'm missing?"*

Employer: *"Does this person know his/her stuff? How much training will we need to provide?"*

Life/Work Roles:

Person: *"How do my experiences prepare me for this career? If I am missing any experience, how can I pick it up?"*

Employer: *"Does this person have the background needed for this position? How much training will we need to provide?"*

Work Connections:

Person: *"Is there work available in this career in the area I want to live? Do I know anyone who can help me in any way?"*

Employer: *"Do we have a need that this person can fill? If not now, when?"*

General Questions:

Person: *"Why would I move towards this career or job? Which of my needs would this career meet? Why might I reject this career?"*

Employer: *"Why would I hire this person? Which of my needs would he/she meet?"*

Person: *"Do I bring anything extra, beyond what is being looked for?"*

Employer: *"Does this person bring anything extra?"*

Person: *"Are there any problems or challenges that might arise if I move towards this career?"*

"If something doesn't match, is it that crucial? Can I pick it up on the job or should I get it before I take the job? If it is something that the career is lacking, is it a deal-breaker for me or can I live without it?"

Employer: *"What problems might arise if we hire this person?"*

"Why might I reject this person? What is he/she lacking? Does he/she have anything that doesn't fit or would be a concern if he/she were hired?"

Activity: Looking down the Path

At some point people need to look down the path; and, even though they don't know all the twists and turns that may come, choose a possible direction, see what it would look like, and map out the best way to get there.

Life/career choice is not a destination but a journey taken one step at a time. There are many steps on this journey. Finding out who they are and what they could do are only the initial steps of their life/career journeys. These must be followed by vision, decision, and action. People will need to take these steps over and over again as they walk their life/career journeys.

Review

People should affirm who they are and what they'd like to express through their life/career. Next they should review what they've learned about their life/career possibilities and then review their initial evaluation of each possibility. They are then ready to choose the most preferred one and write it into the centre circle of the Looking down the Path circle (Figure 38), adapted from *Guiding Circles 2*. If for some reason that one does not work out, they can complete this for their next choices as well.

Vision

After the review, people can visualize their life/career goal. Ask them to see themselves as having reached their goal. *"What does it look like?"* Then ask them to look back and identify the things they did to get there.

At this point, some people may still be unsure about setting a clear vision. Remind them that this is just a final check to ensure that what

Figure 38: Looking Down the Path

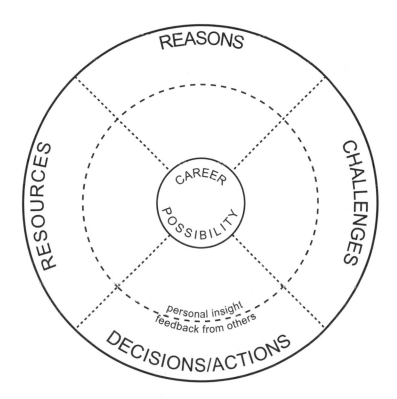

is chosen is the best at the current time. Creative vision/decision/action planning is flexible enough to enable them to fine-tune or revise their goals as they move along.

The Looking down the Path circle can be used as a lens or framework to summarize, organize, and examine their thinking on each life/career possibility at this point. People should clarify four aspects of their vision:

1. The **Reasons** why they think this life/career possibility would be a good fit for them at this time,

2. The possible **Challenges** that they might face on that path,

3. The **Resources** they will have to help them on their journey, and

4. The **Decisions** and **Actions** they will have to make if they are going to reach their **Vision**.

These four aspects will help people recognize any unrealistic goals and/or clarify those that are realistic.

1. Reasons

If people have done a good job of comparing their personal Career Circle with the Career Information Circle, they ought to be able to state reasons why this life/career path would be a good choice for them. If people shift to generalities here, encourage them to state specific reasons. There should be enough of a match between the two circles, that people can go around the sections of the circle and demonstrate how they would be able to fulfill the requirements of the career and that it will balance with their life as a whole. When they actually meet employers in interviews, they should be able to confidently answer the question, *"Why should I hire you?"*

2. Challenges

Challenges must be handled in a balanced fashion. As we have discussed earlier, it is easy for people to take on a negative attitude when they can only see problems. On the other hand, some people only look at the positive side and ignore or deny that there are any challenges at all. They see the new career or position through rose-coloured glasses. Before they actually get in, they are effusive in their praise of the new opportunity, but sometimes within weeks or months, they talk of it as the job "from hell." Both extremes can distort one's vision of a future life/career choice.

If people are to make realistic career choices, they must reflect on the challenges they might face if they pursued that career. Challenges may come in many forms, but they all share something in common: they make it difficult for people to reach their goals. It may be something personal; for example, something may be missing in a career that people will have a hard time giving up or something may be there that they will have a hard time putting up with. It may be that there are obstacles to be overcome before reaching the goal; for example, it may take longer to get the necessary learning or experience than was previously thought. Whatever the form, people need to identify them, accept them, prepare/ practice for them, and then start the journey and deal with the challenges when they arise (*Guiding Circles 2*).

- **Accept**

All life/career paths will have challenges along the way; this is the reality in an imperfect world of work. Challenges are normal, the question is not whether there will be challenges but how people will face them. When people accept a life/career path, they are accepting not only the good but also the "not so good." Challenges are just part of the cost of doing what they want to do. For example, new parents are very excited about a new baby; but along with the angelic smiles, they know they are accepting lots of sleepless nights and bouts of crying. But they still have children, because they know it will be worth it.

- **Prepare and practice**

Once people have identified and accepted the potential challenges they will face, they should prepare and practice just as a mountain climber might prepare for the challenges of a mountain climb. The following are some helpful questions to help people identify how they can prepare themselves:

- *What challenges have you faced in the past? How did you overcome them?*

- *What exactly will be the challenges ahead?*

- *How would you describe these challenges (e.g., like a mountain, a raging river, a deep gully, a blinding storm)? How do you feel about them? What are you fearful of?*

- *What will you need to overcome these challenges? What resources do you already have that will be of help?*

- *What do you need to pick up? What new skills or attitudes could you develop?*

- *What opportunities can you find to practice what you'll need to overcome the challenges?*

- *What self-care could you practice while on the journey?*

- *Since there is usually more than one path on the journey, what alternative paths could you explore?*

- *Who could be a support to you? How? What resources could they share with you?*

- *Do you have any heroes or role models who have faced similar challenges? What can you learn from their story?*

- **Start**

Challenges can ultimately only be faced as people are actually on the journey. People may not see as far ahead as they'd like. They may not have all the answers. They may not feel fully prepared. But at some point, people just need to start walking, keep moving, and deal with each challenge as it arises. As people journey, they can stop at times to rest and enjoy what they have accomplished to that point, to restore energy, to clarify the next stage of the journey, to recommit to the journey, and to revise goals as necessary. The activity The Journey Continues later in this chapter will address this further.

3. Resources

As people move toward a career possibility, they need to take inventory of all the resources they have to help them as they deal with the ups and downs of the journey. If the goal is truly realistic, people should have the resources needed not just to enable them to do what they would like to do but also to handle the various challenges that will arise. *"What needs to be overcome? What needs to be done?"* People need to be specific as they seek to match resources to each step.

Encourage people not to be stingy here. People need all the help they can get and they might have many more resources than they ever thought. Some of the resources they could list include:

- Their own stories of favourite things or past experiences can be full of examples of how they have overcome past challenges.

- Everything they recorded on their Career Circle (skills, interests, personal style, values, balance, learning, life/work roles, work connections) is in fact a resource.

- The various supports (personal, people, activities, places, concepts, things) they identified in the Connections activity are all resources.

- The various life/career possibilities they generated are all resources.

- The examples of others who have followed similar paths are full of motivations and strategies on for continuing on the journey.

4. Decisions/Actions

Finally, people need to plan for the decisions and the actions they will need to take if they are to move toward their vision. Without such decision and action planning, the good intentions represented by their vision may be lost in the confusion of life's moments. When possible, decisions can be made before they need to be made; they can be made ahead at times when life is a bit clearer.

Using techniques such as the Miracle Question (Amundson, 2009), people can map out a path to their goal. Starting from the vision of having reached their goal, they need to ask themselves questions: *"What did I do to get here? What choices did I make to take these actions?"* They need to keep asking the same questions again and again, stepping backwards until they reach the point of the first step they need to take to start moving toward their vision. Again they need to be as specific as possible.

Once people have listed their insights onto the Looking Down the Path circle, they are almost ready to choose a vision to follow at that time. One more activity is important at this point and that is set forth in the next activity, Collective Decision Making. Once they have completed that activity, they will need to choose a direction and start moving.

Activity:
<u>*Collective Decision Making*</u>

The theme of interconnectedness is especially crucial in vision/decision/action planning because people do not do these alone. The Looking Down the Path circle in the previous chapter has an inner ring for personal insight and an outer ring for feedback from others. This parallels the two rings in the Career Circle (Figure 12) used during self-assessment.

This approach recognizes the relationship between individual and collective decision making and equips people with a strategy to enable them to involve others effectively in their career vision/decision/action planning.

This activity uses the same structure as the Insight from Others activity (Chapter Five) so it would be helpful to review that activity. Rather than duplicate the instructions of that activity, we will just focus on the aspects specific to vision/decision/action planning.

Identifying Others to Give Insight

First, people can identify others who should have a voice in their visions/decisions/actions and then use one of the three recommended strategies (talking with others, a talking circle, and/or a simple questionnaire) to gather their insight.

Who should people look to for insight as they look down the path at potential life/career directions? Two types of people should be considered: people who are a source of strength and support (see Connections activity, Chapter Five) and/or people who are significant influences or who are significantly affected by your visions/decisions/actions (see Connections: Influences & Affects activity earlier in this chapter). These may be the same people. By involving others, people will demonstrate to them a commitment to fully involve them in a balanced way.

Asking for Insights from Others

What insight should people be looking for from others? Clearly it is insight that will help them make the most effective visions/decisions/actions as indicated by the Looking Down the Path activity.

The strategies set forth in the segment on Insight from Others can also be used to gather insight for collective decision making. The following questionnaire (*Guiding Circles 2*, pp. 36-43) can be helpful not only as a formal questionnaire but also to guide other types of discussion:

1. *How do you think my career decisions will affect you? How do you think you influence my career decisions?*

2. *As you look at the career possibility (or possibilities) I'm considering, do you think I've missed any good reasons for following this path?*

3. *As you look at the career possibility (or possibilities) I'm considering, do you think I've missed any potential barriers to following this path?*

4. *What decisions or actions do you think I'll need to make in order to reach my career goal?*

5. *What resources or supports do you think I'll need on this path? How do you think you could be a support to me?*

6. *Do you think there are any career possibilities I've overlooked? Which ones? Why?*

Debrief the Insights of Others

As with the Insight from Others activity, it is important to debrief the insight given by others. People should compare and contrast their insight with the insight from others. *"What is the same? What is different? If they are different, why? What new ideas have been raised?"*

During debriefing, record the insights provided into the appropriate sections of the "feedback from others" ring on the Looking Down the Path circle (Figure 38). Encourage people to continue to listen for positive insight from others in their regular contact with them. When they hear something new, they can add it to their Looking Down the Path circle.

The goal at this point is to discern possible vision in such a way that people and the significant others in their lives will all be able to take ownership of it. If people have included others through all the steps of self-assessment, career exploration, vision/decision/action planning, there will be a greater likelihood that others will understand and support the chosen paths. If at this point, it appears as if the chosen path is a good one and yet others still won't support it, you can review the strategies for resolving conflicting values discussed earlier in Chapter Five.

Activity: The Journey Continues

The activities presented so far in this chapter address most of the realities we raised about vision/decision/action planning. However there is still the concern that this process must be sustainable over life's long journey even if people encounter barriers on the path. What is needed is a cyclical model of vision/decision/action planning rather than a purely linear one.

Such an approach would take the emotional weight off the planning process that people sometimes experience. Some people are afraid to set a direction or to take any first steps because they are afraid that if they do so, they will be trapped for a lifetime. Others are reluctant to start moving because they don't have everything all planned out.

But people do not have to have it all planned out ahead in order to succeed. They should try to cover as many bases as possible but life is such that they can't know everything. But they can start by acting on what they know and adjusting as they go. As they travel along their journeys, even if they encounter barriers, they will learn new things that will help clarify future vision and goals. As these are clarified, people can explore the new decisions and new actions needed for the next steps. And so the cycle begins and continues; each new step helps clarify the next steps. The life/career journey is not a destination but a journey taken one step at a time. This approach provides people not just with an initial action plan but an on-going vision/decision/action planning strategy that may be used along every step of this life/career journey.

In *Return on Imagination*, Wujec and Muscat (2002) encourage business leaders that their "returns" will increase if they "return" to more creative and imaginative business practices. They re-visit the various aspects of business, including action planning, from an imagination perspective. Their cyclical approach works well not only for businesses but also for individuals on their life/career journeys. The Journey Continues circle

(Figure 39; see also *Guiding Circles 1* and *2*) adapts their creative model and applies it to a flexible creative vision/decision/action planning model based on four steps people need to take over and over again:

1. Set Goals

After reviewing their vision and the Looking Down the Path circle (Figure 33), people can choose a direction. Encourage them to choose

Figure 39: The Journey Continues

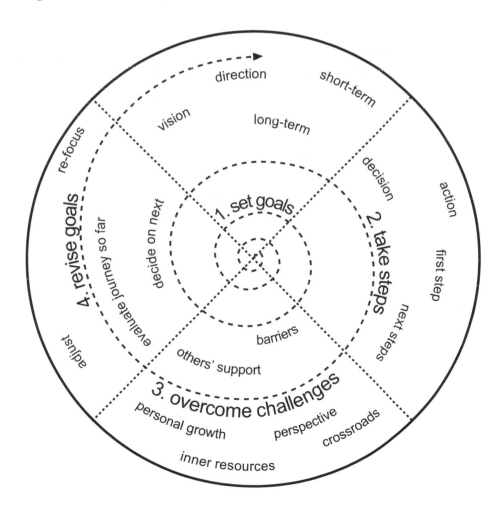

the best they can at this time with the understanding that they can adjust things in the future as needed. At this point, some of the strengths in the traditional action plan model can be utilized. People need to set some initial goals; as much as possible, ensure that they are SMART (Specific, Manageable, Achievable, Relevant, Time-related).

2. Take Steps

Once goals have been set, people need to plan the appropriate decisions and actions that will move them in the direction of their goals and start acting on them. If the steps are too general or are too far in the future, ask people what steps they will need to take to complete the goals or steps they have already identified. The first steps are especially important; these must be clear and easily achievable or people may become discouraged too quickly.

3. Overcome Challenges

As people begin to move toward their goals, they will likely encounter potential barriers. Some may be minor and only slow the journey; while others may be major and divert or even halt the journey for a while. When identifying potential barriers, people walk a fine balance. On the one hand, you don't want to focus on this to the extent that people become discouraged and quit. On the other, you don't want people to be unrealistic and be taken surprise by obvious barriers. Encourage people to identify the potential challenges they may face and be prepared for the ones they don't.

4. Revise Goals

Encourage people to walk as far as they can in the direction they have set and then stop to evaluate what they have learned so far, to reevaluate their current goals, to identify possible alternative paths, and in light of this to revise goals as necessary. There is no simple answer as to when this step is necessary. It may be necessary when people reach the initial goals they have set for themselves. It may be when some barrier has completely blocked that path. It may be when some new opportunity has suddenly come up. It may be just taking time to regularly see how things are going and to allow for new insight gathered on the journey so far to suggest alternative paths.

Once people have taken these four steps, they are in effect back at Step 1 with a new set of goals that they can take steps toward, addressing challenges as they arise, until it is time to pause and to reevaluate and revise goals again, to take new steps, and so forth. This step-by-step process will enable them to keep walking no matter what they encounter on their life/career journeys. In effect, this circular model looks at every segment in the life/career journey as a repeat of the basic linear model (i.e., set a goal, take steps, etc.).

If people still have a difficult time grasping the hopefulness that is generated by this concept of walking by following the same process step by step, the following quick "walk-the-problem" type activity may help. Ask people the simple question, *"Do mazes have dead ends?"* Typically most people say *"yes"* as if it is obvious and irrefutable. Mark off a section of the room as if it were a "dead end" segment of a maze. Pick a "volunteer" to get up and walk down this corridor. When they reach the end, ask them why they can't go any further. The usual response is that they have hit a dead end and, therefore, they can't go any further. Ask the person to come back and place a hand on the wall of the "maze" and then to walk the maze and keep walking as long as their hand touches the wall (This is the traditional way of solving mazes or labyrinths.). As people reach the end of the maze segment, they turn and walk along the end, and then turn and walk back along the wall opposite to the first one they entered the segment by. Bring home the illustration by asking the question, *"Was this a dead end or a curve?"* The answer is clear: *"a curve."* *"What made the difference?"* The answer is just as clear: *"a change in perspective."* This activity can be debriefed by asking people if they have ever taken such curves in their life/career journeys thus far. People always acknowledge that they have walked such curves many times.

The creative vision/decision/action planning model and activities presented in this section hopefully will provide people with a similar change in perspective that they will handle all the twists and turns of real life as curves and not as dead ends.

chapter nine

KEEPING IN STEP WITH A CHANGING CAREER

Between a Rock and a Hard Place

We have had the privilege of facilitating workshops all across Canada and in many other countries. Though expressed in many different ways, a common concern is the increased stress many life/career practitioners face as they try to do their jobs well. Though very committed to the task of assisting people on their life/career journeys, some show signs of the weight of this stress. This can range from a vague sense of weariness to a creeping hopelessness about the value of their work. Some raise questions about the system, the people they work with, and their own selves: *"What is the point? What difference can I really make? Does anyone really care?"*

This should not be surprising since life/career practitioners face the same issues as others in the caring professions. The American Counseling Association's (ACA) Taskforce on Counselor Wellness and Impairment (Lawson & Venart, n.d.) summarizes some of the major issues and calls for increased wellness education for those in the caring professions. They recognize the importance of having an intentional self-care program in order to prevent the damaging effects of compassion fatigue and burnout that result from working long term with emotionally draining situations.

It is not our intention here to review in detail the general discussion on burnout and the need for self-care in the caring professions. Rather we wish to highlight why this should be an increasing concern to life/career practitioners, to suggest some potential elements of self-care, and to encourage further discussion on this issue.

Life/career practitioners share many stress factors with other caring professions. Some of the most common ones:

- Empathy for people who are hurting because of their life situations,

- A deep desire to alleviate the problems and pain of people,

- A cumulative exhaustion (physical, mental, emotional, and spiritual) because of a hesitancy to recognize and/or seek help for the stresses involved in such work,

- Unrealistic expectations for self and the system and for people,

- Repeated disappointments,

- A perceived lack of supportive environments,

- Personal coping styles, and

- Seemingly inadequate levels of training and experience.

We have found the image of being stuck between a rock and a hard place to be a useful metaphor from which to view some of the specific struggles facing many practitioners today. Often when people think about being between a rock and a hard place, the image is static. Nothing could be further from the truth. Life/career counselling takes place in a rapidly changing and chaotic world. It is not surprising that life/career counselling, as a field, is also rapidly changing and chaotic. In this sense, many practitioners experience stresses not dissimilar from the people they work with. It is the changing chaotic nature of the rock and the hard place that can exacerbate the grinding effect on practitioners as they struggle to keep up with a career, that seems to be increasingly out of their control. Life/career practitioners often must find their self-care, while they are on the run, if they are to keep up with such a changing career. Let us examine the hard place, the rock, and the practitioner between them:

1. The Hard Place

The "hard place" is a picture of the increasingly difficult task that life/career practitioners are engaged in. "Often counsellors are told directly and indirectly that they need to work longer, see more clients, produce results in shorter time periods with more multiple stressed clients, and put aside their own needs in the service of others." (Lawson & Venart, n.d., p. 4) It is a hard place for many reasons; the following in not a comprehensive list but it is telling:

- increasing workloads;

- increasing diversity of people, including multi-barriered people, Aboriginals, immigrants, youth, seniors, disabled, etc.;

- difficult real life situations with no quick easy answers, in contrast to many government priorities emphasizing reducing the number of people on social assistance ASAP;

- more time needed but no extra time or even less time allowed;

- distinction between life counselling and career counselling is becoming increasingly fuzzy because barriers to work involve many personal issues (e.g., addictions, disabilities, family issues, mental health issues, cultural barriers, etc.);

- Some people have been in the system so long; they seem impervious to it. The people sitting across from a practitioner may have talked to many practitioners before and will have heard all the questions and know all the answers. They may have high levels of hopelessness because all previous attempts have just led to more failure.

2. The Rock

The "rock" refers to the structures in which most life/career practitioners work; it can be everything from immediate bureaucracy to broad socio-political structures (economics and the labour market, culture, etc.). In addition to increasingly difficult workloads, many life/career practitioners feel that many aspects of the structures are not providing the supportive environment they need; in fact they feel as if the structures are actually making it more difficult for them to do their jobs. While many of the structural changes are intended to help the situation, we have already seen that even the best-intentioned structures can be counter productive. Some of the factors that weigh heavily on life/career practitioners are:

- continuous changing of priorities, goals, expectations, procedures,

- simplistic perspectives oriented to the old labour market,

- lack of consultation,

- increasing accountability without relevant markers for the new counselling situations,

- more directive expectations from funders,

- insecurity as a result of the increasing use of short-term contracts,

- not enough time or resources allocated for increasingly difficult counselling situations, and

- increasing levels of documentation for accountability purposes; more and more of the job is spent just asking questions and filling in computer screens: no time for counselling.

3. The Practitioner in the Middle

In between the hard place and the rock, it is easy to see how practitioners may feel as if they are being ground down between two increasingly difficult realities. This difficult situation may be exasperated by personal issues of life/career practitioners such as:

- Conflicting values (the job they took has been changed around them; the system's values and their values sometimes seem to be increasingly going in different directions),

- Loss of a sense of competency,

- Lack of a sense of control,

- Lack of recognition,

- Uncertainty and insecurity,

- Perfectionism,

- Workaholism; no time for self with increased work loads,

- Lack of training, and

- Lack of self-care.

Possible Responses

There are many possible responses to the realities that life/career practitioners face. MacKenzie (1998) in *Orbiting the Giant Hairball* identifies three basic responses to the struggles of working within bureaucracies that can be applied in this situation.

- **Crash and burn**: Some may just give up and become part of the problem; they may be going through the motions and even doing valid work but the spark is gone

- **Fly off into outer space**: Some may react and just leave, thinking that it is not worth it. For some, leaving the field may indeed be the best response for them, but practitioners must be aware of the danger of knee-jerk reactions that sometimes lead to situations that are even worse.

- **Orbit the Hairball**: Some may accept that change and challenge are to be expected; they aren't necessarily the enemy. Rather than just working harder and longer, they commit themselves to finding creative ways to do their job within the limits they face and to take care of themselves within it. Such creativity, imagination, and hope must be focused toward all three spheres: the hard place, the rock, and self. They realize that though they may not be able to do everything they would like in the way they'd like, there is still value in helping people as much as they can.

The next four segments address some initial thoughts about self-care when working in between the rock and the hard place. Hopefully you will find these perspectives helpful.

Self-Care Possibilities

The previous segment presented some of the challenging realities of being a life/career practitioner. After looking at such realities, one might well ask why anyone would want such a career. But there is more to a career than challenges. It is not ultimately the "cost" of a career that is the issue; it is what people achieve as they are willing to embrace the cost. Though it may be a hard task sometimes, assisting people with their life/career journeys can be incredibly rewarding, especially every time you see a life living to its potential. In addition to the rewards of a career in life/career counselling, there are many excellent resources (personal and professional) that practitioners may draw upon. This has been the focus of much of this book; *Hope-Filled Engagement* encourages us that we may engage people with hope, creativity, and imagination in ways that can overcome many of the challenges on the journey. Practitioners must apply the same hope, creativity, and imagination to their own self-care as they walk their life/career journey. They may draw upon many of the same tools and activities they would encourage others to use for their own personal and professional development and self care.

Self-awareness

The place to start with self-care is with self-awareness. The principle of engaging people where they are engaged in life applies here. *"Where are you now in your own life/career journey?"* You can use the Looking Down the Path circle to reexamine your current situation. In one sense, imagine you didn't have your current job and were only at the stage of evaluating your current career for the first time. *"As you examine the reasons, challenges, resources, decisions/actions that this career presents before you, would you still see this as your vision or would you change your vision?"* Re-establishing vision is a powerful motivator for self-care.

1. Reasons?

Ask questions such as: "Why would you take this path today? Are your reasons the same as when you initially went into it? What things are you thankful for as you reflect on your experiences in this career? Have you lost sight of the reasons why you went into this career in the first place? Is it the same career as the one you initially accepted? What has changed, if anything? What have you been doing for self-care?"

2. Challenges?

"What are the problems, difficulties, concerns you have regarding this career? What do you complain about? How have the challenges changed over time? How is your life balance? How has this career path affected it? In what areas, do you think you need self-care? What is keeping you from pursuing better self-care?"

3. Resources?

"What resources can you draw upon if you were to continue on this career path? Have you recently completed an up-to-date self-assessment for your self? Have you recently completed the Connections Circle to ensure that you are recognizing and drawing upon all of the connections you have in your life? What personal assets do you have to enable you to face your career challenges? What do you have to enable you to find the self-care you need? Who do you know that could walk with you or assist you on your journey?"

4. Decisions/Actions?

"If you were to continue on your current career path, what would you need to do to ensure your self-care? What would you continue doing the same way? What would you change? What would the changes look like?"

In addition to *Hope-Filled Engagement* tools, The American Counseling Association's taskforce on counselor wellness and impairment

(American Counseling Association, n.d.) provides several quick but helpful assessment tools related to counsellor wellness: Self-Care Assessment; Stress Reactions inventory; Professional Quality of Life Assessment (ProQOL measures areas such as compassion fatigue and potential for burnout); and Impact of Secondary Trauma on Organizations.

Self-Care Lifestyle

After a self-care assessment, practitioners can begin the process of creative vision/decision/action planning for their own self-care. This should not just be some side activity but a fundamental lifestyle choice, a commitment to a life of personal wholeness and balance. A vision should be created with self-care as an integral part of the life/career journey. Finally specific actions will need to be identified to move toward self-care being part of daily life.

Generate your own Connections Circle and identify a list of self-care possibilities from the support you already have. A healthy support network is essential for self-care. Take special note of others who can travel with you on your self-care journey.

If you struggle with the issues of conflicting values discussed earlier, review the Balance Circle and Resolving Conflicting Values. The spheres of life on the Balance wheel could be used to ensure that the self-care possibilities being considered are holistic. Much of self-care involves balancing the various aspects of one's life. *"Which aspects of your mental, emotional, physical, and spiritual being will each self-care possibility address?"*

In addition to the ideas in this book, a quick Google search on the internet will produce many other ideas and resources for self-care. For example, the ACA suggests the following holistic strategies for counsellor wellness:

- **Wellness Activities - Cognitive:** Meditation: Journaling ; Reading for pleasure; Hobbies; Volunteering at something NOT counselling related; Going to the movies, theater, symphony, museum, county fair.

- **Wellness Activities - Emotional**: Talk to friends; Laugh; Spend time with people; Participate in an encouragement exchange with a colleague; See a counsellor; Give yourself permission to cry.

- **Wellness Activities - Physical**: Drink plenty of water; Eat regular meals; Exercise regularly; Get enough sleep; Turn off the computer/cell phone; Go for a walk during lunch; Get a massage.

- **Wellness Activities - Spiritual**: Take time for reflection and prayer; Spend time outdoors; Connect with a Spiritual Community.

Engaging in Self-Care

Self-care is not necessarily going to be an easy process to work out. The way may be unclear and there may be many ups and downs on the path, but by using tools, such as the Journey Continues circle, you can start the journey and grow as you go. Once self-care possibilities have been identified, the next step is to choose some initial goals and start moving. Starting points can be identified by balancing urgency with feasibility. *"What really needs to be worked on now? What steps would be the easiest and most effective to start with?"* With experience, it will be possible to fine-tune a self-care lifestyle that is appropriate and sustainable.

Self-care is possible. It is important that you find creative ways to realize your potential for self-care and then turn that potential into reality. Wujec and Muscat's (2002, p. 6) words about approaching our futures with creativity inspire all of us to allow ourselves to believe in possibilities not just for those we work with but for ourselves as well.

Our future depends on the possibilities we define,
The decisions we make,

And the ways we bring our vision into reality.
Real power is the capacity to originate and
Implement the ideas that create lasting and positive change.
We could trust in the power of imagination to
Discover and invent something new.

But how?

Just imagine …
Turn on your entire brain.
Be your whole self.
All of it. Every last little bit.
Let go of the world's relentless rush to formulate,
Slave, and implement.
Stay loose and let little ideas evolve into good ones.
Nurture the ideas that are important.
Give them time.
Give them space.
Let them breathe.

Play with them like Lego pieces.
Not everything of value comes from logic and rational explanation.
Create environments where ideas flow freely.
Build skills for bringing inspiration to reality.
Use tools to stimulate imagination.
Design so the spirit of inspiration
Continues to circulate.
Believe in beauty.
Seek truth.
Dream big.
Think about your place in the world.
Welcome to the world of possibility.
Imagination is what makes all things possible.

Cross Training for Personal and Professional Development

What Is Cross Training?

Cross training is a key strategy for serious athletes. They recognize that if they wish to be the best they can be, they need to train outside their discipline in order to develop all of their abilities in a balanced way.

But cross training is just as applicable in other areas of life. For example, cross training is a strategy that is used within the business world to develop well-rounded leaders and workers. Cross training fits with the theme of life/work balance and the interconnectedness of all the aspects of a life.

One logical consequence of the need to develop holistic concepts and strategies for use in life/career counselling is the increasing importance of cross training. This is especially true in light of the rapidly changing and chaotic world of business and work. There is a wealth of life/career theories and resources available to practitioners today; effective practitioners will strive to become proficient with these. But as we have already discussed, these may not be enough, because the world of the life/career practitioner is changing so fundamentally. Many of the answers that practitioners will need in the days ahead will not be found in that which has already been developed within the career world because the already existing materials were developed for different life/career contexts.

> *"Problems cannot be solved by thinking within the framework in which they were created."*
> - Albert Einstein

This is where cross training can be so effective. The career field may not have answers to all its new questions but other fields are asking similar questions and have already found some effective answers. Through cross training, practitioners can access concepts, strategies, skills, and even activities that can be adapted for use in the context of life/work counselling.

Cross training may be very formal or very informal. Practitioners may take formal courses, attend workshops or conferences, read widely, search the internet, or seek out people in other fields to talk with.

Benefits of Cross Training

In addition to being a rich source of creative ideas for life/career practitioners, there can be several other benefits as well:

- Cross training encourages well-rounded practitioners who are effective with more holistic, integrated, and balanced approaches.

- Cross-disciplinary exposure can increase practitioners' willingness to collaborate with others in other disciplines.

- Cross training can reduce the boredom and weariness that can easily creep in when practitioners find themselves facing the same routines day after day.

- Cross training can help practitioners avoid blind spots in their knowledge and skill base that can occur when there is too narrow a focus in personal and professional development.

- Cross training lends itself to greater flexibility in personal and professional development.

- In the athletic world, one of the most commonly expressed benefits of cross training is that it reduces the risk of injury. Life/

career practitioners may not be at the same risk for physical injury (except for those that come from a job largely tied to a desk), but they are subject to other forms of stress injuries such as compassion fatigue or burnout.

• Cross training is effective at enhancing motivation, as practitioners are energized by new ideas.

Areas for Cross Training

In the world of athletics, a well-designed cross-training program includes a variety of activities that stress different forms of workout and develop all the parts of the body. It is this variety that helps develop a high level of overall fitness.

What areas should life/career practitioners cross train in? One place to start is by identifying the knowledge or skills necessary to be an effective practitioner in today's world, especially those which are changing as a result of the changes in the field. Which of these are not adequately covered by existing life/career counselling theories and skills? Practitioners may do a personal audit to determine which of these is the greatest need for the work they do. These are the areas to begin cross training in. The following are some areas worth considering:

Creativity and imagination

It was reading of the fundamental changes in the labour market in the 1980s and concepts such as Gelatt's positive uncertainty (1989, 1991, 2003) that lead us to focus on creativity and imagination in detail and to explore the world of craft. Books such as *A Whack on the Side of the Head* (vonOech, 1990), *Orbiting the Giant Hairball* (MacKenzie, 1998), or *Return on Imagination* (Wujec & Muscat, 2002) are good places to start. The world of creativity and imagination is a rich source of potential activities that can surprise people while they are having fun. For example, a quick search on the internet on the craft of improv will yield many ideas for helping people to think more quickly and effectively on their feet in formal interviews or in happenstance contexts. The business world has used improv for cross training for years (Mosedale, 2001).

Spirituality

The diversity of material on this subject is as wide as the span from formal religious expressions to informal personal quests. Authors such as Parker Palmer (1998, 2000) have written on areas such as spirituality in education and represent those who have sought to integrate spirituality into practical professions. Allegories such as *Brave work: A guide to the quest for meaning in work* (Tocher, 1998) can be helpful in approaching this area whatever the spiritual orientation.

Change and transition

In a context of fundamental change in the world of work and many imposed changes upon the roles of life/career practitioners, there is great value in equipping oneself to work with change and transition. William Bridges (1991, 2004) has several excellent books on this subject.

Diversity awareness:

With the increasing diversity of people who need life/career counselling, it will be important to read widely on diversity (e.g., culture, race, gender, age, disabilities, etc.). You can start with material on cross-cultural communication or counselling (Amundson, Westwood, & Prefontaine,1995; McCormick & Amundson, 1997; Westwood & Ishiyama, 1991). In addition, check how other fields, such as education, are dealing with diversity issues.

Brief-focused or solution-focused therapy

Life/career counselling may have more in common with brief-focused or solution-focused therapy than traditional psychological counselling that focuses on understanding dysfunctionalities. Within the short time frames that practitioners are working with, it is obvious that any approach that focuses on assisting people to identify and transfer their strengths across the different areas of their life would be very helpful (Amundson, 2009).

Life coaching

Life coaching is becoming increasingly popular because it doesn't carry the stigma of the term "counselling." People aren't seeking coaching because there is something wrong with them (e.g., mental illness) but because they want to grow; they want things to be different. It is an important area to cross train in because it seeks to walk with people as they work through change in their life/career journeys. John Whitmore's description of life coaching (Whitworth, Kimsey-House, & Sandahl, 1998, p. x) certainly fits within the context of *Hope-Filled Engagement*:

> Not only do we live in a changing world, but also the speed of change is ever on the increase and with it come stresses and confusion sometimes beyond our own apparent resources. A personal coach does not remove these problems, but goes two steps further. The coach can help us turn them into challenges and enable us to overcome them by drawing on resources within ourselves that we never knew we had. With our new found confidence we can then face new challenges.

Inspirational and motivational resources

This is a rich source of material for both practitioners and the people they work with. Recent books such as *The Element* (Robinson & Aronica, 2009) addresses many of the issues raised in this book and are full of countless illustrations of people who have found themselves and meaningful life/career paths despite facing incredible challenges. There is a long tradition in the entertainment world of movies that tell the stories of teachers or coaches who were able to connect with and inspire people written off by the system. There are classics such as To Sir With Love (Clavell, 1967) with Sydney Poitier or more recent ones such as Take the Lead (Godsick, et al., 2006) with Antonio Banderas playing the role of real life Pierre Dulaine, a ballroom dance instructor who has helped tens of thousands of New York City students find self-respect and pride through dance.

Recent neuro-science research

One of the most encouraging areas we have found in the last few years has been that of neuro-science research. For example, the best selling *The Brain That Changes Itself: Stories of Personal Triumph from the Frontiers of Brain Science* (Doidge, 2007) introduces neuroplasticity and explores the incredible ability and potential of the brain to heal itself. Books such as *Happy at Last: The Thinking Person's Guide to Finding Joy* (O'Connor, 2008) explores new findings about stress illnesses and new approaches to addressing them. Such books provide a much needed paradigm shift for those who feel stuck, thinking they cannot change.

Rest and Relaxation

Play can be a wonderful form of cross training. Successful athletes know that giving their bodies and minds a break is just as important as any formal training they take. This is just as true for practitioners.

There are many other areas certainly worth considering, such as mediation and negotiation or positive psychology, which could be explored. The important thing is that practitioners step out and stretch themselves through cross training. The benefits both personally and professionally will be more than worth the effort.

Activity: Recognition

Importance to Self-Care

Over the last several years, we have observed that recognition is an important issue for life/career practitioners. Many feel as if they don't receive appropriate recognition for who they are and all they do. This is a troublesome perception because "as social beings, we need to feel appreciated and valued and know that our work matters" (Amundson, 2009, p. 340).

Our *Career Crossroads* workbook (Poehnell & Amundson, 2001) was originally developed while working with life/career practitioners who were undergoing a major change and transition in their work lives. Many were struggling whether to stay or to leave the organization or even the field. Some were stuck at this crossroads. One of the factors affecting them that we identified was that of recognition.

The issue is more complex that just whether practitioners receive recognition or not. Recognition is a part of the dialogue between people and their world. A key to sorting out recognition issues is to recognize that as with many aspects of dialogue, there can be a vast difference between how different people give and receive it. As a result, there can be a vast difference between people's perception of how they are recognized and the actual recognition others are attempting to give them. Ideally we would all learn to give recognition in the forms best understood by others; unfortunately, as many people will attest, this is easier said than done.

A sense of recognition is an important component of our self-esteem and being able to give and receive recognition is, therefore, an important aspect of self-care. The activity that follows is one we have used in *Career Crossroads* workshops to help people see the possibilities for recognition they have in their lives.

Forms of Recognition

We use the same possibilities approach with this activity, as we use with the Connections activities. People often tend to notice the recognition they don't get and neglect the recognition they do receive. This activity helps people broaden the way they view recognition in their lives. The steps are as follows:

1. Brainstorming

Start by asking, *"What are the possible forms of recognition people may receive?"* This question may be better answered by first asking a more foundational question: *"Who gives recognition to people?"* People give recognition to themselves and to others. As well, the forms of recognition that people exchange with one another will to a certain degree reflect the nature of human relationships. People have vertical (up and down) relationships and horizontal (side to side) relationships; therefore, forms of recognition may vary depending upon which direction it comes from. We use a Recognition Chart as a framework to generate and list possibilities generated by two questions; Figure 40 is a sample of a typical chart completed in workshops.

- *What forms of recognition may people give to themselves?*

- *What forms of recognition may a person receive from each of the following 4 types of relationships?*

    a. Vertical Relationships (structural relationships not personal):

    1) Those over us in some sense (e.g., supervisors, mangers, funders, etc.; Kaye & Jordan-Evans, 2002, pp. 158-171).

    2) Those under us in some sense (e.g., clients, customers, students, co-workers accountable to us, etc.).

Figure 40: Sample Recognition Chart

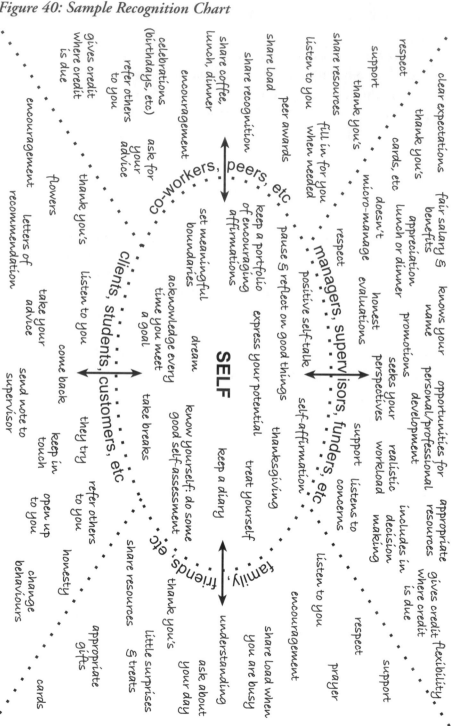

2. Horizontal Relationships:

   a.   Co-workers and peers (e.g., those in the same office, in the same company, in the same field, in associated fields, etc.).

   b.   Family and friends.

2. Initial Debriefing

Once people have listed and posted the possibilities they have generated, facilitate a brief discussion about what they have discovered about recognition. Usually people talk about being surprised about how many different forms of recognition can be given and received. They may also compare and contrast the various forms that come from the different sources.

3. Personalize and debrief

Ask a volunteer to step up to the lists posted on the wall and ask him/her to circle some of the forms of recognition they have received. Ask, *"What types of recognition have you been given?"* Ask other participants to circle them in their head. If there is time and if it is appropriate, you can ask some other key questions:

- *"What types of recognition would you like to be given?"*

- *"Are you satisfied with the level of recognition you are receiving?"*

In the debriefing, ask people, *"What is the personal impact upon them when they identify all the recognition they are receiving?"* Again people are usually surprised by the amount of recognition they are actually receiving. They usually find this to be an incredibly validating activity. People also note that they need to be more intentional and consistent in accepting recognition in different forms, in being explicit to others about the forms of recognition most meaningful to them, and in giving recognition to themselves and to others.

The Potential of the Moment

Over the last few years during our training workshops, we have heard an increasing number of life/career practitioners express frustrations about the limitations they face in their jobs. When they focus on all the challenges before them, as they work between the rock and the hard place and then think about the seemingly insufficient resources to do the job properly (e.g., time, energy, mandate, training, tools, etc.), they ask the question, *"So what's the point?"* It is easy to see how this can happen. But as we have suggested throughout this book, there may be real challenges but sometimes the biggest damage is done by our attitudes and responses to those challenges and limitations. Rather than doing what we can, it is easy to fall into a victim mentality that prevents us from doing anything at all.

When we face the temptation to slip into a victim mentality, it is helpful to stop and reframe our paradigms. The boxes we face can be viewed as traps or as building blocks for creativity and imagination. Let us illustrate with two really discouraging realities for many life/ career practitioners.

Practitioners often feel powerless to change the contexts in which the people they work with live. The contexts may be very personal, such as mental illness or addictions or family. Or they may be broader social-economic issues, such as justice issues, social-economic issues, or labour market issues. These issues can seriously affect the possibilities of people, yet usually the practitioner can do little or nothing about them. They can feel small and insignificant and out of control. It is easy in this context to start thinking at some level: *"I can't change it all, so what's the point?"*

Another common frustration is the limited time practitioners can spend with people. They may only be able to meet with people for a few sessions, sometimes only one. And to make matters more frustrating, the session is usually only an hour or less. We have seen practitioners who are only allowed 30-minute appointments. It is easy in this context to start thinking, *"What can I do in only 30 minutes?"*

So what is the point of meeting with people one time for only 30 minutes, especially when we can't change many of the realities that are influencing their lives? The answer to this question is really a matter of perspective. If you work from an all-or-nothing perspective, you may feel burdened by the weight of trying to carry responsibility for not only these people's lives but the weight of the world's problems as well. It is easy to think that there is no point. But if you work from a possibilities perspective, you may creatively think about each moment as a moment of hope, filled with all the future potential of the people you work with. Then the answer is clear: **we meet with people because each encounter has the potential to make a difference**.

> *Every moment is the chance of a lifetime.*
> - Pir Vilayat

There are many concepts that encourage us never to underestimate the potential of a moment to change a life.

That change may come very quickly as Malcolm Gladwell suggests in his paradigm-shifting book *The Tipping Point: How Little Things Can Make a Big Difference* (2002). Little changes can have big effects and change can happen quickly.

Or the moment may be the starting point of a slower, more gradual chain of events that results in a major change at a later time. The concept of the "butterfly effect," expressed in chaos theory, illustrates this potential. A butterfly in one part of the world flaps its wings; this causes a subtle air movement that ultimately affects a hurricane in another part of the world.

There is an alternative to the all-or-nothing perspective. The journey motif reminds us that we don't have to walk with someone through their entire life or solve all of their problems, let alone solve all the problems of the world. The reality is that we can't wait until all the problems are solved, because they never will be. When we engage people where they are engaged in life, we have to help people in the midst of the realities of their life.

We meet people at the crossroads of life; we are responsible for how we assist them at those crossroads. We can't do it all but we can do something. We ought to meet them with a sense of hope that this might be that tipping point for them. We ought to meet them with a sense that we may be starting a chain of events in people's lives that one day may even change the "big realities." For example, there are many social justice issues that affect the Aboriginal peoples we work with in our Guiding Circles workshops. We cannot change those issues in the workshops no matter how much we wish we could. But we never know whether the person we are helping will be a potential "Nelson Mandela" or the parent of a "Nelson Mandela" who, because of our help, will start on a path that could lead eventually to finding a means of bringing about cultural reconciliation and justice for Aboriginal peoples in our country.

Motivated by the potential of a moment, in hope we can equip people to walk their journeys and we can help them find the best direction to go in their current situation. We don't know which engagements will be as life-changing as we desire; but if we don't try, none of them will be.

One of the greatest steps towards self-care we can take as life/career practitioners is to watch that our own hearts are filled with hope as we engage people.

We can't think of a better thought to close *Hope-Filled Engagement* with than the words of Albert Schweitzer. We trust that this book has helped you see that you can choose to join in saying,

> "To the question whether I am a pessimist or an optimist,
> I answer that my knowledge is pessimistic,
> but my willing and hoping are optimistic."

REFERENCES

?What If! (2002). *Sticky wisdom: How to start a creative revolution at work.* Oxford, UK: Capstone.

Adams, M. (2009). *Change your questions, change your life: 10 powerful tools for life and work.* San Fransico: Berrett-Koehler.

American Counseling Association (n.d.). ACA's Taskforce on counselor wellness and impairment: Assessment tools and wellness programs. Retrieved August 14, 2010 from http://www.counseling.org/wellness_taskforce/tf_assessment.htm.

Amundson, N. E. (1989). A model of individual career counseling. *Journal of employment counseling, 26,* 132-138.

Amundson, N. E. (2003). *The physics of living.* Richmond, B.C.: Ergon Communications.

Amundson, N. E. (2009). *Active engagement: The being and doing of career counselling.* Richmond, B.C.: Ergon Communications.

Amundson, N. E., & Poehnell, G. (2004). *Career pathways* (3rd ed.). Richmond, B.C.: Ergon Communications.

Amundson, N. E., Poehnell, G., & Pattern, M. (2005). *CareerScope: Looking in, looking out, looking around.* Richmond, B.C.: Ergon Communications.

Amundson, N. E., Westwood, M., & Prefontaine, R. (1995). Cultural bridging and employment counselling with clients from different cultural backgrounds. *Canadian journal of counselling, 29,* 206-213.

Angel, D. L. & Harney, E. E. (1997). *No one is unemployable: Creative solutions for overcoming barriers to employment.* Hacienda Heights, CA: WorkNet Publications.

Beck, B., Halling, S., McNabb, M., Miller, D., Rowe, J. O. & Schulz, J. (2003). Facing up to hopelessness: A dialogal phenomenological study. *Journal of religion and health, 42*(4), 339-354. Doi 10.1023/A:1025816827553. Abstract retrieved from http://www.springerlink.com/content/n4j0688814v839w4.

Bissonnette, D. (1994). *Beyond traditional job development: The art of creating opportunity.* n.p.: Milt Wright & Associates.

Bono, M. (n.d.). The best kept secret everyone seems to know - Part 2 of 2. Retrieved August 6, 2010 from http://www.articledashboard.com/Article/The-Best-Kept-Secret-Everyone-Seems-to-Know---Part-2-of-2/711231).

Bridges, W. (1991). *Managing transitions: Making the most of change.* New York: De Capo Press.

Bridges, W. (2004). *Transitions: Making sense of life's changes (Rev. 25th ed.).* New York: De Capo Press.

Businessknowledgesource.com (n.d.). The psychology of an entrepreneur. Retrieved August 14, 2010 from http://www. businessknowledgesource.com/smallbusiness/the_psychology_of_an_ entrepreneur_021604.html.

Chang, J. & Jun, F. (n.d.). The contemporary conflict of values. *Paideia.* Retrieved from http://www.bu.edu/wcp/Papers/Valu/ValuChan.htm.

Csikszentmihalyi, M. (1991). *Flow: The psychology of optimal experience.* New York: Harper Collins.

Csikszentmihalyi, M. (1997). *Finding flow in everyday life.* New York: Basic Books.

Clavell, J. (Producer & Director). (1967). *To sir with love* [motion picture]. London: Columbia.

Cochran, L. (1995). Conflict in career decisions. *ERIC Digest* ED404584.

Cornwall, J. (2005, December 9). The entrepreneur mind: A definition [Web log message]. Retrieved from http://forum.belmont.edu/cornwall/ archives/004165.html.

Davis, E. (2001). Connecting to the problem. *How,* 16(3), 28-34.

Doidge, N. (2007). *The brain that changes itself: Stories of personal triumph from the frontiers of brain science.* New York: Penguin.

Edwards, B. (1989). *Drawing on the right side of the brain* (Rev. ed.). Los Angeles, CA: Jeremy P. Tarcher.

Frank, F. (1973). *The zen of seeing: seeing/drawing as meditation.* New York: Vintage.

Fritz, R. (1989). *The path of least resistance: Learning to become the creative force in your own life.* New York: Columbine.

Gelatt, H. B. (1989). Positive uncertainty: A new decision-making framework for counseling. *Journal of counseling psychology,* 33, 252-256.

Gelatt, H. B. (1991). *Creative decision making.* Los Altos, CA: Crisp Publications.

Gelatt, H. B. & Gelatt, C. (2003). *Creative decision making using positive uncertainty: Rev'd edition* (A Fifty-Minute Series). Boston: NET.

Gilbert, D. (2006). *Stumbling on happiness*. Toronto: Borzoi (Random House of Canada).

Gladwell, M. (2002). *The tipping point: How little things can make a big difference*. New York: Back Bay Books.

Godsick, C., Grace, M., & Nabatoff, D. (Producers), & Friedlander, L. (Director). (2006). *Take the lead* [motion picture]. United States: New Line Cinema.

Henson, D. (n.d.). Beginner's mind. Retrieved from http://www.ironpalm.com/beginner.html.

Hopelessness. (n.d.). Adjective finder. Retrieved August 04, 2010, from Thesaurus.com website: http://www.thesaurus.com/browse/hopelessness.

Human Resources and Skills Development Canada. (2006). *National occupational classification*. Retrieved from http://www5.hrsdc.gc.ca/NOC/.

Imagination (n.d.). Retreived from http://www.greaterhorizons.com/imagination.html.

Kaye, B. & Jordan-Evans, S. (2002). *Love 'em or lose 'em: Getting good people to stay (2ⁿᵈ ed.)*. San Francisco, CA: Berrett-Koehler.

Landin, C. (2008, August 12). The Jante law. Retrieved from http://swedentourism.wordpress.com/2008/08/12/the-jante-law.

Lawson, G. & Venart, B. (n.d.). Preventing counselor impairment: Vulnerability, wellness, and resilience. Retrieved August 14, 2010 from http://www.counseling.org/wellness_taskforce/PDF/ACA_taskforce_vista.pdf.

MacKenzie, G. (1998). *Orbiting the giant hairball: A corporate fool's guide to surviving with grace*. New York: Viking Penguin.

McCormick, R. & Amundson, N. E. (1997). A career-life planning model for First Nations people. *Journal of employment counselling*, 34, 171-79.

McCormick, R. & France, M. H. (1995). Counselling First Nations clients on career issues: Implications for the school counsellor. *Journal of guidance and counselling*, 10, 27-31.

McCormick, R., Amundson, N. E., & Poehnell, G. (2002). *Guiding Circles: An Aboriginal guide to finding career paths, Booklet 1: understanding yourself*. Saskatoon, SK: Aboriginal Human Resources Development Council of Canada and Ergon Communications.

McCormick, R., Neumann, H., Amundson, N., & Mc Lean, H. (1999). First Nations career/life planning model: Guidelines for practitioners. *Journal of employment counselling*, 36(4), 167-177.

Merton, T. (1973). *Contemplation in a world of action*. Garden City, NY: Image Books.

Michalko, M. (1998). *Cracking creativity: The secrets of creative genius*. Berkley, CA: Ten Speed Press.

Moore, T. (1997). *The re-enchantment of everyday life*. New York: Harper Perennial.

Mosedale, G. (2001). A primer for applying improv skills to leadership. Retrieved September 18, 2010 from http://media.www.whartonjournal.com/media/storage/paper201/news/2001/03/26/News/A.Primer.For.Applying.Improv.Skills.To.Leadership-58520.shtml.

Neumann, H., McCormick, R. M., Amundson, N. E., & MCLean, H.B. (2000). Career counselling First Nations youth: Applying the First Nations career/life planning model. *Canadian journal of counselling*, 34(3), 172-185.

O'Connor, R. (2008). *Happy at last: The thinking person's guide to finding joy*. New York: St. Martin's Press.

Palmer, P. J. (1998). *The courage to teach: Exploring the inner landscape of a teacher's life*. San Francisco: Jossey-Bass.

Palmer, P. J. (2000). *Let your life speak: Listening for the voice of vocation*. San Francisco: Jossey-Bass.

Poehnell, G. (2003). Guiding Circles, Booklet 1: Coaches manual. Unpublished document.

Poehnell, G. & Amundson, N. (2001). *Career crossroads: A personal career positioning system*. Richmond, B.C.: Ergon Communications.

Poehnell, G. & Amundson, N. (2002). CareerCraft: Engaging with, energizing, and empowering creativity. In M. Peiperl, M. Arthur, & N. Anand (Eds.), *Career creativity: Explorations in the remaking of work* (pp. 105-122). Oxford, U.K.: Oxford University Press.

Poehnell, G., Amundson, N., & McCormick, R. (2006). *Guiding Circles: An Aboriginal guide to finding career paths Booklet 2 – Finding new possibilities*. Saskatoon, SK: Aboriginal Human Resource Council of Canada and Ergon Communications.

Robinson, K. & Aronica, L. (2009). *The element: How finding your passion changes everything.* New York: Penguin.

Siler, T. (1999). *Think like a genius: Use your creativity in ways that will enrich your life.* New York: Bantam Books.

Stanfield, B. (Ed.). (2000). *The art of focused conversation: 100 ways to access group wisdom in the workplace.* Gabriola Island, BC: New Society Publishers.

Super, D. E. (1990). Career and life development. In D. Brown & L. Brooks (Eds.), *Career choice and development: Applying contemporary theories to practice* (2nd ed., pp. 197-261). San Francisco: Jossey-Bass.

Super, D. E., Osborne, W. L., Walsh, D. J., Brown, S. D., & Niles, S. G. (1992). Developmental career assessment and counseling: The C-DAC model. *Journal of Counseling and Development, 71,* 74-82.

Tocher, M. (1998). *Brave work: A guide to the quest for meaning in work.* Ottawa: Canadian Career Development Foundation.

Vancouver School Board (n.d.). 2004/05 Aboriginal report – How are we doing? Retrieved from http://vancouver.ca/commsvcs/socialplanning/initiatives/aboriginal/tools/directory/education.htm).

vonOech, R. (1990). *A whack on the side of the head: How you can be more creative* (Rev. ed.). New York: Warner Books.

Westwood, M. J., & Ishiyama, F. I. (1991). Challenges in counseling immigrant clients: Understanding intercultural barriers to career adjustment. *Journal of employment counseling, 28,* 130-143.

Whitworth, L., Kimsey-House, H., & Sandahl, P. (1998). *Co-active coaching: New skills for coaching people toward success in work and life.* Palo Alto, CA: Davies-Black.

Wujec, T. (1988). *Pumping ions: Games and exercises to flex your mind.* Toronto, ON: Doubleday Canada.

Wujec, T. (1995). *Five star mind: Games and puzzles to stimulate your creativity and imagination.* Toronto, ON: Doubleday Canada.

Wujec, T. & Muscat, S. (2002). *Return on imagination: Realizing the power of creativity.* Toronto: Financial Times.

Zander, R. S. & Zander, B. (2000). *The art of possibilities: Transforming professional and personal life.* NY: Penguin Books.

ADDITIONAL CROSS-TRAINING RESOURCES

Bright, J. E. H., & Pryor, R. G. L. (2005). The chaos theory of careers: A user's guide. *The career development quarterly*, 53, 291-305.

Bright, J. E. H., Pryor, R. G. L., & Harpham, L. (2005). The role of chance events in career decision making. *Journal of vocational behavior*, 66, 561-576.

David, J. (n.d.). How to learn improv rules and structure. Retreived August 6, 2010 from http://www.ehow.com/how_2304143_learn-improv-rules-structure.html.

de Shazer, S. (1985). *Keys to solution in brief therapy*. New York: Norton.

Feller, R.W. (1995). Action planning for personal competitiveness in the "broken workplace." *Journal of employment counseling*, 32, 154-163.

Foster, R. J. (1978). *Celebration of discipline: The path to spiritual growth*. New York: Harper & Row.

France, H. & McCormick, R. (1997). The helping circle: Theoretical and practical considerations of using a First Nations peer support network. *Guidance and counselling*, 12(2), 27-32.

Fritz, R. (1991). *Creating*. New York: Fawcett Columbine.

Garrett, M. W. & Osborne, W. L. (1995). The Native American sweat lodge as metaphor for group work. *The journal for specialists in group work*, 20(1), 33-39.

Guinness, O. (1998). *The call: Finding and fulfilling the central purpose of your life*. Nashville, TN: Word.

Hall, D. (1995). *Jump start your brain*. New York: Warner Books.

Handy, C. (1994). *The age of paradox*. Boston: Harvard Business School Press.

Hanna, F. J., Bemak, F. & Chung, R. C. (1999). Toward a new paradigm for multicultural counseling, *Journal of counseling & development*, 77, 125-134.

Heath, C. & Heath, D. (2010), *Switch: How to change things when change is hard*. n.p.: Random House Canada.

Herr, E. L. (1999). *Counseling in a dynamic society: Contexts & practices for the 21st century* (2nd ed.) Alexandria, VA: American Counseling Association.

Killinger, B. (2007). *Integrity: Doing the right thing for the right reason*. Montreal, QC: McGill-Queen's.

Krumboltz, J. D. & Levin, A. S. (2004). *Luck is no accident: Making the most of happenstance in your life and career.* Atascadero, CA: Impact Publishers.

Landa, R. (1998). *Thinking creatively: New ways to unlock your visual imagination.* Cincinnati, OH: North Light Books.

Lehrer, J. (2009). *How we decide.* New York:Houghton Miffin Harcourt.

McCormick, R. (1998). Ethical considerations in First Nations counselling. *Canadian journal of counselling,* 32(4), 284-297.

McCormick, R. (1997). First Nations counsellor training: Strengthening the circle. *Canadian journal of community mental health,* 16(2), 91-99.

McCormick, R. (1997). Healing through interdependence: The role of 'connecting' in First Nations healing practices. *Canadian journal of counselling,* 12(2), 27-32.

McCormick, R. (1997). An integration of healing wisdom: The Vision Quest ceremony from an attachment theory perspective. *Guidance and counselling,* 12(?), 18-22.

McCormick, R. M., & Paterson, D. W. (1996). Student counselling in Canadian universities. *International journal for the advancement of counselling,* 18, 235-243.

Mate, G. (2003). *When the body says no: The cost of hidden stress.* Toronto: Vintage Canada (a division of Random House).

Michalko, M. (2006). *Thinkertoys: A handbook of creative-thinking techniques (2nd ed.).* Berkley, CA: Ten Speed Press.

Mitchell, K. E., Levin, A. S., & Krumboltz, J. D. (1999). Planned happenstance: Constructing unexpected career opportunities. *Journal of counseling and development,* 77, 115-124.

Pedersen, P. (1997). *Culture-centered counselling interventions.* London: Sage.

Pryor, R. G. L., Amundson, N. E., & Bright, J. E. H. (2008). Probabilities and possibilities: The strategic counselling implications of the chaos theory of careers. *The career development quarterly,* 56, 309-318.

Pryor, R. G. L. & Bright, J. E. H. (2003). The chaos theory of careers. *Australian journal of career development,* 12, 12-20.

Pryor, R. G. L. & Bright, J. E. H. (2006). Counseling chaos: Techniques for practitioners. *Journal of employment counseling,* 43, 2-17.

Ryan, M. J. (2006). *This year I will: How to finally change a habit, keep a resolution, or make a dream come true*. New York: Broadway Books (a division of Random House).

Seligman, M. E. P., & Csikszentmihalyi, M. (2000). Positive psychology. *American psychologist*, 55, 5-14.

Siegel, D. J. (2010). *Mindsight: The new science of personal transformation*. New York: Bantam Books.

Smalley, S. L. & Winston, D. (2010). *Full present: The science, art, and practice of mindfulness*. Philadelphia: De Capo Press.

Stevens, R. P. (1999). *The other six days: vocation, work, and ministry in Biblical perspective*. Grand Rapids, MI: Eerdmanns.

Thrift, E. & Amundson, N, (2005). Hermeneutic-narrative approach to career counselling: An alternative to postmodernism. *Perspectives in education*, 23, 9-20.

Tharp, T. (203). *The creative habit: Learn it and use it for life: A practical guide*. New York: Simon & Schuster.

Walter, J. L., & Peller, J. E. (1992). *Becoming solution-focused in brief therapy*. New York: Brunner/Mazel.

Weaver, J. (2000). Creativity. *Community banker*, 9(1), 16-19.

Westwood, M. J., & Ishiyama, F. I. (1991). Challenges in counseling immigrant clients: Understanding intercultural barriers to career adjustment. *Journal of employment counseling*, 28, 130-143.

Yapko, M. D. (2009). *Depression is contagious: How the most common mood disorder is spreading around the world*. New York: Free Press.

About the Authors

Gray Poehnell

Gray Poehnell is an experienced career consultant with an interest in holistic approaches that cultivate career integrity and hope through practical spirituality, creativity, imagination. As partner to Dr. Norm Amundson in Ergon Communications, he has participated in the development and writing of numerous career counselling programs and has co-authored several workbooks (including *Career Pathways, Career Crossroads, CareerScope, Guiding Circles)* and now the book *Hope-Filled Engagement*. Ergon books have been translated into 16 languages and are being used internationally, as well as across Canada.

Gray has worked with diverse client populations, such as youth, social assistance recipients, older adults, immigrants, professionals and Aboriginals. As a trainer, workshop facilitator, and keynote presenter, he has equipped life/career practitioners both nationally and internationally. Gray is of Metis descent and over recent years has focused on projects to develop career materials from an Aboriginal perspective and to train Aboriginal career practitioners across Canada and in Australia in the Guiding Circles approach. He is also facilitating Guiding Circles training with a wide range of life/career practitioners who work with other client groups that benefit from a more holistic approach, such as multi-barriered clients or students. He is very happily married, has 2 adult daughters, and currently lives in beautiful Steveston at the mouth of the Fraser River, Vancouver, British Columbia, Canada.

Dr. Norman E. Amundson

Dr. Amundson is a Full Professor in Counselling Psychology / Faculty of Education at the University of British Columbia, Canada. He has given numerous workshops and seminars and also has been a keynote speaker at many national and international conferences. He has over 30 years experience working in the career development field.

In his writings, Dr. Amundson emphasizes the importance of creativity, imagination, cultural awareness, and action as career counselling strategies. His publications include: *Active Engagement* (Winner of the Best Book Award by the Canadian Counselling Association); *The Essential Elements of Career Counseling*; *The Physics of Living*; *Metaphor Making*; and several career workbooks including *Career Pathways*, *Guiding Circles*; *Career Flow*, and *CareerScope*.

Dr. Amundson is actively involved in a number of professional associations and has won a number of awards. Some of his recent accomplishments include: 2004 Best Research Article in the Career Development Quarterly and the 2008 International Leadership Award - National Career Development Association; the Judy Geoghegan-Doi Distinguished Professional Service Award – National Employment Counseling Association; Honorary Life Time Board Member of ENET; Honorary Life Time Member of the Swedish Career Development Association; Lifetime Achievement Award from the University of Regina Alumni; and an Honorary Doctorate from the University of Umeå, Sweden.

To Contact the Authors

To contact Gray Poehnell:

11780 Yoshida Court
Richmond, B.C. V7E 5C6
Tel.: 604.277.4988
Email: graypoehnell@mac.com

To contact Dr. Norm Amundson:

Faculty of Education
University of British Columbia
Vancouver, B.C. V6T 1Z4 Canada
Tel: 604.822.6757 Fax: 604.822.3302
E-mail: norman.e.amundson@ubc.ca

To order Ergon publications, please contact:

Ergon Communications
PO Box 36033
10991 No. 1 Road
Richmond, B.C. V7E 1S4 Canada
Tel./Fax. 604.448.9025
Website: www.ergoncommunications.com